Jumbo

Also by John Sutherland

Thackeray at Work

Victorian Novelists and Publishers

Fiction and the Fiction Industry

Bestsellers: Popular Fiction of the 1970s

Offensive Literature

The Longman Companion to Victorian Fiction

Mrs Humphry Ward: Eminent Victorian, Pre-eminent Edwardian

Sir Walter Scott: A Critical Life

Victorian Novelist, Publishers, and Readers

Is Heathcliff a Murderer?

Can Jane Eyre be Happy?

Who Betrayed Elizabeth Bennet?

Where was Rebecca Shot?

Is Henry V a War Criminal? (with Cedric Watts)

Stephen Spender: The Authorized Biography

Last Drink to LA

The Literary Detective

Reading the Decades

The Boy who Loved Books

How to Read a Novel

Curiosities of Literature

Magic Moments

The Dickens Dictionary

Bestsellers: A Very Short Introduction

How Literature Works

Love Death Sex and Words (with Stephen Fender)

Lives of the Novelists: A History of Fiction in 294 Lives

A Little History of Literature

JUMBO

The Unauthorised Biography of a
Victorian Sensation

John Sutherland

Aurum
Press

First published in Great Britain in 2014 by
Aurum Press Limited
74–77 White Lion Street
London N1 9PF
www.aurumpress.co.uk

Picture credits: ANSP Archives Collection 49: 200; www.cartoonstock.com: 197;
The Natural History Museum, London: 40; © PA Images: 257; Collections and
Archives, Tufts University: 132, 148, 158; ZSL: 59, 60

Every effort has been made to trace the copyright holders of
material quoted in this book. If application is made in writing to
the publisher, any omissions will be included in future editions.

A catalogue record for this book is
available from the British Library.

ISBN 978 1 78131 244 5

1 3 5 7 9 10 8 6 4 2

2014 2016 2018 2017 2015

Printed and bound by CPI Group (UK) Ltd, Croydon, CR0 4YY

To the Last Living African Elephant

Contents

'I AM BECOME A NAME'
(Alfred Lord Tennyson, *Ulysses*)

A Note on the Text

This is not a biography of the world's most renowned elephant nor of its famed owners, the London Zoo and Phineas T. Barnum. Those things have been expertly done elsewhere, and I am grateful and indebted to them. What is offered here is, to borrow a term from the first time I 'saw the elephant' (on screen, that is), a kind of fantasia. Call it elephantasia.

Acknowledgements to a number of authors whose work I have drawn on will be found in the endnotes. But, at the outset, I must express particular thanks to Paul Chambers's *Jumbo: This Being the True Story of the Greatest Elephant in the World* (2009). What follows here does not aim to supersede his masterly biography; my intentions are more free-ranging and egotistical. As has anyone who has opened its pages, I have been consistently delighted and instructed by F.C. Sillar and R.M. Meyler's *Elephants: Ancient and Modern* (1968).

Jumbo: Private Passion, Local Pride

In AD 34 Colchester – 'Camulodunum', as the recently invading Romans called it – was holding out remarkably successfully against the mightiest empire in the world. The invaders had been attracted to the damp, cold, unwelcoming, irritatingly wineless country for its mines and slaves (*non angli, sed angeli,* etc). A rag-bag of blue-arsed warriors, under Caratacus, were keeping the legions at bay outside the ramparts. The town was important to the resistance, the capital of the Catuvellauni tribe. Tribes have always been big in Colchester.

It was the battle which would turn the war. The Emperor Claudius (later to be immortalised by Robert Graves) was impatient. Although not in terrific physical shape he came himself to England. (If you want something done, do it yourself.) With him came reinforcements, artillery (the boulder-hurling kind) and thirty-eight 'war elephants'. Not since the distant prehistoric days of the hairy mammoth had a pachyderm hoof shaken British soil. I myself have seen a train of sad circus elephants attract virtually the whole gawping population of Colchester as they trooped through the High Street to their tents in the Castle Park, the luckless fellow with the big shovel and bucket following. God knows what the goggle-eyed Catuvellauni thought when they saw these monsters. Morale collapsed.

Colchester fell in days, the British tribes surrendered *en masse*, Claudius awarded himself the title Britannicus and went home, leaving the tedious mopping up to his generals and the man with the shovel and bucket. What happened to the elephants was not recorded, although some bones found at the nearby port of Harwich (where boats left for Rome) suggests that at least one did not make it back for the triumphal parade through the capital (some spoilsport palaeontologist claims they are mammoth bones, which I prefer to disbelieve – it would be nice to think my town could claim at least one 'kill').

Civilisation had come to Colchester (subsequently named, oddly, after old King Coel – another story). It had come borne on the back of the largest, most fearsome beast on earth. To this day brochures urge the tourist to 'Visit Colchester, Britain's oldest recorded town and soak up its history. Walk through the Roman streets where Emperor Claudius once rode trium-phantly on an elephant'. It's a bit of a stretch that he actually came in perched on the thing, like Sabu the Elephant Boy – but vivid, and it draws in the punters.

The Romans stayed some 300 years before the tribes, on every frontier, drove them out again. They left behind a castle (later taken down and rebuilt, with the original material, by the Normans), whose defensive walls still substantially stand to this day (I myself, in my barbarous childhood, loved to climb them) and which served the town excellently in its great Civil War siege, coins, and huge amounts of shards and shells. The Romans were particularly fond of the Mersea oysters, for which the town is still famed, and whose world-beating quality it celebrates annually and guzzlingly with the Oyster Feast.

Had the Romans stayed, Colchester would have remained the country's capital, rather than Londinium. Colcestrians are still sore about that, as they are that their football team rarely makes it out of the Third Division and that envious bureau-crats appointed Chelmsford the Essex county town. A certain rueful frustrated gigantism lingers – elephantiasis of the soul.

In 1883, in the great late-Victorian urban boom, the town erected its huge four-legged water tower, at the crest of one of the two large hills on which the town's centre rests. It is (and was) the second-largest water tower in Britain. Over a million locally baked bricks went into its massive construction.

Jumbo, the world's most famous elephant, had a few months earlier been transported, in a large iron box and with country-wide protest, from London Zoo to New York.

England says goodbye to Jumbo

Colchester's water tower was duly named (what else?) 'Jumbo'. The animal had never actually come to Colchester but thousands of the town's children had (delirious with excitement) ridden on his back at the Regent's Park Zoo on days out to London.

Colchester was where, as Philip Larkin wryly puts it, my childhood was 'unspent'. Not a day went past when I did not look up fondly at Jumbo, on my walk to school, drinking for

3

years from its subterranean metallic trunkery. It was absurd but magnificent. Pevsner may well sneer; so does Wikipedia, which claims that the 'Jumbo' appellation is 'a term of derision'. It is not – I vouch for it – we Colcestrians were and are *proud* to call it Jumbo. It's the visible sign of the inner 'bigness' of Colchester.

Jumbo remains the town's dominant skyline feature but, alas, has now fallen into the 'white elephant' stage of architectural existence. As legend has it, the blanched beast (loaded with religious significance, requiring worship as well as care) was what an Indian prince would give a rival, sure in the knowledge that looking after the finicky animal and the attendant priests would lead to financial ruin. Or, at the very least, nervous breakdown.

Water is more efficiently supplied nowadays – from systems that do not require pumping the stuff 120 feet into the air so it can dribble back down again. Anglian Water sold Jumbo to a property developer in 1987. But so 'listed' ('Grade II', insultingly) is the elephantine structure – as one of the marvels of Victorian engineering – that its exterior cannot be defaced. On the other hand, brick buildings of this age are hugely expensive to keep up. Everything feasible has been tried, including making it a lofty fast-food restaurant (selling, inevitably, Jumboburgers).

Having bountifully slaked the thirst of Colchester for a century, Jumbo looks likely to suck out the town's lifeblood. Somewhere in the fields of Elysium Claudius must be laughing. How Jumbo will be safely pulled down is unclear. Where is George Orwell with his elephant gun when you need him?

Nonetheless the elephant remains close to the Colcestrian soul and always will. Colchester Zoo was founded in 1963 and its central attraction is described thus in one of its advertising flyers:

Elephant Kingdom is one of Colchester Zoo's most impressive enclosures and is at the forefront of modern zoo design. The unique concept of our design allows all the elephants maximum sight, sound and physical contact and has specially designed night stalls, a roped off 'safe area' and spacious indoor bull elephant quarters.

The elephants can be viewed in their large outdoor paddocks where they have access to a waterfall and pool area. You will usually find that Tembo, our bull elephant, will often be on his own in his paddock. Tembo is easily viewed by taking a ride on the UmPhafa road train accessed from Familiar Friends. In the wild, bull elephants tend to lead a naturally solitary life.

'Tembo'? Does one hear an echo? The flyer continues:

Tembo is quite easily recognised. He is the largest of all our elephants at the zoo, he also has a much stockier build, thicker tusks and a very smooth rounded forehead in comparison to the three females. Tembo came to Colchester Zoo after being rescued from Chipperfield's Circus in 1998.

'Rescued'. How times change. Those 'sad elephants' mentioned earlier belonged to Chipperfield's travelling circus. Its week's stay was one of the high points of my year – particularly the 'elephant ballet' (inspired by the elephant dance to 'Dance of the Hours' in Walt Disney's *Fantasia*).

Colchester's intimate relationship with the elephant – Jumbo at its centre – usefully focuses the ambivalence we have about this wonderful beast and its omnipresence in our lives – if only as a multi-purpose epithet. It is terrifying (ask Caratacus);

it is, obscurely, holy (ask any Indian prince); it is awesomely big (ask any Colcestrian, gazing up, reverently, at their landmark building); it is as gentle in the flesh as Babar is on the storybook page (ask any child feeding Tembo a doughnut through the bars of Elephant Kingdom).

What follows could be seen as the chronicle of a benign haunting. 'Jumbo', and Jumbo's kind, have been with me for six decades – elusive, but inescapable, like Henry James's *The Beast in the Jungle*. The idea I have is, almost certainly, zoologically misinformed and incorrect. But Jumbo is always with me as I watch Jumbo Jets fly overhead (they should really be called 'Dumbo jets'), put on my stylish jumbo cords, or tuck into a jumbo-shrimp 'starter'. Perhaps he's with you as well.

Blazing the Trail for Jumbo

John Donne has a poem, 'Air and Angels', about loving a woman two or three times before he knew her face or name. He was ready for her. The British people, one can fantasise, before they made their first acquaintance with Jumbo, 'knew' his face and name. They were ready for him. When he arrived, in 1865, he slotted into a groove that had been long prepared for the greatest elephant in history.

John Milton, who almost certainly never saw an elephant, pictures one (as yet mate-less, it would seem) in *Paradise Lost* frisking about Adam and Eve, in their short-lived Edenic bliss, before it all went haywire for everyone and everything, including Jumbo's ancestor.

> Fair couple, linked in happy nuptial league,
> Alone as they. About them frisking played
> All beasts of the earth, since wild, and of all chase
> In wood or wilderness, forest or den.
> Sporting the lion ramped, and in his paw
> Dandled the kid; bears, tigers, ounces, pards,
> Gambolled before them; the unwieldy elephant,
> To make them mirth, used all his might, and wreathed
> His lithe proboscis.

Was the father of all elephants African or an Asian? Recent research by the Institute for Creation Research, conducted by Dr John D. Morris from close examination of entirely trustworthy Biblical sources, comes down definitively for the Garden of Eden being located somewhere around Ethiopia.[1] That would mean the Edenic elephant was an African bush variety – just like Jumbo.

One doesn't, to be frank, see a lot of gambol potential in the hugely popular and recycled early sixteenth-century prints of Pope Leo X's elephant Hanno, which may, along with other much-recycled pictorial imagery, have been in Milton's mind when he wrote the above. And there is a glum look about the eye which suggests Hanno may be thinking about the Fall of Elephant and whether his ancestor's bipedal, short-nosed playmate was entirely wise to eat that apple. Hanno, sadly, expired from eating an injudiciously administered laxative coated with gold.

Glum Hanno

Sir Thomas Browne, possessed of the most lovably curious mind in the annals of English literature, begins the third book of his *wunderkammer*, *Pseudodoxia Epidemica* (*Vulgar Errors*, 1642), with a scholarly cogitation on the elephant's strangely wooden-looking legs (I omit the voluminous footnotes):

> THE first shall be of the Elephant, whereof there
> generally passeth an opinion it hath no joints; and this
> absurdity is seconded with another, that being unable to
> lie down, it sleepeth against a Tree; which, the Hunters
> observing, do saw it almost asunder; whereon the Beast
> relying, by the fall of the Tree, falls also down it self,
> and is able to rise no more. Which conceit is not the
> daughter of later times, but an old and gray-headed
> error, even in the days of *Aristotle*, as he delivereth in his
> Booke, *De incessu Animalium,* and stands successively
> related by several other Authors: by *Diodorus Siculus*,
> *Strabo, Ambrose, Cassiodore, Solinus*, and many more.
> Now herein methinks men much forget themselves, not
> well considering the absurdity of such assertions.

Browne was a man of his time and scholarly background
who sought knowledge in the pages of books rather than the
world around him. Oddly enough, he – the witty castigator
of the vice – was himself in error here. Elephants sleep lying
down. Or perhaps not. There are some unusual elephants
who do, reportedly, sleep exactly as Browne describes. Bolivar
(1859–1908), one of the meanest and most unpleasant circus
animals ever to have trampled sawdust, having killed any
keeper unlucky enough to have to deal with him, spent the last
sixteen years of his life sleeping (or not sleeping) standing up.

As an observer noted:

> Four pronounced depressions in the asphalt floor of his
> apartment mark the spot where night and day the great

beast has shifted from one leg to another. Swaying from side to side and swinging his trunk with the motion like a pendulum of an ancient clock, he marks the flight of time by gradually wearing away the hard floor beneath him.[2]

Sleepless Bolivar

If there was a tree nearby one has no doubt Bolivar would have leaned against it, or, out of sheer grumpiness, pissed it to death. His wary keeper recorded that 'he snores at night'. Very loudly, one must suppose.

Sir Thomas Browne was also well off the mark in his comments on 'joints'. I quote from the Kruger National Park information manual. It was written by people who might not have been all that well up on Cassiodore and Solinus, and sadly lacked the florid Browneian-Ciceronian prose style, but had actually taken the trouble to look at an elephant:

The joints that are perceived as 'knees', are in fact wrists. This is a common misunderstanding due to the belief that a leg joint that bends between the foot and the body must be a knee. The main difference between us and the elephants is that our foot bones and hand bones are separate, whereas those of the elephant are one in the same, and have evolved to suit this four-legged mammal.[3]

It would seem clear that Sir Thomas Browne, alas, is again in error – but not of the vulgar kind. And we still love him for his style.

Apart from Claudius's trip to Colchester in the flesh, Britain's first experience of the elephant was in 1255 when Louis IX of France gave his brother-in-law Henry III an elephant for the Royal menagerie in the Tower of London. The beast was wonderfully commemorated in a design by the artist Matthew Paris, who noted: 'We believe that this was the only elephant ever seen in England.'[4]

Prisoner of the tower

(Paris did two designs – this shows the elephant being fed by its keeper, Henricus de Flor – evidently, from his name, brought along with his beast from France. Henricus seems to be giving it a loaf of bread with one hand, holding a cudgel in the other, ready to deliver a sharp whack on the snout, if necessary.)

The un-named animal was, supposedly, acquired by Louis during one of the many crusades in Palestine. It was brought by ship up the Thames and lodged in a specially constructed cage in the Tower of London. 'We command you,' Henry instructed the Sheriff of London, in his usual royal fashion, 'that ye cause without delay, to be built at our Tower of London, one house of forty feet long and twenty feet deep, for our elephant.' Would that one talk to one's own builder that way.

Henry already had an impressive personal menagerie at the tower. The elephant joined three leopards, and a Norwegian 'Polar' bear which is recorded as liking to take the occasional dip in the Thames – in that day teeming with wholesome fish. The spectacle doubtless allayed the gloom of the noble prisoners in the Tower, awaiting the executioner's axe. Now, alas, only the ravens survive to amuse the swarming tourists.

Henry's elephant did not survive long. It died within three years. The cause of death was given as a surfeit of red wine, for which, presumably, the animal had developed a dangerous predilection in France. It would be nice to think that, as with 'false fleeting' Clarence in Shakespeare's *Richard III*, a fellow occupant of a cell in the 'Bloody Tower', it was a 'butt of Malmsey' which did for Henry's elephant.

Henry's elephant's brief sojourn in England is commemorated on the swinging signboards of innumerable English pubs – most famously the Elephant and Castle (a few hundred yards away from the Tower) in south London. The Cutlers' Company adopted the elephant as their heraldic device – doubtless impressed by the scissor-sharp tusks (incisors, anatomically) which Paris depicted.

'Enough booze to kill a small horse', as the drinking man's slang describes a heavy session. But how much red wine would it take, one idly wonders, to kill an elephant? Given a body weight of 5 tons, it's estimated that a lethal dose would be between half a gallon and a gallon of ethanol: neat alcohol, that is. That translates, by my reckoning, as between ten and twenty gallons of plonk. It must have been a very heavy session indeed that did for King Henry's elephant.

Over the following centuries there were touring fairs and small circuses showing off an elephant or two. But they had the big drawback that, unlike bears and bulls, there was little fun in 'baiting' them. Even the Roman mob, whose tolerance for such things was high, are recorded as being occasionally nauseated by the arena sand being covered with elephantine entrails and carcasses, too heavy to pull off easily, creating tiresome delays and stench[5]. They preferred the faster action of lions and Christians. One does rather wonder, though, how gladiatorial Russell Crowe would have handled an elephant.

The English nation's first serious relationship with the Elephantidae was a beast called 'Chunee'. He was an Asian elephant, brought from Burma around 1809, presumably just out of calfdom. Full-sized elephants are hard to transport even today and, by sail-driven cargo vessel, a trip of 8,000 miles would need at least 10 tons of food. Elephants, their digestion being so inefficient, die in days if they don't get their daily hundredweight or so.

Chunee had been imported for the booming theatre world around Covent Garden and made his stage appearance on Boxing Day 1811 in the pantomime *Harlequin and Padnamaba*, at the Theatre Royal in Drury Lane. It was not a success. He is recorded as 'rumping the audience' – the verb 'dumping' may be more appropriate. His theatrical career ended abruptly.[6]

Chunee was lucky. Elephants in circuses have always had it hard – their 'tricks' involve much behind-the-scenes brutality from trainers. Necessary, these professionals of the big tent tell us, though they would rather we didn't look. When the audience is present, the symbolic whip and chair are all that is on show. Theatrical elephants have it a lot worse, their tricks being that much more protracted and necessarily intricate. In 1829 a female elephant, called Mademoiselle Djek, made something of a hit in a burlesque called *The Elephant of Siam and the Fire Fiend*. The Victorian novelist Charles Reade – who prided himself on writing 'fiction based on fact' – undertook considerable research into the way Mademoiselle Djek was treated to get her 'stage-worthy'. The novel he wrote on the basis of what he turned up, *Jack of all Trades* (1858), makes grisly reading (it is Mademoiselle Djek's trainer, the 'Jack' of the title, writing):

> I walked quickly up to her. I did not hesitate or raise the question which of us two was to suffer; I knew that would not do. I sprang upon her like a tiger and drove the pitchfork into her trunk. She gave a yell of dismay and turned a little from me; I drove the fork into her ear.
>
> Then came out her real character.
>
> She wheeled round, ran her head into a corner, stuck out her great buttocks, and trembled all over like a leaf. I stabbed her with all my force for half-an-hour till the blood poured out of every square foot of her huge body, and during the operation she would have crept into a nut-shell if she could. I filled her as full of holes as a cloved orange.

The image sticks in the mind. What Reade describes is, one suspects, what has always happened to elephants who are required to perform for spectators rather than merely be on display for the public. The cloved orange technique persists in circuses to this day, as PETA, and their earnest spokesman the film star Alec Baldwin, will assure you. You'll find it on YouTube (a word which, like 'trunk call', has always strangely evoked Jumbo for me).

No elephant in captivity has it easy. But Chunee, for twelve years, had it easier than most. After his Theatre Royal debut and debacle he was acquired by Edward Cross (1774–1854), who was running what is historically regarded as England's first public zoo in Exeter 'Change, close by the theatre district on the Strand. The 'Change was a forerunner of the modern shopping mall, with arcades, and various shops and boutiques selling *bric à brac*. In 1773, a man by the fine name of Gilbert Pidcock had the bright idea of setting up a menagerie of 'wild animals' in the larger saloons, charging punters a (whopping for the time) one-shilling entrance fee.

Pidcock was inspired to go into the business, one guesses, by the crowds who gathered on 1 April every year to see the lions of the Royal Menagerie, half a mile down the river, go on annual display. Pidcock picked up various 'exotics' from sailors coming home from voyages to foreign parts, who knew that a parrot, turtle or a wombat would subsidise a few jolly nights in the taverns and houses of easy virtue along Limehouse. He also picked up tatty discards from the Royal Menagerie. Both it and his own menagerie had a high death toll and their animals tended to 'mange' very fast, denied fresh air, exercise, the company of their kind and their natural foodstuffs. But that was the condition for most Londoners at that time in the slums and 'rookeries' bordering the Thames, whose putrid, sewage-thick waters were no longer something a sensible polar bear would care to swim in. It was slums for everyone down at the river, where the 'cloaca maxima' (the 'Fleet' river, which gave its name to Fleet Street, spewing out a higher kind of sewage) debouched into Old Father Thames.

Pidcock's business was acquired by a resourceful Italian showman by the name of Stephano Polito (1763–1814). He had been touring England with a small tented circus and decided to settle down and let the customers come to him (although he still did a bit of touring in the summer). Cross, who had married into the Polito family, took over the running of the establishment and renamed it the Royal Grand National Menagerie (Cross was not one for understatement) in the early years of the new century. Polito died in 1814 and Cross became sole owner.

Over the thirty years before Chunee came along the successive proprietors had built up a handsome little zoo in the 'Change. It included, as the early 1800s advertisement boasted: 'Nero the largest Lion ever seen in the whole world, the Boa-constrictor and the laughing Hyena, Ourang Otang, Birds of Paradise, Ostriches and every living animal from the Jungles in the far East'.[7]

All this in a floorspace about the size of your local Tesco.

Chunee caged

Nero's days as top animal were over once Chunee appeared on the scene. After the shameful end of his theatrical career

Cross went the whole hog (so to speak – he did, actually have the odd hog) and bought the giant thespian for £1,000. A huge expense – and risky. How to look after elephants was a wholly unknown skill in London's West End. How to stable them, humanely and efficiently, in a space the size of an attic, without running water supply, was risky verging on reckless. But it worked out wonderfully – for Cross, at least. Chunee became, literally, the biggest 'show' in London. More to the point, unlike Nero the lion, irascible like all his big-cat kind, Chunee was a great trouper.

Celebrities of the day came and had private sessions (half a crown charge, minimum) with the great Chunee. Drawing on his theatrical expertise he would do his little turns. The most famous was to take a tiny sixpence coin (a 'tanner') from the customer's hand, then return it. In his diary for 13 November 1813, an impressed, despite himself, Lord Byron recorded:

> The elephant took and gave me my money again, took
> off my hat, opened a door, trunked a whip, and behaved
> so well, that I wish he was my butler.

The elephantine Jeeves is a nice Byronic touch. It didn't necessarily cost common folk a shilling. Every Sunday, Cross and a keeper would take Chunee out for an amble down the Strand. More fun than the Lord Mayor's Coach – or matins.

Chunee became much loved over the years, as more and more people could claim to have seen him, or have enjoyed the silver tanner trick. But there was the occasional ominous tantrum. When he scraped his head on a nail carelessly hammered into the wall of his stall, Chunee suddenly turned on the offending keeper and, it seemed clear, would have killed the fellow had not other handlers stepped in with the twelve-foot spears they prudently carried to keep the animal 'in awe'. (Circuses dealing with elephants today prefer the bull hook, one is told, which can usefully claw as well as poke). The animal clearly had a temper. Had Byron been injudicious enough, say, to stub his cheroot on Chunee's trunk the world may never have received *Don Juan*.

It's a nice Stoppardian scenario to imagine Byron meeting a demure little Miss from Hampshire – the anonymous lady referred to on the title page of *Pride and Prejudice* – at Mr Cross's establishment. The confessed Janeite and 'pachydermophiliac', Diana Birchall, astutely picks up a passing reference in *Sense and Sensibility* to children being taken 'to see the wild beasts on Exeter Exchange' and draws speculative conclusions.

Mr Cross's menagerie

In her engagingly skittish article on the subject, Birchall concludes: 'My feeling is that she did.' See the elephant, that is. Feelings, alas, don't carry much clout in the higher reaches of literary scholarship. She is, Birchall says, ever on the lookout for that smoking-gun letter from the novelist to her sister,

Dear Cassandra,

Henry and Eliza and I went to the Exchange today to see the wild beasts, and there was an Elephant that quite put me out of countenance,

Affectionately, Jane

Good luck to Birchall.[8]

Things went disastrously wrong on 1 November 1825. The tale is told most comprehensively by Richard D. Altick in his book *The Shows of London* (1978). Chunee's favourite handler, John Tietjen, came in as usual to clean the cage; he was accompanied by a colleague, carrying the de rigueur 12-foot spear, to keep the animal at bay while Tietjen got to work with the shovel, bucket and broom. Tietjen airily (and fatally) remarked to his fellow handler, 'Never mind the spear, the elephant knows me well enough.' He took the spear and threw it on the floor, and to prove the point that there was nothing to worry about gave Chunee a friendly whack on the rump with his broom. Bad move. Chunee promptly impaled the luckless Mr Tietjen on his tusks, like toast on the toasting fork, killing him instantly.

A coroner's inquest was held the same day. One witness testified that Chunee, in a fit of post-homicidal remorse, had

Chunee kneels for execution

trembled uncontrollably on seeing what he had done. Accidental death was recorded but the court imposed a nominal one-shilling fine on the menagerie. The money (what every customer paid on entry) was nothing, but clearly Chunee was now on probation.

The animal was still much beloved and was kept on public view. However, a little more caution in his interaction with the public was imposed. But things soon went from bad to worse – horribly much worse. For some years now Chunee – a mature elephant in 1826 – had been displaying annual outbreaks of 'musth'. This is the testosterone storm which impels bulls to mate – sometimes violently enough to kill the luckless dam who is the victim of their affection. Elephants are not gentle lovers. When musth happens it's a bad time to be around an elephant, particularly one in a very confined space standing 11 feet, with a 30-foot trunk reach, weighing, as the 27-year-old Chunee now did, 5 tons. The notion of him having a fit of priapic fury on some Sunday in the Strand didn't bear thinking about (another, less reliable, account records that Chunee did suffer just such a fit on his Sunday walk and killed his keeper – details are fuzzy).

Cross and his crew had put their faith, whenever the sinister symptoms of musth made their appearance (fairly unmistake-able: streams of goo down the cheeks, startlingly green urine and the emergences from the animal's bowels of a very large penis), in a home remedy, namely a barrel containing 55 lb of Epsom salts mixed, for palatability, with molasses. It worked for constipation on the human consititution. And Chunee's dose, some mathematically minded wag worked out, would give 4,000 of his Majesty's subjects the runs. And who thinks about sex in that condition?

But, as the years passed, and Chunee's urges became stronger, it was clear that 'the salts' no longer worked for the male elephant's gigantic lusts. It reached such a pitch in the elephant's spring 1826 'fit' that carpenters, remembering what had happened to poor John Tietjen, refused to go into Chunee's cage to strengthen it. It had cost Cross £350 to fortify the 'den' with oak beams and iron rods, but it was obvious, the way things were going, that Chunee would soon batter through them. What then? Massacre in the Strand.

There was nothing for it. Chunee would have to be 'put down'. The most efficient way to do it was to call in the artillery. As Charles Reade gruesomely chronicles, Mademoiselle Djek had died by cannon ball, after she killed one member of the paying public too many (it seems they put some delicacy she particularly relished in the mouth of a cannon, then when she leaned in to fillet it out, let fly).

But the Strand was too built up, and too populated, for cannon balls to be flying around taking the heads off innocent bystanders as well as sex-mad elephants. Poison was a possibility, but elephants have half a million sense receptors in the trunk (half nose, half upper lip) which transfers food to their mouths, and they can smell and taste poison very astutely – a beast which eats 300 lb of vegetation a day has to be wary of all those toxic plants in the wild and avoid or spit out the ones which are a danger to it. On 1 March his keeper tried to feed him 'corrosive sublimate' (mercuric chloride) mixed with his hay, which Chunee wisely declined. In musth, typically, male elephants are, anyway, anorexic. They have other things on their mind than the day's hay.

The redcoats were called in. Two soldiers, from Somerset House (across the way) came, took up a point-blank firing position, and loosed 152 musket balls into their target. Chunee is reported to have knelt, at his keeper's command, to receive the fusillade. One rather doubts it, but it makes a pretty and rather pious picture:

Chunee Agonistes

British bullets may have won the day against Napoleon's Imperial Guard at Waterloo, but they didn't work on Chunee. In the end the musketeers, and handlers, had to stab him to death with long poles with sabres attached to them. Cold steel.

All this was happening with members of the public attracted by the sound of gunfire (the muskets were single-shot muzzle loaders, and the volleys went on, intermittently, for half an hour with calls out for more ammo) and – worse still – members of the press, whose newspaper offices were only a few hundred yards away. It was headline news. To spare the sensibilities of the public it was given out that it was toothache which had driven Chunee into his madness. Drastic dentistry, one might think.

As Altick drily puts it: 'As soon as the shooting was over and the elephant lay huge and silent in the blood-spattered wreck of his den, Cross understandably allowed his concern for his ledger books to overrule his feelings and admitted the public, at the usual charge, to view the grisly scene.'[9]

There was the trickier problem of disposing of 5 tons of fast-decaying elephant meat, bones and skin – preferably for profit. Thank God for the small mercy that it was freezing March. The Bow Street magistrates were quick to instruct Cross to dispose of the remains in a sanitary way, to safeguard public health. He had a week or so to do it. The magazine *London Society* chronicled the dissection, division and disposition of Chunee's mortal remains.

The dissection of Chunee was a mighty labour: the body was raised by a pulley to a cross-beam, and first flayed, which it took twelve active men near twelve hours to accomplish. Next day (Sunday), the dissection was commenced, Mr. Brookes, Mr. Caesar Hawkins, Mr. Herbert Mayo, Mr. Bell, and other eminent surgeons being present; and there, too, was Mr. Yarrell, the naturalist, to watch the strange operations. The carcase being raised, the trunk was first cut off; then the eyes were extracted; then the contents of the abdomen, pelvis, and chest were removed. When the body was opened, the heart—nearly two feet long, and eighteen inches broad—was found immersed in five or six gallons of blood; the flesh was then cut from the bones, and was removed from the menagerie in carts. Two large steaks were cut off and broiled, and declared, by those who had the courage to partake of them, to be a fine relish. Spurzheim, the phrenologist, who was present, was anxious to dissect Chunee's brain, but Mr. Cross objected, as the crown of the head must then have been sawn off. The skin, which weighed 17 cwt., was sold to a tanner for 50/.; the bones weighed 876 lbs.; and the entire skeleton, sold for 100/., is now in the museum of the College of Surgeons, in Lincoln's Inn Fields.[10]

Cat and dog meat suppliers were traditionally called in when a large animal (too large to throw in the gutter or the Thames) died – pets being less fussy about putrefying flesh. Sometimes, one must suspect, meat traders followed the gothic example of Sweeney Todd. Who, to this day, knows what is in a meat pie or hamburger?

Skeletal Chunee

There is no question that in death Chunee was a huge boon to veterinarian and zoological science, dying, as he did, near any number of metropolitan institutions devoted to the 'March of Mind' (not least London University – now known as University College London – set up that same year). There were general lamentations and criticism in *The Times* about Cross's care of his livestock. Bad poems were penned and a play was put on at Sadler's Wells dramatising the event, *Chuneelah; or, The Death of the Elephant at Exeter 'Change*. One is told it had a good run.

The grisly end of Chunee was an important event for Jumbo, forty years later. It proved, beyond question, you could not keep wild animals in converted shop premises for commercial gain – however eager the paying public might be to see them. There had to be regulation and some other arrangement. The explosion of research that Chunee's massive cadaver inspired led, as day follows night, to the highly regulated establishment of the Zoological Society of London, a few months later, in Regent's Park. It would exfoliate, at a later date, into London Zoo, which would be Jumbo's home for 17 years (oddly the same period of time Chunee had spent in Exeter 'Change). Sometimes change needs 152 bullets. But for twenty years the ZSL, mindful of Cross's money-grubbing menagerie, was chary of paying customers. Until 1847 you could only see the animals in the ZSL enclosure with a signed 'order' costing a shilling. The hindrance was a direct consequence of the shameful things that had happened at Exeter 'Change.

What was left of Cross's menagerie went to the ZSL when he sold up, as he did in short order. The 'Change itself was pulled down in 1829. The Strand Palace Hotel now stands where the Royal Grand National Menagerie once stood (do guests, one wonders, hear mournful spectral trumpetings, and faint gunshots, of a late-February night?). Chunee's skeleton came to a sad end in the 1941 Blitz. A direct hit destroyed it, along with most of the Royal College of Surgeons' Hunterian Collection of unusual bones. Shot in life, bombed in death. There should be a very blue plaque for the sad, much-loved, hugely abused elephant.

The death of Chunee left a lasting wound on the English psyche. Young Abraham Bartlett, the man with direct charge of Jumbo thirty years later, when he became superintendent of London Zoo, was physically present at the slaughter of Chunee, and was traumatised by it for the whole of his life. Much as he loved wild animals, he would always be a stickler for propriety in the care of them and, above all, taking no risks.[11]

Dickens, I'm fairly sure, was also there. He was fifteen years old and all eyes and ears for anything that was going on in London. His *Sketches by Boz* essay 'Gin-Shops', written virtually on the tenth anniversary to the day of Chunee's execution, opens:

> It is a remarkable circumstance, that different trades appear to partake of the disease to which elephants and dogs are especially liable, and to run stark, staring, raving mad, periodically. The great distinction between the animals and the trades, is that the former run mad with a certain degree of propriety – they are very regular in their irregularities. We know the period at which the emergency will arise, and provide against it accordingly. If an elephant runs mad, we are all ready for him – kill or cure – pills or bullets, calomel in conserve of roses, or lead in a musket-barrel.

The details in that last sentence (calomel is mercurous chloride, which is very similar to the poison unsuccessfully offered to Chunee), and the remark about 'periodic madness' suggest to me that young Charles either saw the shooting or was an eyewitness to some part of the aftermath. What is more significant is that it imbued the image of the elephant for him with indelible sadness. It surfaces in the wonderful description of Coketown, in Dickens's *Hard Times* (a novel, on one of its many levels, about travelling circuses and the animals in them):

> It was a town of red brick, or of brick that would have been red if the smoke and ashes had allowed it; but as matters stood, it was a town of unnatural red and black like the painted face of a savage. It was a town

of machinery and tall chimneys, out of which interminable serpents of smoke trailed themselves for ever
and ever, and never got uncoiled. It had a black canal
in it, and a river that ran purple with ill-smelling dye,
and vast piles of buildings: full of windows where there
was a rattling and a trembling all day long, and where
the piston of the steam-engine worked monotonously
up and down, like the head of an elephant in a state of
melancholy madness. It contained several large streets
all very like one another, and many small streets still
more like one another, inhabited by people equally like
one another, who all went in and out at the same hours,
with the same sound upon the same pavements, to do
the same work, and to whom every day was the same as
yesterday and to-morrow, and every year the counterpart of the last and the next.[12]

'Melancholy madness': the state of every elephant in
captivity. They 'weave' and 'nod' their heads, like pious Jews
'dovening'. It's an astute observation.

What happened on 26 February 1826 was momentous.
With the death of Chunee – and the huge publicity (not to say
disgust) it provoked – the exhibition of animals in England
split into science-based zoos and entertainment-based circuses.
If you wanted to see animals you went to the former. If you
wanted to see animals perform you went to the latter. Jumbo,
when he arrived, would preside, majestically, over both worlds.

The Many Lives of Jumbo

He was not born 'Jumbo', of course, and he would not acquire that immortal, but intrinsically enigmatic, name for many years. 'The Towering Monarch of His Mighty Race, Whose Like the World Will Never See Again', as P.T. Barnum would call him, began life as a motherless runt, lucky not to end up in a stewpot or eaten alive by desert crows. His remarkable career, from waif to monarch, is symbolic of many things in Victorian life – not least 'rising' in the world. In Jumbo's case, top of the world. Or, at least, top of the big top.

Baby Jumbo's exact place and date of birth is vague. He might, as regards the genealogical record, have been brought in by the stork, from who knows where, like his namesake Jumbo Jr in the film *Dumbo*. His birthdate is most reliably put as sometime in early 1860, or shortly thereafter. The place was indeterminately what was borderland Abyssinia and the Sudan and is now Eritrea. It was, in 1862, a terra incognita visited only by the occasional white hunter, merchant or explorer. They too, legend had it, might end up in a stewpot. It is not a safe place to visit today: you won't find it in the Sunday travel supplements. It is of significance to Jumbo's later career – and his preservation – that this was a region in which France had a colonial interest. It was French money, and the channels it grooved, which rendered him worth keeping alive over the first parlous year of his babyhood captivity.

Elephants, in their natural habitat, roam in loosely organised herds with complex social, linguistic and gender systems which, to this day, are not entirely understood. Jumbo belonged to the more far-ranging of the species, the African branch of the twin family of surviving proboscidea. The other branch was the more docile, smaller eared, smaller tusked, Asian elephant, long a drudge in the service of mankind. *Loxodonta Africana* (the first word means 'slanting teeth', ie. tusks) are not by nature servile and, in Jumbo's day, were commonly believed to be as savage as they were massive. They are, by all accounts, more aggressive and less easily trained. But that may be because unlike the Asian variety they have not been bred for thousands of years for docility and as beasts of burden. Poodles, one recalls, were once hunting dogs.

To the untrained Western eye, the differences are minimal. An elephant is an elephant is an elephant. In the Johnny Weissmuller Tarzan movies (one of my childhood comforts) the apeman hero is always shown alongside or astride amiable Asian elephants – identifiable by their ears (although in some of the films fake ears were draped over the beasts, and fake tusks stuck on – no more of a con than Tarzan's Gillette-smooth chest and chin). Zoological exactitude was not one of Hollywood's strengths at this period, although they did their best and it was good enough for Colchester, circa 1950.

African ferocity (viz Hannibal and his thirty-seven war elephants, which almost brought down Rome) can be harnessed, but for most armies of antiquity it was more trouble than it was worth. Darius's spectacular defeat by Alexander, despite his massed elephant brigades, did not help the animal's military reputation. Rome, after Hannibal had shaken the pillars of its empire, tried them out but chose not to develop them as a central element in its formidable arsenal. Elephants did not, for example, replace the Roman phalanx in the same way that the tank, after 1918, replaced cavalry. But on occasion they could be used to terrify the enemy (as at Colchester, in AD 34).

The author of the classic study of war elephants, John M. Kistler, argues fiercely against the received view that, as Field Marshal Montgomery argued, they are and always have been 'monumentally futile' in any real war, and about as much use as the guardsman's bearskin when the cannon begins to roar.[1] Elephants have indeed won battles – particularly the African elephant (a whole book's worth is chronicled by the partisan Kistler). But, reviewing all the evidence, it seems that their fighting prowess is most useful in battle against each other in their natural habitats.

Jumbo's sub-variety of African elephant is deemed the earth's largest surviving land mammal. Despite all the hype, during his years with the American circus magnate Barnum, Jumbo was never the world's largest individual elephant. In fact, for a fully grown African male, he could be thought stunted. No Jumbo in the Mr Universe sense. Bulls a full foot and a half taller have been recorded in the wild. Jumbo's weight, however, was a full ton and a half more than it would have been had he been obliged to forage for himself in the wild. The African elephant is routinely described as 'lank', and 'lean' for its size. The public's love of giving Jumbo buns and lack of the activities his frame was designed for (finding food, fighting, sex) was the reason. He was obese: Jumboish in the Billy Bunter sense.

Without firearms the calibre of artillery, the elephant, of any species, is not easily hunted. Even with a weapon like Ernest Hemingway's .577-caliber Nitro Express (it weighed 16 lb), or Theodore Roosevelt's 'Double Adolph', elephants are, all accounts testify, hard to bring down. When charging, a mature animal moves quickly and anything other than a precisely placed shot will not stop them. And the nineteenth-century hunter in that situation usually only had one chance. The huge recoil from the gun, and tricky reloading, made it do or die. Many did die. The life expectancy of the 'great white hunters' who specialised in elephant quarry, when that manly profession was still revered as heroic rather than genocidal, was estimated at twenty-nine years – although a surprising number of them survived to write slaughterous books.

In the books and testimonies of these elephant hunters (see Samuel White Baker, or the hunts described by the old Africa hand H. Rider Haggard in his novels – particularly the elephant massacre in chapter eight of *King Solomon's Mines*) the details of every single engagement – even where lifetime 'bags' were in their hundreds – were remembered in minute and precise detail; etched, one presumes, on the memory by fear, thrill and risk. Moments of truth, every one of them.

On open ground, like the grassy plains (savannahs) and desert spaces, interspersed with trees (bush) and glades, where Jumbo was born and lived free for a pathetically few months, it was less fiendishly difficult for hunters lacking fire-arms to kill elephants. Horses, with their superior speed and mobility, could be used. The killing of savannah elephants had been brought to a high art by the Hamran tribes, in the region where Jumbo originated. Their killing techniques rank as the most sophisticated humanity has come up with before the widespread availability of the elephant gun. Who knows, those techniques may have been handed down and refined, generation to generation, from when cavemen first went up against the mammoth.

The Zulu warrior going into the bush with his shield and spear to kill the lion that would make him a man, had it easy compared with the aggageer, with only a two-edged sword and a horse, facing 5 tons of armour-plated, tusked, animal charging towards him at 30mph with slaughterous intent, and a brain larger than a human's and quite as capable of thinking tactically.

Bullfighters who aim for the heights, one is told, train with cows. The reason being that a cow defending her calf keeps her eyes on her human opponent when charging him with deadly intent. Bulls lower their heads to make a better strike with their horns. So too, hunters' lore had it, the most dangerous elephant was a cow with her calf – loving offspring nursed and nurtured for at least two years, and kept always within a few yards to be taught, over that long period of infant care, the ways of the elephant. Mother elephants were wired to protect their young at all costs – even their own lives. It was in a vain attempt to protect him that Jumbo's mother died.

There were brutal methods to kill elephants used in more densely vegetated environments than the Hamrans'. Pit-falls, for example, or setting fire to the woods in which the animals were lurking in order to ambush them with barrages of spears and arrows in their panicked flight from the flames. The Hamran aggageers who captured Jumbo were, by contrast, veritable artists of elephanticide.

The first white man to see Jumbo, something he liked to boast about all his long life, was the explorer, big-game hunter and prolific author, Samuel White Baker (1821–1893). Nicknamed the 'Victorian Nimrod'[2] Baker was himself a famed elephant killer – he had picked up the craft in the wet jungles of Ceylon. The African elephant, particularly in dry habitats, was tougher, and more dangerous prey by far

– something immortalised by a picture of Baker himself in flight from *Loxodonta Africana*.

The Great White Hunter takes flight

Like all great white hunters (and unlike native hunters) Baker was as interested in conservation as in slaughter. He foresaw astutely the dangers of the 'civilisation' of which he was a harbinger. Before Europe became interested in colonising Africa's land and America in enslaving its people, the relationship of man and elephant had been pretty well balanced. Elephants had a good chance of surviving as a species. As Baker put it in *True Tales for My Grandsons* (1883), with the racist condescension of his age:

> Fortunately for the preservation of the elephant from complete extinction, it is not only a formidable antagonist, but its extreme sagacity enables it upon many occasions to avoid, or to escape from, the wily savage.

It was, in other words, a 'fair fight'. But what when the wily savage would be armed as potently as was Baker himself, with a Reilly 10 'elephant gun' with its 'half-pound shell and twelve drams of powder', or, more horrible thought, an AK47? 'Sagacity' and the thickest of hides are no defence against a weapon firing 600 high-velocity 7.62 armour-piercing rounds a minute, so simple that a child can handle it. And they do. Horrors still to come.

It is to Baker that we owe the fullest and most vivid description of the world into which Jumbo was born, in which he nearly died, and from which he was rescued or – as others (including Baker) would see it – taken into elephant slavery as wretched as those African bipeds transported a hundred years earlier to the Americas.

Jumbo was very little game when the big-game hunter saw him in early 1861. In fact, he hardly qualified as game at all. At two years old he was barely 40 inches tall – smaller than a pit pony and barely larger than a great dane. Baker was not, as it happened, in Africa primarily to hunt elephants (although he always did so when the opportunity arose) but in pursuit of that Victorian chimera, the source of the Nile.

In Abyssinia, he fell in with a clan of Hamran Arabs, under their leader, Taher Sherrif, a great man among his people and, like Baker, a 'mighty Nimrod'. Jumbo was a captive of the clan, recently taken from his slaughtered mother, and was being kept penned, along with another baby elephant and rhino, ostriches and other wild animals. It struck Baker as odd from what he knew of the ways of the African Arab. The Hamran were not by nature or tradition Doctor Dolittles but Nimrods – hunters, not keepers, of animals. They had not the slightest interest in 'domesticated' beasts or, perish the thought, 'pets', any more than an eagle would want a canary in a cage to decorate its eyrie. It was a truth observable across the whole dark continent. As Baker observed:

The natives of Africa are peculiarly savage, and their instincts of destruction prevent them from capturing and domesticating any wild animals. During nine years' experience of Central Africa I never saw a tamed creature of any kind, not even a bird, or a young antelope in possession of a child.[3]

Elephants were traditionally valuable to the Hamran solely as sources of food and, with the edible flesh stripped off, semi-precious materials. As Baker records in *True Tales for My Grandsons*:

> The carcase of an elephant is a supply for an entire village; the fat is boiled down, the flesh is smoked and dried for a future store, the hide is prepared for the manufacture of shields; even the skull and the bones are hewn into pieces, from which the oily fat is extracted, and the tusks remain as trophies of the chase, one of the pair being the perquisite of the chief. In many places the tusks are used for making heavy armlets; and for trumpets.

For those on the very edge of civilisation (an ever-infringing edge in the nineteenth century) the tusks also represented a cash crop, ivory, for which there has been, since time immemorial, an international market. Baby Jumbo had no tusks and nothing else of obvious value to the Arabs. Why were they going to all the trouble of keeping him? And why was he penned in a menagerie or small zoo in which the owners had not the slightest zoological interest and tourists, like Baker, could only visit at the risk of their lives?

One thing was certain. He was an orphan. The techniques

by which Jumbo's mother had been killed are described, admiringly, by Baker. The Hamran used a hunting party of four. In this case Sherrif and his three brothers. Their horsemanship was non-pareil:

> Never were there more complete Centaurs than these Hamran Arabs; the horse and man appeared to be one animal, and that of the most elastic nature, that could twist and turn with the suppleness of a snake.[4]

When a likely beast was seen, usually by a waterhole with open space for manoeuvre, one of the party attracted its attention and incited it to charge. The second rider, with the most dangerous mission of the four, galloped at top speed from behind the quarry, armed with a heavy, two-bladed sword, and slashed at the back sinew of the elephant's hind leg, where the hide was thin. One well-aimed (and always lucky) blow would hobble the beast. The other two riders held back to assist if things went badly.

If things went well the elephant would stumble to the ground and bleed out in an hour or so, in a pool of some 500 litres of its own blood (a painless death, the more squeamish Baker was reassured). Once drained, cuts of the animal's meat were more easily carved off and its tusks removed as trophy or booty. This might, of course, be done while the beast was expiring if time pressed (not painless).

Alongside his new Hamran friends, Baker (armed, of course, with his trusty Reilly) killed his first African elephant, to add to the bag he also had to his name in Ceylon. It was thrilling – and dangerous. Baker (writing thirty years later) noted 'every one of the celebrated [native] hunters I was associated with in 1861 has since been killed by elephants'. Including,

one assumes, the virtuosic Sherrif brothers 'the most celebrated aggageers among the renowned tribe of the Hamran'.
It is quite likely Jumbo might have died, or killed, in a good
fight, had he been allowed to grow to maturity.

What Baker admired above all was the manliness of this
kind of engagement. The contest ennobled both elephant
and man: 'The hunting of Taher Sherrif and his brothers was
superlatively beautiful; with an immense amount of dash there
was a cool, *sportsman-like* manner in their mode of attack.'[5]

Baker claimed to have been the first white man to see the
'celebrated Jumbo' cowering in that strange Hamran menagerie, whose purpose would later be explained to him. He also
claimed to have noted how 'scrawny' and puny Jumbo was
– more so than his baby companion who was sturdier, but
who, ironically, did not survive the journey to the coast which
followed.[6]

'Runt Jumbo' who became 'King Jumbo' has entered the
mythology. But Baker was recollecting all this very late in
life, for his grandchildren, and hunters love to talk big when
yarning. How did Baker know *which* of those two baby
elephants (neither of whom yet had names or identifying
adult characteristics) died, and which survived? Despite the
mythology, common sense suggests it was the sturdier of the
two. But the myth is certainly more beautiful.

One thing is certain. Baker despised utterly what his
civilisation went on to do with 'Jumbo'. It was, in his view,
obscene, and wholly unsportsman-like to degrade an animal
which, in its natural habitat, had nobility – a nobility demonstrated to its fullest in the drama of the hunt, in which both
man and beast staked their lives. Better by far to have died
bleeding on the dusty plains of Abyssinia than to have
ended up like the following (the advertisement was drawn

Oscar and elephantine friend

during the period Oscar Wilde was a sensation in his visit to America):

A hundred and sixty years on, Eritrea is now one of the dark places of the earth. So dark that we do not care to think about it too much. The aggageer is as extinct as the dodo. The quotient of human misery, per capita of population in that godforsaken, perpetually war-torn, climate-change-scorched part of the world must be among the highest anywhere on the planet. The region had for eons teemed with elephants. The ancient Egyptians got limitless ivory from the region and the Ptolemaic kings got their war elephants from there in the third century BC. Baker had not the slightest difficulty in picking off an elephant in the few days he spent with the Hamran; they were thick on the ground.

No more. Between 1955 and 1999 there were no reported sightings of elephants in Eritrea. A tiny herd was spotted by helicopter at the turn of the millennium. It is described as a 'relic population' – a bleak phrase.

The Middle Passage and Middle Men

The 'middle passage' is what historians call the journey from African freedom to American slavery that tens of millions of African-Americans suffered. It's appropriate to the little African Jumbo's experience over the next wretched months of his life. Why the Hamran were bothering to create little zoos in the desert had perplexed Baker. Twenty years earlier the only reason for the Arabs keeping a baby elephant would have been as foodstuff, young elephant having, presumably, the same preferable taste that lamb has to mutton, or veal to beef. Jumbo would have been meat stored temporarily in a living larder – himself.

It was explained to the white hunter that the Arab hunters had been commissioned to gather the menagerie for a market so far away it could, for them, have been in the stars. They were getting into the export business: specifically the world animal trade. Railways and steam travel at the coast had made animal export feasible. Obviously mature elephants, rhinos or giraffes are too large and dangerous even for modern transport systems. Babies and juveniles of the species were, however, manageable freight in 1860. But, being immature, they were more fragile. Moving livestock from the deserts of north Africa to Europe was a skill which would be learned by trial and error – error meaning animal death. Jumbo was a small elephant, but a large guinea pig.

It was all down to new patterns of supply and demand. Menageries displaying exotic foreign species had previously been the exclusive privilege of the kingly, the aristocratic rich and the vulgar rich – lords of creation. The Jardin des Plantes, where Jumbo was ultimately destined, had begun as a royal menagerie in Paris. It was no more a zoo, or wild animal park, in the modern sense, than Marie Antoinette's Petit Trianon, with its little lambs, represented a serious effort at sheep herding. This line of trophyism continued in such bizarreries as the Rothschild wild animal park at Tring (the mega-rich owner liked to perambulate in a zebra-drawn carriage) and William Randolph Hearst's exotic animals grazing the hills round San Simeon. Among them, the castle historian tells us were:

Lord Rothschild takes the air

Several species of African and Asian antelope, zebras, both Bactrian (two-humped) and dromedary (one-humped) camels, sambar deer from India, red deer from Europe, axis deer from Asia, llamas, kangaroos, ostriches, emus, Barbary sheep, Alaskan big-horned sheep, musk oxen, and yaks. As many as four giraffes were kept in a small pen located next to the road.[1]

There was, however, another kind of menagerie developing in mid-nineteenth-century Europe: 'people's zoos' – rougher establishments that still had something of bear-baiting arena and freak show about them. They were owned by entrepreneurs, in it for the money, not kingpins and big shots. They catered to the general, entrance-fee-paying populations of towns and cities. The pioneer in the growth of this kind of menagerie for the people was Claus Hagenbeck, the son of a Hamburg fishmonger who had discovered that he could earn a few extra pfennigs buying and selling seals, brought in at the same harbour where his fish were landed. People would even pay to see them, he discovered, and he added a polar bear to his stock. If nothing else, it got rid of the day's unsold fish. The business grew fast from there on and Herr Hagenbeck was soon supplying the zoos which were springing up in European cities.

Claus's son Carl (1844–1913), deciding against the fish option, left school at fifteen to take over the family import of exotic animals. His first major success, aged sixteen, was with an African elephant which he brought to Hamburg, from the Sudan, in 1860. The species was so rare as to enjoy quasi-unicorn status. Carl had already formed what would become a long association with an Austrian animal trader with a name as exotic as his merchandise, Lorenzo Casanova.[2]

Casanova was based in the Sudan – Jumbo-country. He had moved into Africa after his dog and monkey show were destroyed by a disastrous fire at the St Petersburg Imperial Circus in January 1859. Everyone was well insured (Aviva, the British firm who had expanded their business into Russia, lost lots of roubles that year) and the circus was grandly rebuilt as the Mariinsky Theatre. Casanova, however much money he received from the British insurance firm, didn't have anything to show off to the public, and dogs and monkeys take a long time to train, so off he went to Africa to re-stock and, tentatively, try his hand at an export business in the commodity he knew best: exotic animals. Jumbo would be part of Casanova's first major venture in his new line of work. What he and Hagenbeck were doing was laying the tracks for a new trade route which would grow explosively over the next few decades and which would, eventually, seriously deplete Africa's livestock. That bothered no one in the early 1860s, least of all those who stood to make money out of the trade.

Casanova's initial consignment included a range of 'exotics' – rhinos and giraffes, for example. But his two *Loxodonta Africana* were of particular interest. Asian elephants were old news in Europe. They had been around for decades. Africa was still the dark continent. Its elephants were not merely physically larger; they were believed to be the most savage animal on earth. In the Great Exhibition of 1851 at Crystal Palace a stuffed African elephant (the best England could come up with for fifteen years) attracted as much interest as the plaster-of-Paris dinosaurs, and considerable chagrin. The London Zoo, in existence now for 25 years, didn't have one. Why not? Why did the greatest nation on earth have to make do with an upholstered elephant?

During the early months of 1862 Jumbo travelled and voyaged farther than any African elephant ever had before. One pictures Jumbo's transcontinental route like one of those moving dotted lines on the map in an Indiana Jones movie. The first leg, in February 1862, was from Sherrif's camp along dry riverbeds to the small entrepôt of Kassala. It was a former military encampment, occupied by the Egyptian army. The cavalcade took ten days covering about ten miles a day. This would be, for Jumbo, the least distressing part of the long journey.

Sherrif was the proprietor (for a week or two) of the first travelling circus in Africa. It comprised giraffes, rhinos, two elephants, camels, and a miscellany of smaller birds and animals. A sight to see. No one, of course, was there to see it and those who did would probably have made efforts to kill these conveniently tethered beasts and, failing that, their herdsmen.

Sherrif got most of his cargo through and handed it over to a Bavarian trader Johan Schmidt, acting for Casanova. The Arab probably got a measly $50 for Jumbo. From the whole consignment he would have got himself enough to purchase an arsenal of elephant guns and tilt his way any future desert battles with the animals of his desert plains. Casanova now took over. What it meant for Jumbo was an arduous six-week march across baking desert (by night) to the port of Suakin on the Red Sea. A large crew of hired handlers was required, and a whole herd of goats to supply the vast quantities of fresh milk the baby elephants and rhinos gulped down (and, of course, a lot of water and fodder for humans and beasts alike). It was now more like a cattle drive than a travelling circus. The other elephant died; Jumbo survived.

At Suakin, the animals were moved by steamer, in stiflingly inadequate cargo holds, up to Suez, then by train to their port of departure, Alexandria. There followed (again in cramped cages) the long sea voyage to Trieste and then another train journey to Dresden. It would have been prostrating for a tourist, with all Mr Thomas Cook's comforts; for a small confused elephant it was torment.

Casanova received an offer from young Hagenbeck for his animals, but turned it down. He chose instead to sell off the collection bit by bit. Jumbo went to Gottlieb Kreutzberg, the owner of Grand Menagerie – a small, but well-regarded, travelling zoo and circus. Like Casanova, Kreutzberg had been in St Petersburg in 1859 and lost all of his great cats there (he specialised in lions, jaguars, tigers and panthers). Like Casanova he routinely sold on some of his surplus-to-requirement live specimens to municipal zoos. He had a line in 'giant elephants', which featured centrally in his advertisements. But 'Miss Baba', his prize 'Riesen Elephant', had expired in 1857, after unwisely overindulging in frozen sugar-beet.[3]

Miss Baba the main attraction

Kreutzberg may have bought Jumbo as an investment. He was small now, but would, in time, grow into something impressive. But then, for some reason – probably a temporary cash-flow problem – Kreutzberg decided to sell him on. Jumbo was next acquired by the Jardin des Plantes. The date is uncertain – Paul Chambers hazards early 1863, which is plausible. The director of the Jardin claimed, for obscure reasons, to have received Jumbo from the Viceroy of Egypt. In fact, he had been shuttled around between at least five different owners in a year, none of whom had any long-term interest in him, other than his sale value.

Without getting too anthropomorphic about it, it was a traumatic and formative year for the baby elephant. And, indeed, anthropomorphism is not out of place. Pliny, the first historian to write at length about elephants, claimed that 'of all animals, the elephant is closest to man in intelligence'. And closest to the man-child in its capacity to suffer. Many zoologists would agree. Baby elephants spend years in the close care of their mothers, during which time they pick up such useful knowledge as what their trunks are for. In very early childhood they simply whip the thing round like a nasal skipping rope, apparently, unaware of what its myriad sensors and complex organisation can do. Jumbo was probably still getting by on his mother's milk when she was killed.

Elephants are, recent zoology has suggested, quite capable of 'grief'. How grievous would it be to see your mother killed, before your eyes, in the way the ruthless Hamran did their business; bleeding slowly to death, grunting pathetically, shrieking as her tusks were sawn off, as her calf wailed. And then chunks of her, cooked and devoured, within a few yards of her now motherless calf a few hours later, her maternal odours clearly identifiable to nasal membranes infinitely more sensitive than those of the human nose. Hannibal Lecter could not devise more ingenious torture. All the early evidence suggests that

Jumbo never received what Konrad Lorenz calls the necessary 'imprinting' which an intelligent animal species needs to find its animal identity.[4] In other words, Jumbo did not know he was an elephant. An existential quandary which, one suspects, he never cleared up; near human though his brain was.

Alone, losing even his sole companion (probably eaten as well), he was driven by whip and cudgel through unfamiliar terrain and even more unfamiliar locomotive systems, closely confined for long periods. Add it all together and what one assumes is that Jumbo was 'broken'. In two senses. He was broken in the way a bucking bronco is tamed by a horse breaker, brutalised into docilities and obedience alien to his animal nature. He was also broken in the sense one uses the phrase 'a broken man'. He was neurotic and persistently self-harming. He would, in later life, grind his tusks against the wall of his cell at night, until he had only stumps to grind. By day, for the bulk of his adult life, he was a 'pet'. Children who gave him buns fondly believed this was his true, inner nature: the gentle giant. But it wasn't. It was what he had been deformed into.

In his natural habitat, Jumbo, like other young males, would have broken away at some point from the herd, rejoining it only to pair and fight any competitor bull who came between him and his chosen dam. Such bull elephants are not pets. It's instructive to read, at length, Martin Meredith's description about what a bull elephant is when allowed to be what he is:

> On a hunting trip in Southern Tanzania Mike Carroll witnessed a fight between two bulls of similar ferocity. Starting as a scuffle, it developed into a deadly duel. Again and again, the two bulls charged at each other, inflicting deep wounds. With their tusks engaged, one

bull gave a mighty twist with his head, managing to break off one of his opponent's tusks. 'One tusk' struggled on, bleeding heavily from wounds to his chest, but the fight was now uneven.

Suddenly he dropped his head, turning it at the same time, thus aiming his tusk at his opponent's throat. Dropping his head allowed his opponent's tusks to go high on his head, tearing a terrible gash above his eye and ripping a great hole in his ear. But that one tusk thrust home and caught his opponent in the throat, going deep. With a tremendous heave One Tusk raised his head, lifted the impaled bull off his front feet, and ripped a great hole in his neck. As he caught his balance his guard dropped, and again the one tusk went home, this time through the trunk and deep into the head. Both elephants went down on their knees.

The one-tusker immediately arose, tossed his head, and again thrust deep into the head of his opponent. With this blow the stricken bull went over on his side, feet flailing in the air. One Tusk quickly stepped around and repeatedly drove his tusk into the fallen bull's neck, all the while trumpeting and screaming.

Bleeding badly from chest wound, One Tusk continued to gore the dead bull for nearly an hour before moving off to a stream to drink. Climbing up a steep incline from the stream, he fell dead.[5]

Pets? But petdom was where Jumbo was headed. First, however, there would be a sejour at the Jardin des Plantes.

Jumbeau

The Jardin des Plantes was founded as one of Europe's royal menageries and is reputedly the oldest of them all. Sun-kings would certify their grandeur by receiving and giving, to their solar counterparts, exotic animals. It was living trophyism – and indirectly how the first elephant came to England. Their royal gardens confirmed their link with divinity – was not God the greatest menagerie keeper of them all? (And what, one wonders, happened to His Jardin des Plantes when Adam and Eve were kicked out?)

The Jardin des Plantes, at Versailles was constructed in the baroque style. It was circular with a fine pavilion at its centre and an array of carefully laid-out paths, enclosures, and terraced cages; it was beautifully unnatural. It was graced in 1775 with its first elephant and a two-horned rhino. After the revolution, when kings themselves became not merely an endangered but (in France) a wholly exterminated species the *jardin* was taken over by the revolutionaries who – in their enthusiasm for *liberté* – liberated the animals (except the exotics: even the most radical *sans-culottes* didn't want a two-horned rhino wandering around the streets). For a few weeks, some strange birds were doubtless seen winging across the Parisian skies and I'm sure the hawks feasted well.

In 1792, after the revolutionary mood had cooled somewhat, it was resolved to establish a people's zoo and an adjoining Museum of Natural History. The surviving royal animals formed its nucleus. The site was moved from Versailles to stand, as a municipal institution, near the present Gare du Nord. Napoleon's victories, and the neo-Roman public display which he encouraged, filled the Paris zoo with spoils of conquest. Whole collections of foreign countries were confiscated. 'Famous', the chronicler tells us, 'was the 23-month journey to Paris and arrival, 23 March 1798, of an elephant pair from the menagerie of Het Loo, seized by French forces from the Stadtholder of Holland, Willem V'. If, for Louis XIV, his Jardin des Plantes proclaimed his royal divinity for Napoleon (who took a particular interest in the establishment) it proclaimed his imperial potency.[1]

The Jardin proclaimed, even in its post-revolutionary location, its origins in its classic, geometrical *jardinière* layout. It was, in 1862, about as unlike a wild animal park as Versailles is unlike a giant teepee. The elephants were housed in the octagonal Rotunda – *La Rotonde* – for 'large herbivores', at the garden's centre. It had been commissioned by Napoleon himself and was the Jardin's oldest structure, designed to replicate the cross of the Napoleonic Legion of Honour. It was not designed for its residents. The herbivores, alas, were larger than their rotund habitation. Jumbo would be afflicted – after his three-year stay in Paris – with morbid claustrophobia all his life from his enclosure in *La Rotonde*.

The Jardin retained in the 1860s much of its original character as a place where exotic animals could be shown off in grand style. But it was also a scientific institution which sponsored high level research. Frédéric Cuvier, the most distinguished zoologist of his time, became warden of the menagerie in 1803. In this respect it shared a mission with the London Zoo – the place where Jumbo was destined to spend his happiest (least unhappy, that is) years. But the English establishment had begun its existence as the Zoological Society of London – not a monarch's playpen.

For twenty years only 'fellows' could look at the animals – it was first and foremost their laboratory. The fellows themselves were a scientific elite (Charles Darwin became a fellow in 1837). They did not want gawpers. This despite the fact that the public dearly wanted to gawp. In the first seven months of the ZSL's existence no less than 30,000 people paid the hefty fee of a shilling to purchase the signed 'orders' which would permit them to walk around the animal enclosure. It was a gold mine waiting to be dug.

The ZSL finally surrendered and opened itself to the public as a zoo in 1847. There were two reasons. The low-minded motive was to generate revenue; the high-minded motive was to educate a population woefully ignorant of animal biology. Public libraries were being established round the country with the same benevolent motives (fiction was largely banned as it was 'too exciting' for working people: it infuriated Dickens).[2]

It's a matter for zoological historians which of the two great metropolitan institutions, London or Paris, sponsored the most commendable research. But there is no question that the Jardin was ahead of its counterpart in devising, for the (paying) public, an animal theme park, designed to delight and entertain. Whatever the wellbeing of the animals. London retained a rather stuffier character – formaldehyde and do-goodism aromatised the place.

Research at the London Zoo – always its *raison d'être*, if you peeled everything else away – could be a dauntingly heavy business. Abraham Bartlett, the superintendent during Jumbo's long seventeen-year residence, recalls being called in as a young taxidermist in 1847, to skin the corpse of London's long-serving, much-beloved Asian elephant, Jack, for inspection by the pre-eminent animal anatomist of the age, Richard Owen (1804–1892). Owen was the man who invented the word 'dinosaur' and designed the model menagerie of them which still delights children (including mine, I recall, nostalgically) at Crystal Palace Park. Owen, one of the great unsung heroes of English science, was also 'prosector' for London Zoo, which meant he was charged with dissecting, or preserving (hence the taxidermist Bartlett) any animals of interest that died in captivity. As Owen's biography recalls:

> This gave him vast experience with the anatomy of exotic animals. It also caused him some domestic difficulties, since he had to do this work at his own house. His wife Caroline recorded in her diary how, one summer day, 'the presence of a portion of the defunct elephant on the premises' rendered the house so foul-smelling that she 'got R. to smoke cigars all over the house.'[3]

In other ways Jack's was an eventful post mortem. As Bartlett records the body was hoisted up but,

> by the accidental breaking of the tackle used in lifting the body of this ponderous brute I was nearly crushed to death, and Professor Owen, while endeavouring to remove the brain, so lacerated one of his hands against the jagged edge of the skull bones that an alarming and dangerous illness was the result; in fact it was thought for some time that his life was in danger. Since this event I have had considerable experience in skinning large animals.[4]

And, as it happened, caring for them better than his French counterparts when, twelve years later, he took over management of the London Zoo. Bartlett did not love elephants or any other wild animal. He was singularly unsentimental. But he regarded them as specimens, to be handled with care and respect, for the knowledge that could be extracted from them – during life and after death.

In the Parisian Jardin des Plantes, Jumbo was shamefully neglected and ostracised by man and beast. No one seemed interested enough to keep him in good condition, or even alive. The reason, manifestly, was that he was 'worst in show'. He was puny – belying the fearsome reputation of the African elephant – he was scruffy and his skin was disfigured by disease. Bits of him were actually rotting off. He was wholly unwilling to frisk and frolic and amuse paying customers. Or even come out, stand still, and be wondered at. He was neither terrifyingly large nor *chic*. All he seemed to want to do was cower in his uncomfortably small cell. Moreover, he cost a fortune to keep alive. The Jardin was acutely short of money and attendants at this period, and it had more comely elephants in its five-strong herd. Jumbo was a dud and a waste of money. The Jardin was in the business of showing animals, it was not a rest home for runts any more than the Folies Bergère (established in 1869) was a rest home for superannuated sheep.

Jumbo, at this early point in his life the ugliest of ducklings, was wholly upstaged by the Jardin's star attractions, Castor and Pollux, male and female respectively, who were everything that he wasn't. These two African calves named, archly, after the mythical twin brothers of Helen of Troy, delighted the Parisian population. They were thought to be siblings. Genealogy, as always with elephants bought from dodgy

The end of Jack

traders, was a bit hazy. It was hoped they might one day mate. Incest, after all, was common enough in Greek mythology.

More importantly, the elephant duo were what Americans call 'cute' and the French found *charmant*. They were described as being as 'playful as kittens', and as pretty and harmless as those little bundles of fur. Ladies delicately proffered them specially baked honey cakes called *plaisirs*, which were as delicately received. They were reputed to enjoy hearing patriotic songs and would jig to the *Marseillaise*. Children rode them, on improvised little howdahs. It was a groundbreakingly innovative use of elephants as contact entertainment. The brain behind it was a manager of the large herbivores, M. Devisme. Under his regime you did not merely view the elephants, you touched and interacted with them. Their rasping trunks rubbed your hand; you bonded. Ladies and children were specifically targeted and it was the wave of the future. Jumbo was no part of it. But he would be used to develop Devisme's innovations in the not too distant future. Assuming, that is, he survived the Jardin des Plantes.

Matthew Scott, the keeper sent to pick up the 'elephantine toddler' who would become the great love of his life, had his own, defiantly Anglo-Saxon explanation for why Jumbo had been so shamefully neglected in the Jardin. The French, goddamn their eyes, were a cruel race with no natural love of animals. As he recalled, years later, still fuming, after eighteen months' care by Devisme and his ilk: 'A more deplorable, diseased and rotten creature never walked God's earth. His condition was simply filthy. He had been in the care of Frenchmen for several years, and they either did not know how to treat the race of elephants, or culpably neglected his raising.'[5]

Of course the French knew full well how to treat the race of elephants and get the best out of them – the gambols of Castor and Pollux demonstrated that. As a rational choice, they had decided that French time and money was better invested elsewhere, giving the paying public what they wanted. They were not fools about animals, unlike the Anglo-Saxons, who could not even bring themselves to eat horse, frog or the delicious 'variety cuts' from those animals who did end up on their tables.

Despite national differences, money was still determining Jumbo's fate. The ZSL, and its scientists, dearly wanted an African elephant. They had Indian elephants aplenty – after all, the country owned India, where it was a thoroughly domesticated breed, insofar as elephants can ever be wholly domesticated. But they had never had one of the other breed. They made a bid for one of the Jardin's African elephants, which was accepted. What they offered in return was an Indian rhino. These animals were almost as common as rabbits in the subcontinent. Long-serving British officers there, with nothing to do since the Mutiny had been settled, would come back claiming 'bags' of two hundred or more (needless to say, it is now an endangered species).

The exchange, with the *douceur* of some cash, was accepted. So grateful was the Jardin des Plantes to get rid of this worthless lump of living meat that it threw in a couple of anteaters. The ZSL reciprocated by accompanying their rhino with some dingos, a pair of eagles and a possum – the small change of great zoos. But when they saw what they had bought the English institution must have regretted their rashness. It seems they did not look over the commodity they were buying – hence Matthew Scott's shock on first seeing it, after the deal was clinched. It was the old pig-in-a-poke trick – and it was a very tatty pig which the ZSL acquired. As Scott, the junior keeper who was sent over to collect Jumbo, later recalled:

> When I met him in France, I thought I never saw a creature so woe-begone. The poor thing was full of disease, which had worked its way through the animal's hide, and had almost eaten out its eyes. The hoof of the feet and the tail were literally rotten, and the whole hide was so covered with sores, that the only thing I can compare it to was the condition of the man of leprosy spoken of in the Bible.[6]

Scott was thinking of the apostle after whom he was named and whose gospel was drummed into him at Sunday school:

> When he was come down from the mountain, great multitudes followed him.
> And, behold, there came a leper and worshipped him, saying, Lord, if thou wilt, thou canst make me clean.

And Jesus put forth *his* hand, and touched him, saying, I will; be thou clean. And immediately his leprosy was cleansed.

The elephant, soon to be Jumbo, had found his saviour – and he was English. Scott had no previous experience in dealing with elephants, but it was love at first sight. Had he not appeared on the scene, to become Jumbo's mahout and surrogate 'mother' (Scott's own term), Jumbo would probably not have lasted more than a few months.

A long feud between Bartlett, the superintendent, and Scott, the keeper, with Jumbo at the centre would simmer over the next decade and a half. At this stage, the two men acted in concert to save Jumbo's life. As Bartlett recalled in his memoir, *Wild Animals in Captivity*, Scott brought Jumbo to the zoo on 26 June 1863. They travelled by boat and boat-train (the luggage van) to Waterloo (the name would have given the Francophobic Scott a little patriotic thrill). Then, Jumbo being too big for a cab or a horse-drawn cart, they walked through the London streets to Regent's Park.

It was, the newspapers announced, the first African elephant to set hoof on English soil since Claudius's expedition. But in other ways it was not a day to remember in British zoological history. On arrival, the animal was, Bartlett recorded, 'about four feet high and in a filthy and miserable condition':

The first thing was to endeavour to remove the accumulated filth and dirt from his skin. This was a task requiring a considerable amount of labour and patience and was not to be done in the space of a moment. The poor beast's feet for want of attention had grown out of shape, but by scraping and rasping, together with a supply of good and nourishing food, his condition rapidly improved.

Improvement, however, brought its problems.

He soon became very frolicsome and began to play some very lively tricks, so much so that we found it necessary to put a stop to his gambols, and this we accomplished in a very speedy and effectual manner. Scott and myself, holding him by each ear, administered to him a good thrashing. He quickly recognized that he was mastered by lying down and uttering a cry of submission.[7]

An entirely Victorian proceeding. As any *paterfamilias* (or father of the zoo) would affirm: spare the rod and spoil the elephant. In fact, the rod used to 'master' the elephant was cruel, and kept out of public sight, as was the whipping –necessarily brutal because even a young elephant's hide is so thick (circus hands routinely use sledgehammers, one is told). The rod used by handlers normally has a sharp spear at one end, which can be directed at some tender part of the anatomy, and a pointed hook, or 'gaff', at the other, which is used by riders or handlers to pull the inside of either ear or jab the creature to indicate which way it should move. Scott must have used one (inexpertly at this stage of his career, one assumes) in the amble from Waterloo to Regent's Park.

Bartlett's phraseology 'frolicsome . . . very lively tricks' suggests Dumboish friskiness and pranks but it was something very different. Paul Chambers, who has examined the ZSL archive, tells us that from the outset Jumbo was given to furious explosions of wrath in which he would charge at the walls of his cell (doubtless the whip, spear and hook warned him not to charge at humans). It caused the fabric of his stall regular damage. It became routine for the zoo's carpenters to be brought in of a morning to repair, strengthen and – as Jumbo began his phenomenal growth spurt – band with steel and iron the walls that confined him at night.[8]

The walls were continuously damaged, but so, more poignantly, was Jumbo. His tusks – the crowning glory of a fully-grown male of his species – were snapped off when he deliberately drove them into the bars of his cage. When they began to grow again (an elephant's tusks grow throughout life), he ground them against the walls. They looked what they were: stumps. Even in America they were worn down as fast as they grew – it was a kind of elephantine nail-biting, but much more painful.

The amount of self-inflicted pain in Jumbo's years at the London Zoo, despite all the hype and syrupy love of the English people, must have been phenomenal. But it was a thing of the night and all out of sight. From Bartlett's point of view (Scott evidently concurred) it had to be. If it ever became public it would be disastrous for the two of them:

When in this condition and in his house, none of the keepers except Scott dare go near him; but, strange to say, he was perfectly quiet as soon as he was allowed to be free in the Gardens. I was perfectly well aware that this restless and frantic condition could be subdued by reducing the quantity of his food, fastening his limbs by chains, and an occasional flogging; but this treatment would have called forth a multitude of protests from kind-hearted and sensitive people, and, in all probability, would have led to those concerned appearing before the magistrates at the police court charged with cruelty; and the result might have been very unfavourable and disastrous.[9]

In other words they would be prosecuted, but it had to be done to ensure that Jumbo did not run amok leaving a trail of infantile blood, crushed currant buns and pennies in his wake. The nocturnal 'overpowering' (as Bartlett euphemistically calls it) worked. By day, Jumbo was docile, calm, 'the children's pet'. It recalls that great Victorian monster – the literary image of schizophrenia – Dr Jekyll and Mr Hyde. In the light the good doctor, in the dark the savage monster.

Put another way, Jumbo was mad and so too were his two principal carers. They had, in public and by day, to go along with the popular image of jolly parent figures, with a 'frolicsome' five-ton pussycat to show off. Like Chunee, Jumbo was trained to do little tricks with Scott's bowler hat and take buns and pennies (the pastries for himself, the coppers for Scott) from little paws whose owners would remember it as a magic moment all their lives. Both Scott and Bartlett liked to be photographed in front of 'their friend', their relaxed posture expressing the fact that there was nothing whatsoever to fear from Jumbo: he loves us, he loves you, he loves the world. He

Burton's cramped elephant house

is happy. Bartlett released, for publicity purposes, innumerable stories to the press about the zoo's 'children's pet'. Meanwhile, out of sight, they were doing things which could, as Bartlett says, have led at the least to dismissal and at worst to prison. It was the traditional Victorian hypocrisy, but, given the situation, it was necessary.

Chambers ascribes Jumbo's chronic madness to festering claustrophobia, incurred in the Parisian rotunda. There is surely something in this. When he arrived Jumbo was impounded in the 'stables', designed in 1835 by Decimus Burton, the great exponent of 'exhibition architecture'.

It was wholly inadequate. The newer elephant house, designed by Anthony Salvin and constructed in 1869, was barely more accommodating. As Chambers wryly notes, Jumbo 'warmed' his new home the only way he knew how, by hurling his tonnage furiously against its walls.

Both these quarters were what North Tower was to Prisoner 105, Dr Manette, in Dickens's *A Tale of Two Cities*. They drove him mad and kept him mad. But manageably mad.

Salvin's cramped elephant house

The truth was, London Zoo would not solve its 'elephant accommodation problem' until 2001, when it came up with the obvious solution: no elephants. You cannot, experience in zoos suggests, safely fence them in. Breaking a five-year-old animal, 'civilizing' it, as described by 'Elephant Bill' (J.H. Williams, who came by his expertise in the 'elephant corps' of the Fourteenth Army in Burma in World War Two), is a long and arduous task and needs skill. Claustrophobic enclosure (the 'crush') plays an important part, as does tethering – but only as a transitional phase in the training/domestication process. It is not a permanent condition.[10]

No one at London Zoo had the necessary elephant-handling skills in 1865. But they were lucky. So much ill treatment had Jumbo received that, one assumes, there was no real elephant spirit left in him – except in his pathetic self-punitive outbursts in the darkness of his cell in which only he incurred hurt. Try breaking your incisors on a stone or bashing your head against a wall as hard as you can. No sane person would do it, but this, presumably was Jumbo's control mechanism. Self-harming is what it is called nowadays and it is familiar to any prison warden. Prisons, one darkly suspects, condone it because self-harming is self-controlling. Cut your arms and you won't cut the warder's throat.

Like Winston Smith at the end of George Orwell's *Nineteen Eighty-Four* ('We shall squeeze you empty, and then we shall fill you with ourselves', says O'Brien) Jumbo had been 're-educated', as totalitarian states impudently call their programming procedures. Oddly, like Winston, rats came into the programme. One of the things impeding Jumbo's recovery after his arrival was the fact that at night rats came and gnawed at the raw, rotting flesh around his hooves.

Zookeepers testify that keeping rats away from elephants

is a chronic problem. And poor Jumbo's diseased extremities had the attraction of rawness. Rats gnawing at their hooves can, apparently, kill elephants. That may be the origin of the legend that elephants fear the mouse – something first propagated by Pliny in his otherwise well-informed treatise on the elephant. It's untrue, but they quite likely fear what look like unusually large mice.

One of the structural problems of zoos is that they are veritable paradises for rats. The zoo environment provides innumerable places for them to burrow and stay safe. Poison is too dangerous to the specimen animals and birds to disperse around too promiscuously – particularly inside cages – and there are vast amounts of droppings from the animals to keep the rat population burgeoning (zoo animals, perversely, are universally disinclined to mate). It is an age-old problem that, apparently, not even the modern state-of-the-art zoos have solved. In 2004 the whole staff at the Paris zoological gardens in the Bois de Vincennes walked out on strike because there were so many rats scampering around the place. Human feet were at risk.[11]

Jumbo, it is recorded, had a phobia of rats all his life. His life, hitherto, had been one long Orwellian Room 101 and they were the crowning horror, though he had a larger 'cage' than that threatening Winston. But it served up the same unbearable terror, one can surmise. Jumbo, one guesses, dealt with his many terrors, like Winston, by doublethink, controlled madness and desperate love of Big Brother – in this case Matthew Scott. If so, it would explain some other things. One of the many mysteries about Jumbo's life is that under the ostensibly less caring regime of Barnum and Bailey (as Barnum's outfit eventually became known) he seems to have outgrown his night terrors.

Circuses have a long history of mistreating animals and they have none of the official disciplinary control ordinances that metropolitan zoos have. Bartlett – despite what he later did with Jumbo – was always reluctant to sell any unwanted animal to a circus as they would mistreat the animal, he believed.

But Jumbo, on the basis of what one knows, was manifestly less disturbed during his two years with 'America's Greatest Showman'. No nocturnal, self-harming rages are recorded (although his tusks persisted in not growing – he still ground them). A number of explanations suggest themselves. A plentiful supply of tranquillising booze, companionship (Barnum had up to 50 elephants), more movement? Among all those changes of regime, one can add 'fewer rats'.

Circuses, not having fixed sites, had no resident, promiscuously breeding, rodent populations under the menagerie's feet. There were no rats at all in the 'Palace' railway car which Barnum supplied to his prize exhibit, in which he spent much of his time (and was killed getting into).

The Battle for Jumbo's Soul

Bartlett and Scott had pitched in manfully, shoulder to shoulder, to save Jumbo's life on his arrival at London Zoo. Abraham Bartlett was never a superintendent afraid of getting down on the shop floor, proud as he was of his elevated station in life. His years with the skinning knife made him very much a hands-on superintendent. But whatever camaraderie was generated by the 'save Jumbo' project soured and went rancid over the following years, degenerating into mistrust, loathing and eventually an open feud. It reached a pitch of crisis in 1881 when Bartlett found himself in two minds as to whether to shoot Jumbo or sell him to a circus. He probably felt the same about his turbulent keeper. (He eventually sold both of them to Barnum.)[1]

Jumbo, after his inauspicious first few months, quickly became the zoo's flagship specimen. Scott was, from their first encounter in Paris (less romantic, perhaps, than the phrase sounds) the elephant's 'mahout'. When the relationship 'takes' it establishes, elephant experts inform us, a bond as intimate as marriage, and quite as monogamous. One elephant, one keeper, till death do they part.

From the first night on, Scott regularly slept with Jumbo. The emotional/erotic dimension of their union is explored in

Emma Donoghue's short story, *Man and Boy*.[2] It can only be deduced from dry archival evidence, expertly sifted from Paul Chambers's research, but Donoghue's fiction rings true. There was something 'going on'.

A few months after Jumbo arrived at the zoo, Casanova supplied a 'wife', Alice, via an English middleman. She too was African – but named after the heroine of Lewis Carroll's recently published children's story. Carroll returned the compliment with an elephant episode (elephants the size of bees – using the trunk as an insect proboscis) in *Through the Looking-Glass* (1871) and the delightful nonsense verse which, like Dickens's 'elephant in a state of melancholy madness', captures that strange air of gloom ('grandmotherly', Orwell called it) which hangs perpetually over Jumbo's kind:

> He thought he saw an Elephant
> That practised on a fife:
> He looked again, and found it was
> A letter from his wife.
> 'At length I realize,' he said,
> 'The bitterness of Life!'

Bartlett describes Alice – perhaps some fizz put into him by the creator of Wonderland – with more than his usual vivacity:

> The African elephant 'Alice' was purchased of the late Mr. C. Rice (who at the time had an establishment in St. George's Street, E.) for the sum of £500. At that time she was under 4 ft. in height. She was very tractable. So small was she that it was suggested that she should be put in a cab and taken to the Gardens. Being anxious to remove her that same afternoon I determined to walk

her through the streets. This I managed in spite of the trouble and annoyance caused by a crowd of two to three hundred of the London mob, composed as a London mob usually is of a lot of dirty, ragged, noisy boys, and not a few of that nomad, the London rough, the curse to modern travellers about town. Notwithstanding these difficulties I reached the Gardens just as it was dark. Finding my dinner awaiting me, I introduced my companion 'Alice', who seated herself by my side at the table and evidently enjoyed the bread, apples, etc., with which I supplied her.[3]

Jumbo was now, to the world, a happily married man. Newspapers loved the idea, as did the visitors to the zoo, of the 'married couple' who were routinely brought out side by side – the biggest Darby and Joan in the world.

It was, of course, a complete sham. They were too young to mate, and for elephants the act itself is nasty, brutish and short. The only important relationship in Jumbo's life was, and always would be, the one he had with Scott. The relationship was permanently cemented when, in late December 1867, Jumbo fell very ill. The animal was, the veterinarians solemnly reported, at death's door. The zoo must prepare itself for the worst; Bartlett's hand twitched for his taxidermist's scalpel.

Scott demanded to be left alone with Jumbo and he moved in with the apparently expiring animal for two weeks over the holiday period. When he emerged, Jumbo was once again fit as a fiddle. How had it been done? Was Scott an English witch doctor? Rumours abounded. Scott, it was clear, had strange powers. He and Jumbo were 'known' (insider gossip confirmed it) to communicate via signals, sounds and vocables which only they could understand. Elephant language, zoologists currently researching the phenomenon confirm, is indeed strange, complex and beyond human hearing ('infra-acoustic') although elephants themselves pick up the 'silent thunder', as it has been beautifully called, over huge distances.[4]

Had Scott learned to speak elephant, Berlitz style, by closeness with his 'friend'? Did he have Svengali-like powers? What had actually happened in Jumbo's den? Scott fended off questions as to how he had done it with the facetious (or was it?) and punning answer: 'Bucketfuls of Scotch.' Mystery became mystique: Scott was 'special'.

Over the years Scott consolidated sole, and wholly unsanctioned, ownership of Jumbo's body and soul by virtue of the fact that, when the animal was in one of his 'moods', Scott was the only person who could approach him without risk of death or, worse than a keeper's death (something that when it happened was covered up), a scene in front of the public which would get sensational press attention ('Elephant runs amok in Regent's Park. Many dead,' for example).

Mahoutism – man-animal bonding – is common where elephants are used for war or hard labour, or, in a looser way, in circuses where there will be a designated handler. It is not the kind of thing a zoo finds easy to live with. The official mind sees employees as servants of the institution, not exclusive attendants of some cranky four-legged animal with whom they have a paranormal connection and who, in Scott's case, took it upon himself always to do what he thought right for 'his' animal.

Bartlett, a company man through and through (and the 'superior' in the firing line), saw things differently. He had, of course, a responsibility to Jumbo, to be balanced with his greater responsibility to the zoo, the ZSL, paying customers and, of course, Abraham Bartlett. He was an ambitious man.

But he found himself in an increasingly impossible position. He had the power to hire and fire and no one above him on the council would stop him. But infuriating and insubordinate as the man was, he couldn't fire Scott as he had so ruthlessly fired Scott's predecessor, an elephant keeper with thirty years' faithful service to the zoo, who committed some minor infraction. Scott was committing major infractions, but was untouchable.

If Bartlett did grasp the nettle and dismiss Scott there was the strong possibility that Jumbo, furious at the separation, would be uncontrollable and would have to be put down. And if Jumbo went, the zoo receipts would go down precipitously with him. There would be awful newspaper coverage, ugly questions from the governing council, complaints in Parliament, lamentations from everyone from the Queen down to the last little girl to give Jumbo a currant bun, and – at the end of it all – it might well be Bartlett who got the boot. The superintendent was frozen in a condition of paralytic fury. He could not 'superintend' because the keeper had 'kept' so cunningly well. Stalemate.

Who were these two men, embattled for a decade and a half over a pachyderm? Scott's life, until he met his elephant love, had been almost as bereft of the companionship of his own kind as Jumbo's life. He was born in 1834 and brought up the son of two humble servants on the estate of Edward Smith-Stanley, thirteenth Earl of Derby. Smith-Stanley fathered the fourteenth Earl of Derby, who was three times Prime Minister, but he himself had no interest in politics. He was by nature a passionate amateur zoologist and he lavished his considerable family wealth on the kind of menagerie which a certain kind of rich man has always loved. There are much worse things for rich men to do with their wealth.

Smith-Stanley's collection, located at the family seat, Knowsley Hall, in Lancashire, was spectacular. It was home to 1,272 birds and 342 mammals and it cost the equivalent of a million pounds a year in modern currency to keep the place going. He was constantly enlarging and varying his herds, unique specimens and aviary flock from the most enterprising and trustworthy explorers. He financed expeditions, was a scholar of modest repute and was for five years president of the Linnean Society. A man of great cultivation, he was the patron of the nonsense writer Edward Lear, with whom he shared a quirky humour about animals, when not presiding over the crusty Linneans. Lear was the creator of such imaginary animals as the elephantoid 'Dong with a Luminous Nose' and his omnium gatherum poem 'The Quangle Wangle's Hat' about the 'crumpetty tree', where animals even more exotic than those roaming the Derby acres, congregate, is a compliment to the proprietor of Knowsley. Lear also had a fine artistic eye for the elephant (the illustration below was done in 1871, at the height of the Jumbo craze).

Edward Lear does the elephant

Young Matthew Scott was observed to have, from earliest childhood, stronger relations with animals than humans. There were, to be honest, more interesting animals than humans around him as he grew up. He was the fifteenth child of seventeen. If one does the domestic mathematics there can have been little maternal or paternal warmth to go round to a brood that large. Scott left school at ten and would be a loner all his life, but resourceful, and – that favourite British word – plucky. The metaphor is derived from fighting cocks and, from his earliest years, Scott was a bird lover. Had Jumbo not come into his life he might well have gone on to be head keeper at the ZSL's aviary.

No relationship with a woman (or man) is recorded; Scott seems, from what scant evidence there is, to have been a zoophiliac. It's a rare condition, depicted with charm and humour in Gerald Durrell's delightful *My Family and Other Animals* (1956). Most of us casting our minds back to school will recall one or two among the pupils who were 'mad about animals'; they were not always the best of company.

While still a juvenile, Scott was taken on to work on the Derby estate – first in the aviary, then with the Earl's herd of elands (an elegant variety of antelope). His ability to bond with animals, to the exclusion of most things that preoccupy young males, was observed and approved and encouraged. It was useful.

When the thirteenth earl died in 1851, his successor had no interest in animals and simply wound down and sold off, or gave away the magnificent menagerie with brutal haste and applied himself to the important things in life. The elands trooped down to the London Zoo and Scott, now their chief herdsman, went with them; he was now seventeen years old. The zoo, still newly opened to the public at large, experienced a surge of visitors with the Great Exhibition of 1851; it was boom time in Regent's Park. Scott was given a wage of £40 per year with bed and board, and installed in one of the zoo's lodgings. The work was hard, but it was, by the standards of the day, a living wage and the job was manifestly what young Mr Scott desperately wanted to do in life. He is not recorded as having had an interest in anything apart from 'his' animals and the occasional drink.

Abraham Bartlett came to London Zoo, as its superintendent, eight years later, when he was in his late forties. In 1858, Scott was at the bottom of the heap and Bartlett was at the top. Bartlett's route to the top had been unorthodox. He had no university training; he was that archetypal Victorian thing, 'a self-made man'. He had been born in 1812 the son of a London barber ('tonsorial artist', as he preferred to put it). One of his father's clients, lived in the Strand by Edward Cross's Exeter 'Change menagerie – home of Chunee. Cross, an amiable fellow by all accounts, took to the young Bartlett and gave him free entrance to the show-rooms and cages whenever the little fellow liked. No shilling was required from Abe. As Bartlett recalled in his fragmentary memoir: 'Almost before I could walk, I was allowed to crawl about in the beast-room of that menagerie, playing with young lions and other animals that were not likely to harm me.'[5]

As he grew older, Cross offered him carcasses of dead animals. His father's business meant access to an array of barber's tools and a plentiful supply of some of the best hair in London, so he taught himself to skin and stuff animals as a hobby. At fourteen, Chunee's gory death by firing squad had a life-long effect on him. When he was old enough Bartlett was apprenticed to his father's trade and hated it. When he reached his majority, in around 1834, and was out of his articles, he threw away his barber's brush and went full time into the animal-stuffing business. He was supremely gifted as a taxidermist and was soon running his own business. There was at the time a huge 'parlour' market for British animals under glass (my grandmother, I recall, had a red squirrel inherited from her mother) and a growing demand for the stuffed specimens of larger and more exotic exhibits in municipal museums. The supply of dead carcasses from natural causes was unpredictable and, if delayed, putrefaction complicated things. Bartlett killed most of the smaller animals he went on to stuff. Customers did not complain, so long as the stuffed beast they ordered looked 'natural'.

Bartlett prospered, married and bought himself a large house in Camden – within walking distance of the ZSL. He did, as it happened, often walk there. He was a respected man among the fellows for his taxidermist expertise. His moment of glory, like England's, was the Great Exhibition of 1851 in which, as he complacently records:

> I was fortunate enough to be awarded the first prize for my specimens of taxidermy which I exhibited, viz – Eagle under glass shade, diver under glass shade (the property of her Majesty the Queen), snowy owl, Mandarin duck, Japanese teal, pair of Impeyan pheasants, sleeping Orang-utang, sun bittern, musk deer, cockatoo, foxes, carved giraffe, dog and deer; crowned pigeons; leopard and wolf.[6]

His *pièce de résistance* – for which the name of Bartlett will forever be revered among his stuffing craft – was a 'restored' dodo. Among his clients over the years were the British Museum, Queen Victoria and, most importantly, the ZSL.

He built up a sideline in live animals and those which he did not immediately need for business he sold on. Many bought for his knife escaped it (one hopes he used the newly invented chloroform – but he probably didn't) to live on in Regent's Park. He had built up a particularly warm relationship with David Mitchell, the secretary of the ZSL, who thought the world of him. Mitchell took advice from Bartlett, when the zoo opened to the general public as to what the admission charges should be. They obviously could not charge the shilling which the privileged 'orders' had cost in the days before 1847. Bartlett suggested a penny a day and sixpence on Mondays. It was a rock-bottom price but volume would make up for that. His sensible advice was taken.

Although he had nothing more than basic school education, his hands-on expertise (and friends in high zoological places) led to Bartlett being offered the superintendency of the zoological gardens in Regent's Park, London, in 1859. It was a pragmatic choice, in the 'best man for the job' Anglo-Saxon tradition, and, as it proved, he was indeed the best man. The position was worth £400 per year and came with a fine house. He was proud, as Victorian self-made men felt they had every right to be, of his rise in life. From barber's assistant to director of the finest zoo of the world. Around 'his' zoo he wore a top hat and tails, marking him out from the keepers (like Scott) in their bowlers and cutaway serge.

The difference between Scott and Bartlett boiled down to one thing. Scott had developed his remarkable skills with live animals, Bartlett with dead animals. This did not mean that Bartlett was cruel – he was not. He was severe on unnecessary mistreatment, or humiliation; he never forgot the horrors of Chunee's 'murder'. Philosophically he divided animals into those that could be domesticated, and those that were too savage to try to domesticate. Elephants, interestingly, he regarded as 'semi-domesticated'. He seems never to have been sure they really belonged in his zoo, but the proof was in the entrance tills – they were what the public wanted. He went along with it.

These two men would be at daggers drawn over the years of Jumbo at Regent's Park – 1865–82.

The Name's Jumbo

It was decided, small and scabby though he was, that Jumbo should go on display at once. The public was eager to see an African elephant and, if they were disappointed when they did, too bad. It was after they had stumped up the penny entrance fee. To begin with, Jumbo was just a standing exhibit – along with Alice or some Asian fellow inmate (there was one in the zoo with the memorial name 'Chunee').

It was necessary, even at this early stage, to find a unique, anthropomorphising name. This was traditional with elephants. There were usually so few of them in captivity, and they were so big, that any names stuck. For those close to them, 'identities' and 'characters' associated with the name would also stick.

Nomination is a big thing among humans. The Christian name involves one of the major ceremonies in the Church and it goes back to the Bible. The first task Adam is described as carrying out in the Bible is naming the animals – God's bountiful menagerie:

> And out of the ground the LORD God formed every
> beast of the field, and every fowl of the air; and brought
> *them* unto Adam to see what he would call them: and
> whatsoever Adam called every living creature, that *was*

the name thereof. And Adam gave names to all cattle, and to the fowl of the air, and to every beast of the field.

Of course *Elephas* must have been there among the noisy ruck. But since we don't know what tongue our primal ancestor used we are at a loss to know what Adam came up with for the (two presumably) elephantidae. 'Behemoth' is sometimes suggested. Creationists tie themselves in knots as to whether it would be possible, even on a slack sixth day of Creation, Saturday, to rattle off the new names of 30 million species, let alone without writing tools remember them.

Anyone who has had to come up with a name for their as-yet-unborn child will have been haunted by the conviction that names are, in some small part, destiny. One is willing a future on one's as-yet-nameless offspring. Research has shown, for example, that a disproportionate number of children forenamed 'Dennis' go on to become dentists. But the problem is that 'Jumbo' 'is a name which seems to have come from nowhere. It has provoked much owlish speculation as to provenance and origin. If, for example, you read Wikipedia you'll find the following confident statement: 'The London zookeeper association leader Anoshan Anathajeyasri gave Jumbo his name; it is likely a variation of one of two Swahili words: *jambo*, which means "hello" or *jumbe*, which means "chief".'

It fits. What doesn't fit is that Swahili was a tongue much in use among the lower hands at the zoo, some of whom, one suspects, could barely speak English. Nor can one find out anything about Anoshan Anathajeyasri (Professor Google is not the slightest help) or any evidence that he had contact close enough to the elephant to award him the name which would be entered on his documentation. And would the scabby runt, not long for this world apparently, who arrived at the Regent's Park in June 1865, have warranted the title 'chief'?

Elsewhere the name is as confidently asserted to derive from the phrase 'mumbo jumbo' – a compound associated with the incantations of African witch doctors. It's hard to see any relevant semantic connection. I, personally, dismiss it.

The truth of the matter is to be found in that incontestable fount of knowledge, the OED (*Oxford English Dictionary*). The entry on Jumbo has, heading its list of historical usage: '1823 "J. Bee" *Slang, Jumbo*, a clumsy or unwieldly fellow'.

'John Bee' (i.e. John Badcock) was the author of the magnificently entitled: *Slang. A Dictionary of the Turf, the Ring, the Chase, the Pit, of Bon-Ton and the Varieties of Life, Forming the Completest and Most Authentic Lexicon Balatronicum Hitherto Offered to the Notice of the Sporting World*. A very busy bee, to have sampled all those slangs. Badcock's lexicon of 1823 slang does indeed contain the word 'Jumbo'. The definition fits the young, unprepossessing calf much more neatly than Wikipedia's 'hail to the chief' thesis.

But not the least of Jumbo's accomplishments was to change the meaning of a word, as Badcock defined it. As he grew into grandeur, what the word 'jumbo' meant changed with him. No longer carrying associations of unwieldiness, it became synonymous with hugeness, geniality, above all cosiness. One felt safe in its orbit. Who, for example, would want to fly in a jet plane trailing the epithets 'clumsy' and 'unwieldy'?

There is a further mystery about elephant names which seems to run counter to the fact that they are so observably intelligent – the nearest in animal kind to us, Pliny plausibly asserts. And yet, as 'Elephant Bill' (J.H. Williams), who spent decades with the animals, tells us: 'The name given to a calf sticks to it for life, but it never *knows* its name, as a dog does.

The real reason why they are christened is so that men can talk about them to each other."[1] I said earlier that Jumbo did not know he was an elephant. Neither did Jumbo know he was Jumbo or why people kept making that particular sound in his presence.

Evolution or Intelligent Design?

Jumbo was very much entertainment for children and it was their pennies that primarily swelled the zoo's coffers so welcomely. But small children are not allowed into zoos unaccompanied by an adult (it's nicely turned on its head in the Coram's Fields little petting zoo in Bloomsbury into which, it is signposted, no adult will be permitted entrance unless 'accompanied by a child'). Like many of my parental kind I took my son, when he was a child, many times to the London Zoo and spent hours doing nothing, while he played and looked at the elephants (they were still there then) doing their wonderful tricks (he was too late for a ride), happy as all the birds in the air (and happier, one could not but note, than those luckless specimens in the abysmal Snowdon aviary). I would pass the time idly speculating. It was not unpleasant if the sun shone.

What, in Jumbo's day, did the thoughtful Victorian father think about during those long hours at the zoo, keeping one watchful eye on the apple of his eye? Evolution, one can plausibly surmise. 'How did all these animals, and how did I myself, "happen"?' Darwin's 1859 bombshell had put huge fizz into the science of zoology, and made it a matter of universal curiosity and wonderment. Much of his initial research was at the

ZSL, where he had been a fellow since 1837. People of a reflective cast of mind, post-Darwin, took a new and urgent look at the animals on display at Regent's Park. The whole question of what the universe was, and what they were, had been turned upside down by *The Origin of Species*. Some answers, it was forlornly hoped, might be forthcoming in those cages and enclosures.

Darwin himself used the elephant as a way of explaining some of the complex mathematics of evolution and science. Every species aimed, instinctively, to displace every other species and monopolise its environment. Why, given its generative habits, was it the elephant population, when left in a state of nature, static? Why weren't there either no elephants, or 19 million elephants trampling over the globe? How were these 'balances of nature' achieved?

The elephant is odd in that it can be drawn to support Creationist as well as Darwinian argument. Surely not even in its zaniest moments would 'natural selection' come up with something as unnatural as Jumbo, who looks as if he could fit in the *Star Wars* barroom scene without raising an eyebrow. It must have been intelligent design, surely. Milton was right: the elephant had been created in one of God's more whimsical moments – like the duck-billed platypus or the unfortunate dodo whom He absent-mindedly forgot to equip with wings.

And yet, evolution could also make a convincing case for Jumbo. True the proboscidea (the 'long nosed ones') had not thrived over the eons. Indeed you could argue that they were, in the eternal struggle for survival, a spectacular dead loss. Martin Meredith makes the point succinctly with a catalogue that seems straight out of Edward Lear:

One million years ago, some twenty species of proboscideans – mammoths, mastodons, gomphotheres,
stegodonts, dinotheres, and modern elephants still
inhabited most major land areas of the world. But
climate change and natural disasters, together with
human evolution, led to mass extinction. The African
branch of Elephas disappeared about 35,000 years ago;
the American mastodon about 8,000 years ago, hunted
heavily by Stone Age peoples, became extinct about
4,000 years ago. Only two proboscideans survived:
Elephas in Asia and Loxodonta in Africa.[1]

All these Cyranos, bar two, had gone the way of the dodo.
If it was the survival of the fittest, it would seem, a monster
conk was not fit for purpose in the ever-lasting struggle.

And it was the trunk, the proboscis, which was at the heart
of the issue. Was this fine appendage an advantage or a disad-
vantage in the great fight to keep from going under? And why
had it evolved (or been created) so odd? Just how, asked Kipling,
in his jolly little *Just So* stories fable, did the elephant get its
trunk? The answer the story offers is that going too close to the
water to drink, the baby elephant's snub nose was grabbed by
a crocodile (this encounter, incidentally, has been observed to
happen – odds usually favour the crocodile). There ensued a
tug of trunk, the organ was elongated and stayed that way.

Kipling goes on to list all the evolutionary advantages: the
baby elephant can swat flies, shower itself, grub in the dirt for
food or pluck it from trees, 'spank' other animals which annoy
it and make music through it. It has what the mechanic calls an
all-purpose tool. But it's a very strange tool. What auto-repair
man would want a wrench you could play 'Yankee Doodle
Dandy' on?

Hilaire Belloc wrote one of his little whimsical effusions on the same wonderful strangeness of the trunk:

When people call this beast to mind,
They marvel more and more
At such a little tail behind,
So large a trunk before.

Pre- and post-Darwinian theories set out to explain the trunk's strangenesses in a more scientific (if less enjoyable) way. Lamarckian theory, which was very popular throughout the nineteenth century, held to a simple utilitarian principle. If a characteristic were useful, it could be 'passed on' to succeeding generations, giving them an advantage. It can be summed up in the proverb 'the higher up the tree you go, the sweeter grows the berry'. Hence the giraffe's long neck.

The trunk, though, is ridiculously over engineered. It's hard for the layman wandering through the zoo to see anything quite as extravagantly, as unnecessarily, versatile. Dr Johnson's mind, it was memorably observed by his patroness Mrs Piozzi, was like the elephant's trunk, 'strong to buffet even the tiger, and pliable even to pick up the pin'. Johnson's own definition in his great dictionary is relevantly verbose:

ELEPHANT: *elephas*. The largest of all quadrupeds, of whose sagacity, faithfulness, prudence, and even understanding, many surprising relations are given. This animal is not carnivorous, but feeds on hay, herbs, and all sorts of pulse; and it is said to be extremely long lifed. It is naturally very gentle; but when enraged, no creature is more terrible. He is supplied with a trunk, or long hollow cartilage, like a large trumpet, which

hangs between his teeth, and serves him for hands: by
one blow with his trunk he will kill a camel or a horse,
and will raise a prodigious weight with it.

The trunk brought with it the survival bonus that, unlike
the giraffe's elongated neck (they would starve were there
no high trees), it could reach up and down without moving
the head – and it can do much else. To quote another, more
zoologically observant, authority than the Great Cham:

> With the two finger-like points on the end of its trunk,
> an African elephant can pick up fruit the size of a marble
> – or a branch a foot thick. This elongated proboscis
> is an incredibly versatile tool: it provides a means for
> smelling, breathing, and touching, not to mention
> drinking and eating. Mothers caress their young with
> their trunks; infants use theirs to investigate everything
> from plants to playmates.
>
> The trunk also acts as a hose, whether for a drink
> or a dust bath. (A coating of dust, like mud, repels sun
> and insects.) To drink, an elephant sucks water into its
> trunk, pokes the open end in its mouth, and releases the
> water to let it drain down its gullet.[2]

In war, and in defence of his territory, the elephant's trunk
(the word is related to 'truncheon') is a mighty weapon. As
Kistler informs us:

> He defends himself with his trunk, and picks up and
> squeezes the life out of a man, or throws him against
> trees, or puts his foot on him and with his trunk tears
> him in two, or holds him in his trunk and batters him

against any hard substance near at hand. The trunk, which is constantly used for heavy work, is very highly developed, muscular, massive and very active; quite different from the flabby, withered trunk seen in a zoo.[3]

But then comes the catch – over-engineering. For the evolutionist the trunk demonstrates the short-term advantage and the long-term liability of the overspecialised organ. The many functions of the trunk rendered it vulnerable in certain life or death situations. It was also indefensible. In battle the Romans quickly realised you could lop it off and equipped their men with long slashing swords.

It was impossible to armour the trunk effectively against even these crudely manual weapons. Thackeray (a writer obsessed with elephants, for the mixed reasons of having been born in India and having been around London when Chunee died) wrote a burlesque, *The Tremendous Adventures of Major Gahagan* (1839) about a long-serving officer of Irregular Horse in India. Goliah is hugely boastful (he is, of course, Irish – a nation Thackeray always satirised for their big talk). One of his yarns is about being under siege by a fearsome native force with massed war elephants ready for the assault. How does the wily Gahagan win the day? This is how he explains it:

> The elephants were, as I said, in a line formed with admirable precision, about three hundred of them. The following little diagram will explain matters:-
> .... G |
> E |
> | F
> E is the line of elephants. F is the wall of the fort. G a gun in the fort. Now the reader will see what I did.

The elephants were standing, their trunks waggling to and fro gracefully before them; and I, with superhuman skill and activity, brought the gun G (a devilish long brass gun) to bear upon them. I pointed it myself; bang! it went, and what was the consequence? Why, this:-

x

...... G |

E |

| F

F is the fort, as before. G is the gun, as before. E, the elephants, as we have previously seen them. What then is x? x is the line taken by the ball fired from G, which took off ONE HUNDRED AND THIRTY-FOUR ELEPHANTS' TRUNKS, and only spent itself in the tusk of a very old animal, that stood the hundred and thirty-fifth!

It's fanciful verging on surreal. But there is a kernel of zoological plausibility at its centre. As boxers like to say, go for the body and the head dies. With elephants in combat it's 'go for the trunk'.

The mystery remains (for me, at least) how those two trunky species survived and all those other proboscidea went the way of the dodo. Creationists would say that, like us, God loves the elephant and wants to keep the animal around. Evolutionists would say – who knows? Evolution moves in a mysterious way and plays a very long game. Deciding who you go along with would take more hours standing in the zoo than most of us have to spare.

Jumbo: The Greatest 'Show' of London

Dressed for the occasion

Zoos cost money. Importing animals was expensive, keeping them in good condition was even more expensive. Jumbo coincided with the flowering of the ZSL into what would be the greatest 'show of London' – and that too cost money. Founded in 1828 as a centre of research for 'fellows', its grounds were

opened twenty years later to the public as a centre of entertainment (and instruction). An influx of women and children
could now wander free in the fellows' former preserve.

The aim of admitting the public into the park – with all
the disturbance of the animal residents it involved – was,
primarily, to raise funds for the science wing, which it did,
magnificently. It also soothed any anxiety on 'selling out' and
'circusing' that the zoo could legitimately be presented to the
world as a worthy educational institution. To this day a similar
'soothing' is supplied by the signposting, all over the place, that
the zoo is in the business less of 'exhibiting' than 'conserving' –
a biological Noah's Ark, not a Roman Colosseum *de nos jours*.
It's doubtful whether many customers, then or now, handed
over their money in the good causes of self-education or the
preservation of the world's endangered species in a zoo ark
close to Camden Town tube station. For most it's a day out,
pure and simple, and most of all for the children. When I walk
alongside the perimeter fence on a warm weekend afternoon,
the yells of the hyenas and the squawks of the birds are often
drowned out by a cacophony of children's shrieks.

Any visit to a modern theme park confirms the centrality of
the 'rides'. It's why people go there. The London Zoo was also
quick to see their appeal. Camel rides were one favourite – and
safe, as they say, as houses. Jumbo was soon strong enough to
carry children on his back and a saddle was ordered for little
passengers, ascended to by a step ladder. Scott would assist the
ascent, pocketing the pennies as he did so. More pennies would
be passed over for the ritual 'buns'; the transfer from Scott
to purchaser, and purchaser to trunk, was carefully moni-
tored, lest any nails, razor blades or other malicious objects
were inserted. For some reason it was common. Most of the
ride and bun revenue stayed in Scott's pocket – to Bartlett's

impotent fury. Scott, it was estimated, took in not far short of £500-worth of copper in a year, rendering him better paid than his superintendent. But it was a small fraction of what Jumbo brought to the zoo.

As Jumbo grew in size a larger 'howdah', or platform (sometimes called a 'tower'), was constructed. Wild reports claimed it could carry sixty passengers – as many as the top deck of a London omnibus. About eight, plus driver, was the usual maximum load.

Under Scott's care, Jumbo gained health, bulk and maintained a placid good temper – at least by day. Strategic news leaks sugar-coated the image of the children's giant pet. Jumbo was a little bit of funfair in the Zoo, the elephantine version of the fairground roundabout or swing boat.

The managers of the ZSL had noted the Jardin des Plantes success with the ill-fated twins. Jumbo was installed as the zoo's magnet attraction – as had been Castor and Pollux. No one who visited the Regent's Park grounds would want to leave having not seen two things: the 'snake house' (a house of horror and fascination to Charles Dickens – especially at feeding time, when live mice were thrown into the herpetarium) and Jumbo. Children, as it happened, might well be shielded from the horrors of the snakes tearing live squeaking rodents apart and the simians masturbating in the monkey house, but Jumbo was a 'must' for the juvenile visitor – and totally 'safe'. A wild animal that was in no sense wild. He was the 'children's pet', in ways that the rhino, gorilla or hippo never could be. Children were kept a safe, barred and barriered distance from those monsters.

Jumbo pioneered what remains now the zoo's main attraction – I see it over the fence every day walking my dog in Regent's Park – the 'petting' zoo. One rather feels for the long-suffering animals; groped, pawed and child-handled as they are. Jumbo, too, suffered children and adults to touch him, caress him, stroke him, pet him. Cats may like it; wild animals in captivity don't, one assumes.

Humans have an odd need to 'touch' the elephant. When the skeleton of Jumbo was taken out and put on display again, in 1993, in New York's American Museum of Natural History, it was noted that the legs, up to as high as a tall man might reach, were varnished with all the 'for luck' touching it had received. It was a tactile ritual similar to that which came close to destroying the stuffed Jumbo at Tufts University. Jumbo, while alive, was touched and touching. No one, other than reckless little Albert Ramsbottom, in the Stanley Holloway monologue, would touch a lion. This is how it goes (it's funnier when Holloway does it, but you'll get the drift – *noli me tangere*, kid):

There were one great big Lion called Wallace;
    His nose were all covered with scars,
He lay in a somnolent posture, With the side of his face
    on the bars.
Now Albert had heard about Lions, How they was
    ferocious and wild,
To see Wallace lying so peaceful, Well, it didn't seem
    right to the child.
So straightway the brave little feller, Not showing a
    morsel of fear,
Took his stick with its 'orses 'ead 'andle And pushed it
    in Wallace's ear.
You could see that the Lion didn't like it, For giving a
    kind of a roll,
He pulled Albert inside the cage with 'im, And swal-
    lowed the little lad 'ole.[1]

But with Jumbo, there was no infanticide; even if some little Albert dared poke him in the ear. It was penny buns and tuppenny rides all the way. He was the children's 'giant pet'.

Big Jumbo and his little friends

It wasn't only children who rode Jumbo. Dignitaries and future great men and women (although Victorian skirts, and particularly bustles, posed a problem) had him under their buttocks. It was not only a thrill, it said something about the supremacy of the species – lords of creation – Homo sapiens. Winston Churchill and Theodore Roosevelt – great warriors both when they grew up – rode Jumbo. Who knows what seeds that twopence worth of bum-bumping planted to sprout, decades later, changing world history.

Jumbo, in his seventeen years at the London Zoo, boosted immeasurably that peculiarly English 'love of animals' which marks the second half of the nineteenth century. It took a political form in the anti-vivisection campaigns (especially attractive to early feminists) and the formation of the RSPCA, which sponsored the epoch-making Cruelty to Animals Act of 1876. There are those who think this English zoophilia is morally unbalanced. The English, said snide Vladimir Nabokov, feel sorry for the blind man's dog.

Jumbo the 'giant pet' was, most who know about elephants concur, a giant con. Tame elephants, one is told, simply don't exist. They can be broken, they can be trained into different forms of cooperation with man, but at heart they are always wild and wilderness is the only place they can be themselves. In spite of that unassailable fact, Jumbo fed the fantasy – so persuasively that it became a kind of truth – that man and elephant, children leading the way, could enjoy an authentically cosy relationship of the kind prophesied by Isaiah: 'They shall do no harm on my Holy Mountain. The lion will lie down with the kid . . . And a little child shall lead them'. Happy myth – and nonsense.

There was another important factor playing into the British love and veneration of Jumbo – the Queen. She did not herself, of course, ride anything much larger than a Shetland pony when going over the Scottish hills with her faithful gillie Mr Brown. But in 1876, she had, by Mr Disraeli's advice, proclaimed herself Empress of India. Not a place, of course, she ever deigned to go to.

At the first 'Durbar', on the first of January, her viceroy, Lord Lytton, made his entrance on a magnificently plat-formed elephant (later viceroys chose more western modes of carriage for their Durbars – horses and Rolls-Royces). The following is the account given by Field Marshal Lord Roberts of the event:

The chiefs and princes were all settled in their several camps ready to meet the Viceroy, who, on his arrival, in a few graceful words welcomed them to Delhi, and thanked them for responding to his invitation. He then mounted with Lady Lytton, on a state elephant, and a procession was formed, which, I fancy, was about the most gorgeous and picturesque which has ever been seen, even in the East. The magnificence of the native princes' retinues can hardly be described; their elephant-housings were of cloth of gold, or scarlet-and-blue cloths embroidered in gold and silver. The *howdahs* were veritable thrones of the precious metals, shaded by the most brilliant canopies, and the war-elephants belonging to some of the Central India and Rajputana chiefs formed a very curious and interesting feature. Their tusks were tipped with steel; they wore shields on their foreheads, and breastplates of flashing steel; chain-mail armor hung down over their trunks and covered their backs and sides; and they were mounted by warriors clad in chainmail, and armed to the teeth. Delhi must have witnessed many splendid pageants, when the Rajput, the Moghul, and the Mahratta dynasties, each in its turn, was at the height of its glory; but never before had princes and chiefs of every race and creed come from all parts of Hindustan, vying with each other as to the magificence of their entourage, and met together with the same object, that of acknowledging and doing homage to one supreme ruler.[2]

Lytton was riding what was reputed to be the largest elephant in India (what could be more majestic for the new Empress?). It was loaned for the occasion by the Raja of

Benares. It all went slightly askew when the musketeers' *feu de joie* panicked the various lesser regiment of elephants on parade who stampeded. Several of the 70,000 spectators apparently were killed. All Indian – but nonetheless loyal servants of the crown, or they would not have been there to be killed.

The new imperial role of Victoria, and the centrality of elephants to the image, stimulated a little elephant mania – a mania which involved a lot of dead elephants. There ensued an industrial-scale production of carved ivory combs, ivory-handled umbrellas and brushes, and cigarette holders. Tusk-legged footstools and side tables, and elephant hoof walking-stick holders became all the rage. All which meant, at the far end of the supply line, massacre.

Bartlett was immensely proud of his connection with the Queen and Empress. She was a known friend to Jumbo, a clandestine visitor (it was rumoured) and her children enjoyed privileged rides and contact on private visits. Not a royal infant rump, until the black year of 1958, did not enjoy contact with the 'lead elephant' at London Zoo. And the leader of them all was Jumbo.

Jumbo's Lucky Escape

As events five years later proved, Jumbo was lucky to have been exchanged with that Indian rhino in 1865. One immediate piece of luck, of course, was that he was nursed back to health in England and would probably have been left to expire miserably in France. The second piece of luck was that he didn't end up as Jumbo cutlets (the currently popular jumbo-burger not yet being invented).

During the 1870–1 siege by the Prussians, the animals in the Paris zoos were slaughtered for food for the starving citizens. Castor and Pollux gambolled no more. But their end was one of which any truly Parisian animal could be proud – they inspired a new dish for the gourmand's menu.

Much as Paris loved the two elephants, they loved their bellies more. The siege lasted five months – not long enough to cause starvation, but long enough to stretch the ingenuity of Parisian cuisine to new, surreal heights of gastronomic invention and savoury disguise. Cats and dogs, easy to trap, were first to be culled. The odd rat found its way into the larder and out again on to the table, unrecognisable. Then horses, then the Jardin's beef-like herbivores. Then, last on the menu of the day, the exotics (the primates were spared, as too humanoid).

And, just a few weeks before the siege was lifted, around Christmas, the prized elephants: including the famous duo. The slaughtering – never an easy thing with elephants – was done by an English butcher, named Deboos, who paid 27,000 francs for the pair. Monsieur Devisme, the keeper whose darlings they were, the man who had made them famous, implored and wept in vain. Paris was hungry.

Castor faces the firing squad

The following lively account of the slaughter of the infant elephants is by Christine Baumgarthuber (*New Enquiry*, 10 July 2012):

Deboos admitted he knew nothing about slaughtering elephants, but, sensible to the caprice of the rich, he saw it as in his interest to learn on the fly. Enlisting the help of a zookeeper and a gunsmith, he settled on Castor as his first victim. The keeper commanded Castor to kneel and rest his head on a wooden block. The elephant obeyed.

The gunsmith meanwhile raised a carbine to his shoulder, took aim and fired. The explosive steel-tip bullet it discharged struck home, but it did not kill Castor. Blood gushed from the wound it made. The elephant appeared surprised and somewhat confused, perhaps thinking he had suffered some accident. Yet he continued patiently to rest his head on the block. It took two more shots to the skull to fell him. 'Love, in animals, has not for its only object animals of the same species, but extends itself further, and comprehends almost every sensible and thinking being,' writes David Hume. 'A dog naturally loves a man above his own species, and very commonly meets with a return of affection.' Pollux received a more humane dispatch than that granted her brother. She died of a single shot behind the ear.

The abundant meat these animals rendered – some 1,500 kilograms – commanded the princely sum of sixty francs per kilo. Restaurateurs printed new bills of fare to advertise the exotic new dishes. 'The discovery of a new dish does more for human happiness than the discovery of a new star.' The *bon viveur* Jean Anthelme Brillat-Savarin records being offered: *Eminceé of elephant! Elephant vinaigrette! Stewed elephant with camel's hump!* These dishes the *beau monde* of Paris downed with gusto.

Gusto, perhaps, but not with universal relish. Victor Hugo was among the first to sup on elephant steak and pronounced it inferior to bear and much inferior to antelope. The English journalist Thomas Gibson Bowles (famous for ingeniously sending his dispatches out of the besieged city by balloon and pigeon – birds lucky enough to escape the *rotisserie*), wrote that of the zoo cuisine he too liked elephant least. The English politician Henry Labouchère (famous for the 'amendment' proscribing 'gross indecency' which later dished Oscar Wilde), another Englishman, concurred:

> Yesterday, I had a slice of Pollux for dinner. Pollux and his brother Castor are two elephants, which have been killed. It was tough, coarse, and oily, and I do not recommend English families to eat elephant as long as they can get beef or mutton.[1]

Oddly Labouchère is also remembered by posterity for his political advocacy of legislation to prosecute cruelty to animals – doubtless the RSPCA has a dusty sepia photograph somewhere on its HQ walls. That still didn't stop him tucking in to his four-legged friends.

The supplies of elephant held out for a couple of weeks but ever more ingenuity was required to offset putrefaction. As late as New Year's Eve, Edmond de Goncourt (famous as the man after whom the premier literary prize of France is named) wrote in his diary: 'Tonight, at the famous Chez Voisin, I found elephant black pudding and I dined'.[2]

For the second time in his life, Jumbo had escaped the cooking pot. Whether the Indian rhino who took his place in the Jardin went the way of all other animal flesh in the desperate days of 1870, or what exotic dish it inspired, is lost to gastronomic history.

Postscript

The Paris gourmand's verdict seems to have been down-thumbs on elephant meat, whether steak, consommé, or as black pudding (I think they're called *andouillettes* in France:

I ate one once, it was like sausage stuffed with sausage skins). Thailand has recently come round to a widespread – dangerously widespread – taste for another elephant delicacy. *The Huffington Post* ran a story in January 2012, headlined 'Elephant Meat In Thailand Poses Extinction Threat', which reported that 'A new taste for eating elephant meat – everything from trunks to sex organs – has emerged in Thailand and could pose a new threat to the survival of the species'. Soraida Salwala, the founder of Friends of the Asian Elephant foundation, claimed 'the estimated value of an elephant's penis is more than 30,000 baht ($950).' With which fact on to the next chapter.

Jumbo's Private Life

It was not the Prussian jackboot which came close to prema-
turely ending Jumbo's life, but 'sex', that omnipresent Victorian
snake in the grass. For a decade and a half he had served as
the big 'draw' in the zoo. He was world famous. Hundreds
of thousands of bottoms, small and large, had ridden him. No
'incident' had marred his service. There is no report of him
even urinating or defecating indecorously.

His name had become proverbial – a brand. There were
innumerable porkers and other beasts of the field and animals
of the Victorian parlour named after him, as were enough
commercial products to fill the shelves of Selfridges (they had
the occasional Jumbo-themed window display). It was slang
usage for anyone more than svelte. Time passes and Jumbo
was, in 1880, twentyish: a significant age for a bull elephant.
He had grown immensely and was now over 10 feet tall and
5 tons in weight.

The arrival of Alice had allowed the construction of a
protective layer of Victorian domestic myth. He was a respect-
ably married man (elephant). There was, every account affirms,
no sex at all between Jumbo and his 'wife', or much interest
of any kind: just the occasional touching of trunks – which
may seem thoroughly Victorian. But neither did Jumbo, like

many Victorian married men, go tomcatting on the tiles. His next owner, Barnum, evidently had some hopes of mating him with a cow called Hebe (named, promisingly, after the goddess of youth, and the mother of the first baby elephant born in America, Columbia). This match-making failed as well.

Jumbo's emergent sexuality, which only insiders at the zoo knew about, was extremely disturbing. It was not on view – he was gentle and asexual enough during the daylight hours and faithfully went through the old ride-and-bun routines. But there was an unexploded-bomb feel about him, which Scott and (more nervously) Bartlett were getting very antsy about.

The disinclination to confront, and never, never, to publicise the fact, that Jumbo had become a sexually mature entity with normal adult desires is something archetypally Victorian and it was modesty which, in this case, was a recipe for disaster.

Elephants have a long, sexless childhood adolescence but when Eros comes to call, it's volcanic. Musth had been well known about as long ago as 1681. Robert Knox, who explored Ceylon and wrote intelligently about elephants from what he saw there, reported:

> At some uncertain seasons the males have an infirmity comes on them, that they will be stark mad, so that none can rule them. Many times it so comes to pass that they with their Keepers on their backs, run raging until they throw them down and kill them: but commonly there is notice of it before, by an Oyl that will run out of their cheeks, which when that appears, immediately they chain them fast to great Trees by the Legs. For this infirmity they use no Medicine, neither is he sick: but the females are never subject to this.[1]

The tsunami of testosterone which floods the male elephant typically lasts a short time – six to twelve weeks, although it can hang around for up to a year. As Knox notes, secretions are produced from swollen temporal glands and urine dribbles from greenish-appearing penis. The penis itself is a fearsome thing for lesser species. To quote one authority, 'It's typically about 4 ft long, it bends in a S-shape when erect, and that it is able to writhe about independent from the elephant's body because of special musculature'.² The 'green penis syndrome' is, one reads, even today not fully understood in the African varieties of elephant. It was certainly ill-understood in nineteenth-century Camden.

It seems clear that in 1881 Jumbo, now twenty-two, was experiencing his first full-blown musth. There is an alternative theory, which is less plausible, that a new set of teeth (his third) were agonising him. But why an elephant who would snap his tusks off would worry about toothache is not clear. The fact was Bartlett and his superiors were face to face with a basic contradiction of the zoo concept – writ large in the body of their largest exhibit. A 'giant pet' with a 4-foot erection. The word 'menagerie' is etymologically related to 'manage'. This situation was inherently unmanageable.

Samuel White Baker was scathing on the topic of what the ZSL purported to do with 'that fine specimen of the African elephant, Jumbo' (his friend from way back in the 1860s). It proved for him the utter pointlessness of zoos. There wasn't space enough in them – nor the right kind of company – for a wild animal like an elephant to be fully adult, to be fully 'itself'. As Baker put it:

It is to be regretted that the architectural arrangements of the Zoological Society are insufficient to control a male elephant when under the influence of periodical excitement. Such periods have a scientific interest, and should be carefully observed and noted. The elephants of the Zoological Society have been regarded as play-things for the amusement of children; if they are to be thus used, common sense would suggest that the Society should restrict their purchases to females.[3]

Hard words, but true. A compromise would be a long time coming – Whipsnade, the free-range ZSL park, established in Bedfordshire in 1928. And even the wild animal park was not a complete solution, and it was hard to get to. And even if the ZSL had taken the WAP route in 1882, the public – after fifteen years of physical contact with Jumbo – did not want to look at him through opera glasses and lob the currant buns by mortar.

What could the zoo do with a sexy elephant? He could, of course, be kept well out of the way during the most difficult times. (The thought of ladies and children seeing that 4-foot monstrosity was not to be borne.) By mid-December Bartlett was convinced that Jumbo was certifiably insane. In his report to the council, he wrote:

I have for some time past felt very uncomfortable with reference to this fine animal, now quite, or nearly quite, adult, and my fear of him is also entertained by all the keepers except Matthew Scott, who is the only man in the Gardens who dare enter this animal's den alone.[4]

If he were a horse, of course, there would have been an obvious solution. Stables and stable hands knew exactly what to do with a wayward stallion: fetch the gelding shears and some stout ropes. But with elephants the necessary parts were buried deep in the body and anaesthesia was still an infant science. And who would be brave enough to put a chloroform pad the size of a bed pillow on Jumbo's trunk? Unrestricted space and physical exhaustion might have helped, but letting Jumbo gallop at randy will over the Regent's Park was not an option.

Bartlett recalled what had happened to Chunee, all those years back and sadly, but bravely, asked the management committee of the ZSL to remit him funds to purchase an elephant gun. And so they did.

Enter the Greatest Showman on Earth

As luck and good fortune would have it, Bartlett did not have to pull the trigger on Jumbo. By miraculous good fortune there arrived, on 13 December 1881, out of the blue, a telegram from the proprietor of 'P.T. Barnum's Traveling World's Fair, Great Roman Hippodrome and Greatest Show on Earth' – also known as the Prince of Humbugs. As was necessary in telegramming (10¢ a word) Barnum was very much to the point: 'What is the lowest price you can take for the large male African Elephant? Barnum, Bailey and Hutchinson.'[1]

He had, he later claimed, 'no hope of ever getting possession of Jumbo' – it was a stunt, like his bid for Shakespeare's birthplace in Stratford, to be transported, brick by brick, to his local Stratford, Connecticut. The phrase 'lowest price' offered plenty of wiggle room.

Barnum was now a venerable seventy-two years old and keen to construct his legacy as the greatest living American. He had put huge effort over recent years into projecting himself not merely as a 'showman' but as a philanthropist and political player. He had demonstrated himself a great American institution in the American Centennial of 1876. The previous year he had been elected mayor of Bridgeport, Connecticut, the town in which he lived and where he had constructed four massive Xanadu-mansions for himself. On one of them he had an elephant drawing a plough along-side the railroad track which ran through his land, as an advertisement for P.T. Barnum. When farmers wrote asking where they could acquire these clearly powerful animals (McCormick power-driven tractors being a year or two off) Barnum archly replied that elephants were only useful for farmers who also owned circuses. He was never short of a wisecrack – something that made Americans love him even more.

BARNUM'S ELEPHANT PLOUGHING IN 1855.

Barnum's elephantine farm animal

One of Barnum's larger houses and its grounds is now the campus of the University of Bridgeport. During his tenure as mayor he improved the town's water supply and beefed up the liquor and prostitution laws (he was an abstainer, moralistic and no friend to bordellos, which sponsored a more squalid form of entertainment than he favoured). And he got a municipal hospital founded – with his name, as always, prominently on it.

There was, there is no more appropriate word for it, a certain 'elephantiasis' of the spirit about the elderly Barnum, the man who was soon to own Jumbo. He was still the great (greatest in his estimation) showman – hence his interest in Jumbo, an acquisition which he said he lusted after 'wistfully' for many years.

In these patriarchal years he had become involved in a fratricidal war with his great circus rival, Adam Forepaugh. A big element in their rivalry was the size and grandeur of their elephant herds: as many as fifty on either side. Barnum had caught wind of Jumbo's being the very biggest example of the biggest variety in captivity. And the elephant's name was universally known: it was well on the way as an epithet for things which were big, big, big. It was an elephant to trample the hated 'Fourpaws' into the sawdust of his second-rate three-ring circus.

Barnum's reputation, taking the long view, was not such as to recommend him to any conscientious custodian of animals. He is credited, plausibly, with the remark 'A sucker is born every minute'. Even if he didn't invent it (there are arguments for and against), it was undeniably his philosophy of showmanship.

He had begun professional life as a huckster with a travelling variety troupe of freaks and 'novelties'. His first coup was in 1835 when he purchased a part share in Joice Heth, an aged former slave whom he promoted, shamelessly, as the 161-year-old nurse of George Washington. He knew full well she wasn't, but his brazen advertising drew in the suckers by the thousand. Barnum, at this start of his showman career, had hit on a great truth – most people *want* to be humbugged. They are fascinated by what his disciple, Robert Ripley, called the 'believe it or not' situation. Another truth sustained Barnum – that there was no such thing as bad publicity.

His hoaxes bordered on the preposterous – pre-eminently the 'Feejee Mermaid', allegedly brought back live by a sailor from the South Seas. Those who paid their quarter to see her expected to see something live, exotic and (hopefully for the male customers) bare bosomed and erotic. What they saw was a monkey's shrunken head and torso stuck on a fish's mummified tail, the whole thing soldered with papier mâché.

The Feejee
Mermaid

It was outrageous. But that word never bothered P.T. Barnum. He hadn't hoaxed them, they had hoaxed themselves. At this early stage of his career Barnum would have been as happy exhibiting Joseph Merrick, the tragic 'Elephant Man', as what he would later (with some justice) call the 'greatest elephant on earth'. His chosen territory, in this early period of Barnumism, was ambiguously between freak show and funfair – leaning strongly towards the former. His sideshow exhibits were in fact outright freakish: mammoth-fat infants, through bearded ladies, to 'the beautiful Circassian girl' (although, puritan that he was, he went easy on sex) and Siamese twins. His most successful exhibit was the dwarf Tom Thumb.

The Great Showman and his
friend Tom

It was one of the more honest of his exhibits, but even
here there was shameless hoaxery. Barnum got him as a four-
year-old and passed him off as fully grown – made plausible
with cigars and whisky. He was, among all else, a child abuser.

Barnum moved on to 'museums', so called: they were
more in the nature of chambers of curiosity and horror than
institutions of scientific record. They made him money, but
kept burning down. His career was a roller coaster of vast
wealth and total bankruptcy. He made close on $200,000 from
promoting the tour of the Swedish nightingale, Jenny Lind,
in 1850 and lost it all in two years. When his second museum
burned to the ground he turned, at the age of 61, to circuses.
He was soon running a three-ring monster – the 'Greatest
Show on Earth'. It was based on Roman models. Spectacle, not
'curiosity', was now the theme and 'big' the keynote. A special
Barnum train took the show round the continent and it was a
holiday for whichever town he stopped in.

The circus world was fast evolving in the US, particularly in the 1880s, and Barnum, long in the tooth, was in constant danger of being outdone. When he made the bid for Jumbo he was at the climacteric of his personal life and in some critical tangles in his professional career. By a series of canny mergers he had seen off a couple of rivals and emerged as the conglomerate 'Barnum and Bailey' (a brand name which survives to the present day). He dearly wanted a 'trophy' acquisition for this new enterprise, something to rock America on its heels.

From Bartlett's embattled point of view, if the American offer were genuine it would blessedly solve two problems: insubordinate Matthew Scott and uncontrollable Jumbo. He leapt at it. Without wasting time on rigmarole with his superiors he fired back a telegram: 'Will sell him for £2,000'. Barnum must have muttered 'sucker' or, possibly, 'peanuts'. He had, a year earlier, offered $100,000 for Columbia, the first elephant to be born in America. He seems not to have known the real reason for Bartlett's knockdown price. The deal was struck and the show was on the road by January 1882.

Bartlett released a notice to *The Times* on 25 January 1882 under the headline, THE GREAT AFRICAN ELEPHANT. The radioactive word 'Jumbo' was scrupulously avoided by Bartlett, who may have hoped no one would notice:

Barnum, the American showman, has bought for the sum of £2000, the large male African Elephant, which has for many years formed one of the principal attractions in the Gardens of the Zoological Society in the Regent's Park.

The purchase has been made upon the understanding that the animal is to be removed and shipped to America at the risk of the purchaser. To those who know the size, weight, and strength of this ponderous creature (certainly the largest elephant in Europe), the undertaking is one of serious difficulty and not unattended with some danger.

The 'danger' that Jumbo was currently in need of a straitjacket was not proclaimed, but Bartlett had covered himself. The ZSL had no liability once the elephant passed through their gates. Barnum had been warned (this was the purpose of the news release) that it was 'not unattended with some danger'. If Jumbo, as was not unlikely, ran amok (sank the boat carrying him to America, perhaps) it would be Barnum who carried the can. Who would be the sucker then?

Jumbomania

Over the early months of 1882 there was played out an episode in which Barnum cunningly hoaxed a whole nation. It was one of his life's greatest coups. The transportation by sea of England's most famous African elephant, bound in chains and behind bars, to what was still regarded as smirched with the shame of having recently been the world's largest slave state, made many in Britain uneasy. Specifically some fellows and the council of the ZSL. Was Barnum – the Prince of Humbugs – a proper recipient of an animal for which the zoo had moral responsibility? And was it wise to part with this goose that laid so many of the institution's golden eggs? Jumbo pulled in, it was estimated, as much as a £1,000 a week in high summer when the nation's children were out of school.

Bartlett found himself in an exquisitely awkward position. He hated circuses for the way they mistreated animals. They were Cross's awful menagerie under canvas. But he could not come clean as to why he was acting against his principles in selling Jumbo. He could confide in the council, but to explain to the nation that it was sex which was at the root of it all would have been, well, un-Victorian.

Protest mounted over the next weeks as the carpenters and ironsmiths constructed, to Barnum's specifications, the vast box which was to carry off Jumbo. Visitors flooded into the gardens – despite the freezing February weather. Why was this happening? It was everywhere asked. Bartlett ventured another mealy-mouthed letter to *The Times* in which he waffled about some of the physiological aspects of adult male elephants at certain times. But he couldn't be too frank, lest he hand Barnum loaded weaponry for a countersuit, on the basis of damaged goods, if things did indeed go wrong. And Barnum was putting big money into the enterprise – $50,000, as he later claimed.

The English people and its tribunes, the London press, were having none of it. Their righteous disgust was expressed in *The Pall Mall Gazette*, a high 'liberal' organ:

> After all the children Jumbo has so patiently carried, all the buns he has so quietly and graciously received, is he to be turned out at last to tramp the world homeless and unbefriended, the mere chattel of a travelling showman?[1]

The assumption being made here was that Regent's Park Zoo was the 'natural habitat' for *Loxodonta Africana*. Barnum's riposte was that Jumbo had not been born in England and, like any immigrant seeking refuge in a better place, was free to 'naturalise' in the US. Chauvinist rage was vented at the Yankee abductor, but less of it, oddly, at the ZSL, whose decision it had been, through their superintendent, to do this shabby deal. Barnum was not kidnapping Jumbo. He had bought him fair and square, paying the sum asked. There were nonetheless death threats, which the Prince of Hokum was only too pleased to publicise.

Although relations between the two countries was warmer

than earlier in the century, British irritation was exacerbated by a growing (and historically correct) sense that America was somehow edging Britain off the world's top-nation spot. Slightly mumbled, 'Jumbo' sounded like 'John Bull'. John Bull/Jumbo in chains, draped in the Stars and Stripes, was not a pleasing image to Victoria's subjects. The *Telegraph*, using the lordly rhetoric of the leader writer through the ages, lamented that:

> Our amiable monster must dwell in a tent, take part in the routine of a circus, and, instead of his by-gone friendly trots with British boys and girls, and perhaps luncheon on buns and oranges, must amuse a Yankee mob, and put up with peanuts and waffles.[2]

A newspaper complaining about waffle?

There were dark references to *Uncle Tom's Cabin* and slavery's cruel separation of families. Was Jumbo to be parted from Alice – put, as it were, on an auction block, while his spouse wept elephantine tears? There was a song sadly warbled by the little ones Jumbo had loved and who had loved him:

> Jumbo said to Alice, 'I love you'
> Alice said to Jumbo
> I don't believe you do.
> If you really loved me
> As you ought to do
> You wouldn't go to Yankeeland
> And leave me in the zoo.[3]

Since money was everything to Barnum, what would he take to cancel the deal, the *Telegraph* asked. A hundred thousand wouldn't do it, the showman stoutly replied. National honour was at stake, he proclaimed. Fifty-one million Americans were *demanding* Jumbo (or would be, when he finished whipping them up into a reciprocal transatlantic frenzy). But, he taunted, after he had acquired him, Jumbo would go on a worldwide tour and, who knew, it *might* well take in 'every prominent city in Great Britain' (Jumbo never did revisit the old country alive – his stuffed cadaver did, but that simply reignited the bitterness of 1882).

The *Telegraph*, which led the exchange of fierce words with Barnum, prided itself on being the largest newspaper in the world: Jumbo-sized, no less, with a circulation in the 1880s of a quarter of a million. But even its clout could not save their beloved 'amiable monster'. Nor could an ill-conceived court action brought on the grounds that the ZSL was infringing its Royal Charter by putting an animal into danger. The sale, the judge pronounced, was perfectly legal. Britain could buy the Statue of Liberty, if the Americans were willing to sell it, and vice versa. More fool the ZSL.

The *Telegraph* finally conceded, tearfully, that 'Jumbo will never come back to us alive. His mighty heart will probably break with shame and grief.' They solemnly reminded Mr Barnum, and the American public of what had happened to the Philistines, when they made Samson a circus display. Nemesis awaited the hooting American masses in their three-ring canvas colosseum: 'We hope Mr Barnum fully realises what ten and a half tons of solid fury can do when it has a mind'.[4]

It was, of course, fear of just such a rampage in the leafy precincts of Regent's Park, where even Pekinese were required to be on a lead, which had led the ZSL to sell Jumbo, although no one outside the institution was privy to the fact in 1882.

For the general public Jumbo was the 5 tons of pussycat he had always been. The British press, it was clear, was enjoying the episode as much as Barnum, milking the 'mania' for sales. They too, in their way, were playing the Great British public for suckers. Reader rage sells newspapers; it had become mock war. In the zoo itself Jumbomania had reached clinical pitch. An anonymous woman, it was observed, had posted herself, like Joan of Arc at the stake, outside Jumbo's stall, apparently conducting a prayer or a fast until death. She was distributing leaflets, asking for the public's as well as the Almighty's intervention. The zoo could have ejected her for causing a nuisance and upsetting children, but they didn't. Attendance records were smashed, despite the season. As Les Harding records:

> Gate receipts were up £2,000 a day . . . It seemed as if the whole population of London were determined to have a gander at Jumbo. On March 8, 1882, a total of 16,632 visitors came to the gardens compared with 1,043 on the same day a year before. By March 13, 24,007 people visited Jumbo, a 14000 per cent increase over the previous year.[5]

Alice's prospective 'widowhood' (with a discreetly deferential glance at that other widow, in Braemar) was everywhere alluded to in the uproar. How could poor Alice bear it? It was put about (not by the Palace) that Victoria herself was upset (or, as *The New York Times* put it, her heart was 'wrenched'). In fact there was no royal pronouncement and, one suspects, no wrenching.

There were, as the ominous departure date approached, mass write-ins by children to the newspapers, Barnum, the London Zoo and Parliament. They testified to the efficacy of the 1870s universal Education Act in rendering British children almost as literate as their American counterparts. Petitions were drawn up. Grandees as eminent as John Ruskin expressed their grand displeasure.

The ZSL mildly, and reasonably, pointed out that there were now three elephants in the zoo offering rides and accepting any buns that happened to be put their way. Moreover, a replacement Jumbo, 'Jingo', was en route from Africa, who promised to be even larger than Jumbo. In the fullness of time he was.

Things reached a climax when Jumbo declined to move out of his cell into his crate to be carried off by his new owner. He simply would not budge. Chains were put round his legs and neck and pulled by the mightiest tug-of-war team the zoo could recruit, without success. It was immovable object and resistible force. It all reached a hilarious pitch when, bypassing the obnoxious crate (everyone could see it was too small for an elephant known to be a claustrophobe), Jumbo was led to the garden's gates. It was intended to walk him out of the zoo and, once outside his habitat, slam the gates behind him and coax him into the box, thence to the docks, thence to his new home. But Jumbo stopped at the exit to the zoo and resolutely refused to move over the threshold. Slamming the gates on his massive rump would merely damage the ironwork. A huge crowd was by now watching the show and Alice, playing up her part, was trumpeting mournfully in the distance (Barnum had hinted to the press that she was pregnant, poor cow).

Scott was ostensibly helping in all this frustrating business. But it was clear to Bartlett and – doubtless – anyone else who thought about it that he was playing a very deep game indeed. Scott, notoriously, could get 'his' Jumbo to do anything he wanted, or in this case not do something. Their famous secret code was at work – a shibboleth, or semaphoric signal was passing between them. It could be plausibly deduced from this pantomime that Scott was clinching his own deal with Barnum and Bartlett – feathering his nest.

He had to go with Jumbo, of course, to America. If he remained behind he would no longer have his trump card to play. Bartlett would get rid of him before his feet touched the ground. Retaining perpetual 'ownership' of Jumbo against the American's 'Elephant Bill' Newman was probably an issue between Scott and Barnum. Another was compensation for the huge amount of annual revenue he would be losing from the sale of all those tuppenny buns – up to £800 a year, Bartlett reckoned. Then he wanted right of return, if something went badly wrong (most bad would be the death of Jumbo in transit). The ZSL agreed to keep his position open for some months until he made his decision. Scott was technically on temporary leave with the strong expectation that once gone, he would be gone for good. It would be the best of riddance from Superintendent Bartlett's point of view.

The new American owner of Jumbo was suspiciously unperturbed by his agent's report that Jumbo was passively resisting all attempts to move him and would not even get to his feet. 'Let him lie there a week,' cabled Barnum 'if he wants to. It is the best advertisement in the world.'[6] There were other boats if he missed this one. The suspicion must be that he was firming up his deal with Scott, and revelling in the publicity.

Finally, after two weeks (in which Jumbo made any number of farewell appearances in the zoo, giving farewell rides), he was coaxed by Scott into his box on 22 March and from there, via road and Thames barge, to the Millwall Docks. The deals were done and the show was on.

Farewell to England

Jumbo left his home of seventeen years at 2 a.m. on a cold March morning to avoid obstreperous spectators. They came nonetheless and were duly obstreperous. He welcomed the crate which would be his quarters for the next three weeks in his traditional house-warming way, battering his head against the iron-banded teak walls and scraping what was left of his tusks against the small barred eye-level vent to produce a shower of ivory. He was ready – and damned angry.

The flatbed wagon pulling his crate required a team of ten dray horses, with men in front and behind carrying oil lamps. The route was chosen in advance to avoid low bridges. Jumbo contrived to get his trunk through the small barred vent to tweak the nearest horse's tail, nearly provoking a capsize. It was not going to be an easy trip.

Despite the dark and the cold there was a large crowd accompanying the lumbering, slow-moving wagon, keeping up a non-stop chorus of hoots and insults. They were particularly directed at gun-toting 'Elephant Bill', who had unwisely threatened to shoot Jumbo if he was obstructed by any angry English mob and leave them the corpse if they wanted the damn thing that much. It did not endear him.

The barge on to which the crate was transferred was cheered to the echo from the banks by schoolchildren and following rowboats as it drifted downstream to where the *Assyrian Monarch* steamship was docked and waiting to receive its unique cargo. Jumbo was loaded on board and deposited in a forward hold without incident.

In the first-class saloon a celebratory dinner was held. There were speeches and 'Elephant Bill' Newman was presented with a gold medal from the ZSL to show there were no hard feelings (as Chambers notes, Bartlett didn't get one, which must have meant some extremely hard feelings around Regent's Park).[1] The ship made a final stop at Gravesend, where the Baroness Burdett-Coutts (Dickens's patroness and sworn friend to Jumbo) boarded to take her adieux. She was the richest woman in England. There was more banqueting and the Baroness, before disembarking, ceremonially presented Jumbo with his last English bun. It was a sacramental moment. The *Assyrian Monarch* (apt name) was a British vessel, but loyally hoisted the Stars and Stripes as it went out to the open sea.

The crossing to New York took thirteen days. Jumbo is reported to have bellowed continuously for the first two days and nights, until exhaustion took over. He was given plentiful beer and whisky (soaked in biscuits, easier to digest). The Baroness had left a supply of his favourite sweeties and sacks of buns. Scott fed him vast quantities of onions 'to warm his stomach' and the plug tobacco for which Jumbo, now adult, had developed a taste. A stream of first-class passengers came down to look and give him canapés and champagne (he was probably drunk for most of the trip). Three hundred steerage-class passengers were permitted to shuffle past one day.

'The Great London Pet', as newspapers called him, made landfall in New York on 9 April. Cannily, Barnum had filed documents certifying he was being imported 'for breeding purposes'. This sidestepped any pesky demands US customs might make for a property valued – as Barnum claimed and probably entered on insurance forms – at $100,000. 'Look after the cents and the dollars will look after themselves' was always his motto.[2]

Jumbo was fortified with even more whisky and port wine for the ordeal of unloading by swing crane at Battery Pier (another apt name for the great batterer). Once on land (and now officially an American) his crate was placed on a specially constructed wagon drawn by sixteen horses for the journey up Broadway to Madison Square Garden, where Barnum and Bailey had their New York winter headquarters.

Thousands of spectators lined the way – which proved a problem. Barnum's original thought was that Jumbo – to get the wrinkles out of his legs – might walk. It would be a fine sight. But it had been noted that his behaviour on board had not been consistently 'lamb-like'. Americans liked parades up Broadway and often enlivened them with firecrackers. Jumbo could not be entirely trusted not to trample a few New Yorkers en route if they, so to speak, got up his trunk.

He was prudently kept in the crate. But that too proved difficult. Under his 5 ton weight and that of his iron-bound, hardwood container, the wheels had sunk into the mud (it had been raining). Sixteen horses and 500 of New York's lustiest men could not move the wagon: it was stuck. Never himself stuck for a spectacular solution, Barnum commanded a couple of elephants to be brought from the Garden. It was done, as the hours passed. They lowered their heads and their massive push-power proved successful. The caravan finally made it to the Garden at one o'clock in the morning.

It was a memorable arrival. And New York had its first

glimpse of its latest immigrant. 'He is not a handsome beast,' *The New York Times* coolly reported. But 'massive', Barnum everywhere insisted, adding 2 feet to Jumbo's height in his bulletins to the press ('museum measurement,' he would explain, when challenged).

It all added to the hoopla. Barnum later claimed that he recouped every cent of the $30,000 it had cost him to bring Jumbo to America in the first two weeks after his arrival, and ten times that amount in two months. Americans were queuing round the block to see him at Madison Square Garden. They didn't want him to *do* anything – Barnum's circus-trained animals could do things like stand on up-turned tubs with fezes on their heads, trumpeting 'The Star-Spangled Banner'. They just wanted to 'see' Jumbo. He was the Great Showman's great show.

Barnum stoked the patriotic fire, always simmering, by putting into circulation such 'now it can be told' information as that printed in *The New York Times* (a more sensational rag in those days) that after she became Empress of India in 1876 Queen Victoria was in the habit of bringing Jumbo clandestinely to Buckingham Palace, where she would ride him round the palace grounds in a special royal howdah with Disraeli acting as mahout.

They swallowed it. The suckers always did.

Among his paraphernalia, Jumbo's actual howdah, straps and step ladder, on which he had given so many rides in the zoo, was brought along with him. The experience was now offered, Scott superintending, to New Yorkers and their children. It was as popular as it had been in the London Zoo. And how much, one wonders, was Scott pocketing? He is recorded as finding America much to his taste and he never took up the safety-net offer of a return to London. One suspects he was earning handsomely, one way or another. And he had what he most dearly wanted: sole intimate contact with his elephant.

About one thing Barnum was inflexibly strict. Jumbo was not a performer – no tubs and fez for him. He was a 'show' animal. Why did he never perform, he was asked? Because he's too dangerous, the Prince of Humbugs would reply. It added to the mystique of the 'savage African'. Jumbo wasn't savage (except against himself – he never stopped grinding his tusks even in America) but it was impossible to train an adult elephant. He was too old to learn. The truth was Barnum could do nothing but 'show' him – and offer the rides, of course, where things could be conveniently managed.

The occasional stunt was in order. The most famous was in late spring 1884, in the dead season between winter quartering and when the summer railroad touring began in earnest. The great Brooklyn Bridge had opened a year earlier, in May 1883. It was one of the wonders of the world – the longest suspension bridge ever constructed and it said something important about America. It constituted the only surface connection between Brooklyn and Manhattan and was, from its opening day (when some 1,800 vehicles and ten times as many pedestrians crossed it), a main artery for the city's pumping lifeblood. It still is.

But six days after its opening there was a sudden panic that it was about to collapse. There was a stampede and a dozen people were killed in the crush. Doubts about the stability of this modern marvel persisted, shadowing its achievement. On the first anniversary of its opening, 17 May 1884, Barnum led Jumbo and twenty-one of his lesser elephants over the bridge. Proof positive. Barnum had, in fact, secretly offered to do the same thing a year earlier, on opening day, for a 'toll' (payable by him) of $5,000 – big bucks. But the directors refused. It would, they felt, cheapen the magnificent structure. When Jumbo performed in Brooklyn, as he often did, he had to do so by ferry boat, which he hated and he almost drowned on a crossing in 1882. A bridge would be a comfort to him.

The May 1884 elephant parade generated huge publicity and cost Barnum nothing in toll. The directors were duly grateful; New York was reassured. Jumbo was always a winner for the Prince of Humbugs. Ironically engineering experts have since established that the pioneering Brooklyn Bridge was too far ahead of its time and, indeed, not architecturally sound. Jumbo might conceivably have drowned in the East River – 'taken a Brodie', as it is called after the most famous jumper from the bridge who, unlike most other jumpers, survived the fall.[3]

A special double-doored train carriage had been constructed to Barnum's specifications for the touring season which would start after winter was properly over. Called 'Jumbo's Palace Car', it blazed with gilt and crimson varnish, and contained every elephant comfort (railway station arrivals were important for drumming up audiences). Jumbo would travel like the monarch he was.

Jumbo drew in the crowds wherever he went or stayed, from railway arrival to railway departure. He repaid Barnum's huge outlay and upkeep expenses many times over and his appeal never faded. But his most powerful impact on the American psyche was via advertising. He was used to hype everything from sock suspenders to laxatives. No longer an elephant, he was a byword and a 'brand'.

Yankee Doodle Jumbo

Wherever he laid his hoof Jumbo was always as much symbol as a pachyderm. And, symbolically, he meant something significantly different for Barnum and the American people from what he had meant for England and the English people. He was, the moment he came ashore at Battery Pier, an 'American'. Empire and imperial trappings were no longer part of his baggage. It was his sheer animal 'bigness' which attracted Barnum and Jumbo's world-beating bigness was a co-emblem of America. And, along with it, the raw power of America.

Other minor symbolisms rather escaped the newly naturalised Jumbo's fellow Americans. He was secured, for the passage, with chains. He was an African being transported to America in a cage. It was – what else? – an image of the slavery which hundreds of thousands of Americans had died fighting over, within living memory. The wounds of the Civil War were still suppurating. It was a confused echo, with historical discords. But indubitably an echo. 'Am I not an elephant and a brother?' Jumbo might have pathetically trumpeted, echoing the abolitionist's slogan. It seems not to have crossed many minds, but it was there somewhere in the background.

The children were still suffered to come to Barnum's elephant. He was still their 'pet' and the most widely circulated poster showed him being touched by a child. But whereas the London advertisements had children and elephant more or less in proportion (10 foot the one, 3 foot the other) in Barnum's picture it's Lilliput and Brobdingnag. Gigantism is the visual theme. American Jumbo was Jumbissimo:

Jumbo supersized

W.A. Starrett, the patriarch of the American skyscraper, observed, with a mixture of pride and ruefulness, during this 'Progressive' period, as it's called: 'We Americans like to think of things in terms of *bigness*; there is a romantic appeal in it, and into our national pride has somehow been woven the yardstick of *bigness*.'[1]

The mind toys with dates. What is considered to be the first skyscraper in the world, the Home Insurance Building in Chicago, was erected in 1885, the year of Jumbo's death. It was started the year of his arrival in the US. The skylines of

America's cities were Jumbo in ferroconcrete. All of which would have a Wagnerian climax, in the first year of the new millennium, when two planes (loosely called jumbo jets) crashed into what were once the two tallest buildings in the world. An apocalyptic collision of two species of American bigness.

One of the oddities of Jumbo's short stay in America is that there were none of the 'difficulties' which had made his last years in London so difficult. A number of reasons suggest themselves. Scott may have had a freer hand and have exercised a more soothing effect; Jumbo may have been less claustrophobically cramped and have seen more open spaces than in the ZSL; he may have had a better balanced diet; perhaps his intake of strong drink was strategically upped to keep him happily 'merry'.

The most likely explanation is that, despite their historically poor reputation where animal care is concerned, a circus like Barnum's really knew its elephants and how to manage them. In the 1880s the larger circuses had veritable herds of the beasts (in itself tranquillising – elephants are gregarious by nature). And, given the large numbers, they dealt with senior handlers like 'Elephant Bill' Newman, and his crew had learned how best to handle an elephant in musth, or otherwise cranky. They had expertise lacking in Regent's Park – particularly where big and dangerous animals were concerned. Barnum's establishment was, in fact, so knowledgeable about elephants that it was at the cutting edge of breeding the animals in captivity. Even university zoology departments hadn't cracked that problem yet.

The key to pacifying these massive beasts was, Barnum and his handlers seem to have learned over the years, to give them each other's company, not 'put them in solitary', which was the London Zoo practice. Barnum's has been called the 'prison yard' technique and is discussed at length by Susan Nance in her 2013 monograph on elephant maltreatment in America. She quotes the evidence of a reporter for *Harper's New Monthly*, who visited Barnum's elephant compound in the circus's winter quarters in 1882, a few months after Jumbo's arrival. Twenty elephants were crammed into a space about 'one hundred feet square, nearly all moving about in the restless manner so peculiar to them . . . Nearly all the animals have a characteristic motion. The elephants move their heads in and out, from side to side, with a kind of figure eight motion ... we call it "weaving" explained one of the elephant trainers.'[2]

The reporter in 1882 saw nothing inhumane in this. We probably do, guessing that these animals were in distress. That was the significance of their weaving. But it was controlled and unthreatening distress – it worked. There were other techniques. When on tour Barnum's crews were assiduous about taking the elephants to nearby rivers or ponds to 'cool them off'. The only time the herd, including Jumbo, is recorded as stampeding dangerously at this period was when harassed by a gang of young boys on the way to just such a dip. Youngsters were always a hazard around circus animals – they were better controlled in zoos, where they were not admitted without adults – but in all those years in ZSL, Jumbo was never taken to a river, the nearby canal, or any of the large ponds in Regent's Park.

Accepting that Jumbo was treated marginally better by Barnum than he had been by Bartlett, was he a *happy* elephant in America? It begs the question: can any elephant be happy in either a zoo or a circus, however enlightened those establishments are? It's further complicated by the fact that Barnum's famous three-ring circus proclaimed itself a direct descendant of the Roman circus – or 'ring'. A glamorous genealogy, but not one that brings with it any associations of kindness to animals.

With their vast imperial territory and still undepleted herds under their administration, the Romans had access to an inexhaustible supply of elephants to bring to their capital. They had tried using them, like their great foe, Hannibal, as weapons of war. But it was never their military style. For Rome the elephant was valued as a trophy (a proud spoil of war), or tribute (a submissive gift from a subject people, or from one rich potentate to another), or – most usefully – something exotic to be woven into the spectacles they loved to put on in the Circus Maximus and its lesser places of entertainment.

Barnum's ponderous 'Elephant Race', one of the highlights of his big-top programme, was manifest homage to the races for which the Circus Maximus was famous. Rome did not, as far as one knows, mount such elephant races, but elephants certainly featured in its circus displays. At one carefully staged event in the second century BC some forty bears and elephants were theatrically put to the sword. Occasionally disembowelled elephants, fighting to the death, weltering in their own blood and guts, are recorded as disgusting even the callous Roman crowd. But on the whole it was the kind of show business which went down well with the Empire's citizenry.

Centuries later Phineas T. Barnum, with Jumbo and his other elephants, offered his customers a sanitised Romanism (as modern cage fighting is a kind of sanitised gladiatorial combat). His elephants, under his canvas three-roofed colosseum, like the Romans', proclaimed man's total mastery over the animal kingdom, even its largest denizens. But was he as cruel as his Roman precedessors?

The American Society for the Prevention of Cruelty to Animals once upbraided him for the ubiquitous use of the handling spike by his elephant handlers. He serenely pointed out that the elephant's hide was two inches thick and it meant no more than the touch of the rider's whip on the horse's haunch. But he was careful to give instructions when any of his elephants died that it should be cut up immediately and the hide disposed of, lest 'do-gooders' come and examine it for wounds. In the end the ASPCA never got the better of Barnum. He always managed to run rings (three rings, one is tempted to say) round them.[3]

The suspicion remains that circuses, in whatever place and at whatever date, cannot be but cruel places. The only question is whether the cruelty is visible to the public – and relished by them, as in bear-baiting or cockfighting – or whether it is out of sight, so as not to horrify the soft-hearted public. The question blew up in America, explosively, in 2011–12 and the circus at the centre of it all was, inevitably, the Ringling Bros and Barnum & Bailey Circus.

The great protector of circus-abused animals in the present age is the covert mobile-phone camera. Animal activists, under the PETA (People for the Ethical Treatment of Animals) aegis had got hold of a series of shots revealing, in heart-rending sequence, what 'training' in this premier circus meant.

PETA spokesperson Tracy Reiman pulled no punches:

> Ringling trainers and handlers routinely beat and gouge elephants with bullhooks – weapons that resemble a fireplace poker with a sharp steel tip ... Kids would run screaming from the big top if they knew how baby elephants are violently forced to perform difficult, confusing, and sometimes painful tricks.[4]

The film actor Alec Baldwin weighed in with a four-minute video urging Americans to boycott Ringling Bros and

Barnum & Bailey and every other circus in America. In the video he claims (with supporting camera evidence) that elephants are 'stretched out, slammed to the ground, gouged with bull hooks, and shocked with electric prods'. This is not solely training technique, he said, but everyday management practice. 'Having worked with actors for many years, it's hard to believe that anyone would have to be dragged kicking and screaming into show business,' Baldwin quipped, 'but for the elephants for Ringling Bros and Barnum & Bailey and other circuses, that's exactly what happens.' Interestingly, Baldwin adds that circus elephants are 'kept chained and confined to cramped boxcars. The lack of mental and physical stimulation results in severe frustration, and is the reason why you frequently see elephants in circuses swaying back and forth.' The circus vigorously denied cruelty, although it did not deny that a few months earlier it had paid a fine of $270,000 (the largest sum on record) for alleged violations of the Animal Welfare Act – without admitting to any wrongdoing.

It all added fuel to the campaign PETA had been conducting for years. At their instigation a Traveling Exotic Animal Protection Act, or TEAPA, was introduced in Congress in November 2011. It would have banned the showing of any exotic species in travelling circuses. It was not enacted but was reintroduced in April 2013. The chances are, with the formidably lobbying muscle of PETA and PAWS (Performing Animals Welfare Society) and high-profile backers like Mr Baldwin behind it, the measure will keep coming back to Congress's door until it does pass.

So was Jumbo cruelly treated? Yes. Did Barnum know he was mistreating Jumbo? Probably not. But if he did, he did not lose any sleep over it.

The Death and Afterlives of Jumbo

Jumbo's death was, like everything else, greater than life. And, like everything in his life, it was strange, with something of the parable about it. It occurred on the night of 15 September 1885, in St Thomas, Ontario, Canada. St Thomas was then a booming railroad town; nowadays it booms rather less, but it remembers that night and always will, if its memorials mean anything.

On that warm evening Barnum and Bailey's men were loading the menagerie onto the circus train, man and beast having come back, exhausted, from a performance in the town. They had done one the night before in nearby Chatham; the railroad tours were gruelling.

To facilitate the embarkation the safety fence alongside the track had been pulled down, with permission from the railroad allegedly. This was an infraction – it meant crossing the tracks. The animals should have been brought into the marshalling yard and conducted into the circus train, well away from any rails and through traffic.

The twilight scene must have been oddly reminiscent of loading the ark. Jumbo's 'two-by-two' partner was not his 'wife' Alice (still pining, allegedly, for him in Regent's Park) but a diminutive clown elephant, Tom Thumb, named in honour of Barnum's star-attraction midget. He and Jumbo were pals. Barnum liked to couple them, to make Jumbo's size look the more massive.

A small crowd of the St Thomas population gathered in the nearby field to watch the circus animals leave town. It was a traditional parting event (W.B. Yeats, of all people, wrote a poem about it). Present in the crowd was seven-year-old Ruby Copeman, allowed to stay up beyond her bedtime. She would live another hundred years, to be the last surviving eyewitness of the awful thing about to happen that night.

What happened was dramatic, tragic, and – perhaps – suspicious, at least for anyone who knew the ways of Phineas T. Barnum.

Jumbo does battle against the train

Having cumbered up the embankment, Big J and Little T were making their way to Jumbo's gilt and chrome 'Palace Car' and Tom's less grand accommodation. They were the last pair of the thirty-nine-strong herd, all the others were now safely installed in their cars. Timetables had been checked and there were 'flagmen' in position, as regulations required. But everyone was tired and instead of waiting until 10 p.m. the animals had begun loading at 9.20 p.m. It was an unlucky change of plan. Special Freight train #151 came thundering down the tracks towards where the string of animals were still crossing. It was unscheduled, but the circus should not have been moving live-stock at that time. The track on which the train was coming was called, with uncanny appropriateness, the 'Grand Trunk'. It was a through train, which would normally speed past with only a warning whistle to clear the tracks.

As Scott and the two animals ambled along, Scott saw the headlight of train #151. 'My God!' he shouted, 'is this train on our track?' It was. 'Run, Jumbo, run!' shouted Scott – but where to? Scott tried desperately to push him back down the embankment. The elephant, fatally confused, trumpeted wildly and ran towards the oncoming train, the circus train and its track on his right side. If he could reach the end of it, and turn, he would be safe. He didn't, by six cars' length. At any point he could have turned left, to the embankment, and safety.

Driving the train, the man destined to be the killer of the Greatest Elephant in the World was engineer William Burnip. A keen-eyed fellow with all his wits about him, Burnip saw through the gloom what must have been a rare and night-marish sight for any Canadian train driver: 'elephants on the line'. He sounded a warning and slammed the wheels into reverse. Too late.

An eyewitness, Edgar H. Flach (a jeweller and citizen of St Thomas of high standing) recorded what happened next:

> The flagman was frantically waving his lantern, trying
> to stop the oncoming train . . . Scotty realized the danger.
> "Run, Jumbo, Run," he cried, half sobbing . . . I could
> see Jumbo running down the tracks. His trunk was

held high in the air and his trumpeting sent paralyzing shivers down either side of my spine. At that moment the locomotive struck the small elephant, hurtling him down the embankment and against a telephone pole. Jumbo in the meantime had kept on at a break-neck speed. He remembered the opening in the line of cars, but ran two car lengths past the opening before he realized his mistake. He stopped and turned. Then it was that the pilot of the engine struck him.[1]

Little Tom was sideswiped by the inappropriately named 'cow catcher' at the prow of all North American trains. He sustained a broken leg, was thrown off the track into the adjoining ditch, and lived. His relatively small weight and the angle of impact saved him. His leg was put in splints and he was good to perform the next day in London (Ontario). The show must go on.

But not for the star of Barnum's Circus. He would entertain for years to come – but it would not be a live show. Jumbo's massive rump had taken the full impact (he must have turned slightly, at the last moment), throwing the train off the rails. Jumbo's skull was crushed, and one of his short tusks driven back into his brain, injuring him fatally. A desperate Scott managed to make his way through the debris, ignoring any danger to his own life, to tend the mortally wounded animal. He is reported to have wept as he stroked its head. Eyewitnesses related (and doubtless did so, boringly, for the rest of their lives) how Jumbo reached out and gently embraced his beloved mahout with his broken trunk. Jumbo lasted only a few minutes more. The scene is described (embellished, one must suspect) by Flach:

134

The animal reached out his long trunk, wrapped it around the trainer and then drew him down to where that majestic head lay bloodstained in the cinders. Scotty cried like a baby. Five minutes later, they lifted him from the lifeless body. That night Scotty laid down beside the body of his friend. At last exhausted from the strain, he fell asleep.[2]

Matthew Scott and the corpse of his beloved Jumbo

The business with the caressing trunk is almost certainly fictional – a tusk through the brain does not encourage deathbed gestures of affection – though Scott's grief was certainly genuine.

Barnum was not there to witness the carnage, pathos (and, in the short term, money loss). He was in New York and didn't learn of the tragedy until the next morning when his breakfast at Murray's hotel was interrupted by the awful telegram. One visualises the fork stopping, frozen, between plate and mouth.

Up in Canada, nothing could be done overnight. Police were posted. The next morning citizens gathered from the grief-stricken, and morbidly curious St Thomas populace and a wreck crew was mobilised to clear up the debris and haul the massive carcass off the line. The pulling power of 200 men was needed to do so. The local men gaily joined in for this tug of war: man versus mammoth. It was becoming something of a death carnival.

What was left of Jumbo ('six tons of elephant hash', *The New York Times* irreverently called it) needed round-the-clock close protection from souvenir hunters. Scotty stood guard all night. It wasn't every day an elephant died in St Thomas, and they wanted to remember it. One fleet-footed boy escaped with a memento chunk of ear and a number of citizens hacked off lumps of hide, when they could dash in and evade the guards. Scott is reported as weeping with rage at such desecrations. One recalls Hemingway's Santiago – the old man of the sea – defending his marlin against the predatory sharks.

Unguarded, the carcass would have been stripped clean down to the glistening bone, like fallen carrion in the jungle, and it nearly was. Mr Flach himself somehow sidled up and carved off a few chunks of the tusks, which he then mounted into stick pins, sold at $1 apiece for months thereafter, in his local shop. One wonders how many were genuine at that giveaway price. But, as in everything, it is the thought that counts. Flach also got one of Jumbo's toenails, which he fashioned into an ashtray for his office desk. Elsewhere in the city's apothecaries there would be a thriving trade in 'Jumbo Jelly', allegedly rendered from the flesh of their eminent visitor. It did wonders for 'male weakness', it was delicately hinted. Jumbo Viagra, *avant la lettre*.

The ever-opportunistic Barnum tried, initially, to overlay the tragedy with another, more fanciful, version of his own devising, centred on the elephantine humanity displayed in Jumbo's last moments. As A.H. Saxon records:

Less than three days later Barnum was proposing to Harper Brothers that they publish, in time for the [Christmas] holidays, an illustrated children's book on the subject, to be entitled *The Life and Death of Jumbo*; and he was soon circulating among journalists a highly fictionalized account of Jumbo's last moments which had the elephant heroically pushing his keeper and Tom Thumb to safety then, unable to save himself, defiantly charging the locomotive head-on.[3]

In his head-to-head combat (in fact head to rump) with the 'metal leviathan', Barnum reported, Jumbo, the flesh and blood leviathan, had met his end 'with a becoming dignity and fortitude'. The clash of the two had a fine symbolism about it: Nature versus the Machine.

One thinks of King Kong, atop the Empire State Building, clawing at the buzzing biplanes – magnificent, but doomed. This last link with the lost mammalians of the prehistoric era, often himself called 'mammoth', fell prey to the wheels of the 'iron horse' – the same thing which was indirectly responsible for the genocide of the Native American. Symbolisms everywhere. Those of a literary disposition may have recalled the death of Anna Karenina. Translations of Tolstoy's novel were making their first appearance in 1885, but the main moral to be drawn from Jumbo's death was the obvious one: not even elephants can stand in the way of progress. Not even if the elephant was, as one admirer called him, the 'greatest, gentlest and most famous and heroic beast that ever lived'.[4] Barnum paid a local reporter (allegedly an eyewitness), Walter Wilkinson, $500 to circulate the 'heroic Jumbo' story and syndicate it nationwide. It worked. Suckers, suckers, suckers.

Jumbo's brave combat with the train was another dollop of the Prince of Humbugs' trademark hokum. But, *se non è vero è ben trovato*. It's a pretty picture and elephants are famously benevolent – none more so than this one. It would not, one likes to think, have been entirely out of character for Jumbo to have laid down his life for those he loved.

The death of 'Great Jumbo' was headline news in papers all over the world. No news is bad news for the owner of a three-ring circus, but financially it was a heavy blow for Barnum. Given the species' normal lifespan Jumbo might have been expected to live another half-century. Barnum's first public statement was stoic: 'Such a trifle never disturbs my nerves'. But the inner Phineas was mightily disturbed. He saw a mountain of silver dimes and quarters melting away in front of his eyes. His first response was the classic American one: 'Sue the bastards'. He shot off a claim for $100,000 damages against the Grand Trunk Railroad: a trunk for a trunk. (Privately he referred to what had happened up there in Canada as 'murder'.)

Barnum valued the property of Jumbo at $50,000 (five times what he had paid England for the beast three years before). The suit went nowhere. The Grand Trunk's lawyers pointed out that if they paid damages they could lay claim to the remains. That did not suit Barnum one little bit. He already had interesting plans for dead Jumbo. He settled with the 'murderers' for a measly $5,000 and free railway transportation for a year.

That story too has an interesting epilogue. The rail travel was valuable to Barnum – his train expenses were ruinously heavy. But in the contract between them, the railway's cunning lawyers had left some stations out of the detailed annexe of Canadian routes and stops. Barnum suddenly found himself landed with a bill for $5,000 to go a few miles down the track. It was 'legal' – those stations were not in the settlement agreement and the railroad could charge what it liked – and Barnum had no alternative means of travel. He declined to cough up and the compensation agreement was voided. Barnum decided to 'look big' and conceded that he was 'dished', but so what? You win a few and lose a few.

An intelligent and thoughtful man, particularly when his mind turned to money, Barnum had ruminated on the story of 'Old Bet' – supposedly the first elephant to be brought to the United States, in 1796. It's an interesting story for those interested in elephantine curiosities. This (with the inevitable encrustations of myth) is how it goes.

Old Bet, then young Bet, had been brought over on one of the American vessels (named, patriotically *The America*) that plied between the eastern seaboard and Calcutta. The she-calf, the captain recorded, was about the size of an ox. She would fetch, he reckoned, $500, 'at least', and would probably have to reside in the southern states, where it was semi-tropical. He did not realise what a treasure he had. The elephant fetched $10,000 (some accounts say more). She was sold to a series of showmen and circus owners on the cold easterly seaboard. None kept her long.

'Old Bet', as she came to be called, was originally intended by her last owner, the magnificently named Hachaliah Bailey, to be converted into a beast of burden – or so he later claimed. Barnum himself had toyed with that idea in earlier days, when he used an elephant to plough his fields in Bridgeport – visible, as he intended, by passengers on the nearby railroad. Good advertising.

Bailey, the story goes, found that Old Bet was so interesting to his neighbours, who showed themselves willing to pay good money to look at her close up and touch her, that he put together a travelling menagerie. It comprised four wagons, a trained dog, some pigs, a performing horse and an elephant – the star of the show. Dates are fuzzy, more so as there may have been more than one elephant named Old Bet around at the time, cashing in on the act. Bailey's 'circus' went on the road in around 1804. Coincidentally, Hachaliah was a remote ancestor of the Bailey, with whom Barnum was currently in partnership and going round America. Small world, the circus world.

On his regional tours on the thriving Eastern seaboard Bailey pulled in audiences to his tent for a payment of a quarter or 2 gallons of rum, to 'see the elephant' (no one wanted particularly to see the pig). The phrase became proverbial. Young Americans who went west, in the great 1749 gold rush, said they were going to 'see the elephant'. There was a thriving newsstand trade in elephant postcards in California to send to the folks back home.

Old Bet came to a sad end. Let George G. Goodwin, a scholar who has looked closely into the career of Old Bet, take up the story:

> What, we ask, became of Old Bet? Bentley was at the exhibit of 1816 when an elephant was killed, and he mentions the killing of the poor beast by a crank in Maine who felt that the animal was taking money from the public. 'A boy was induced,' he writes, 'to secrete himself as she passed on the road and to test the story that her hide was bulletproof. He did so, the shot hit her in the eye and instantly killed her.'[5]

Old Bet was stuffed and continued touring – earning handsomely for Bailey in death as she had done in life. And there was a huge saving on hay. Her hide, and other memorabilia, ended up in Barnum's 'museum', in the late 1820s. Bailey got another Betty, but injudiciously claimed publicly that her hide was bulletproof and in 1826 five young tearaways took up the challenge and proved him wrong. Betty's perforated hide was of no interest to any museum.

The life and death of Old Bet made crystal clear to Barnum, when he recalled it, what a showman might do with an elephant corpse other than bury it. But this was for the future and would require all the resources of his stagecraft. In the immediate aftermath ugly accounts of the death of Jumbo circulated, which needed to be put down by Barnum's lawyers. One newspaper printed the allegation that the owner had discovered Jumbo was fatally ill with TB, and had staged the death deliberately. It was first-degree elephanticide. Barnum, ever ready with a writ, sued for libel. But at this stage of his career anything could be believed about a man who had palmed off the Feejee Mermaid and Washington's 160-year-old wet nurse on paying customers.

Barnum didn't get his $50,000 libel damages, and there is an interesting letter which survives in the Tufts College archives, which hints at possible skulduggery. It was from the taxidermist friend of Barnum's, Henry Ward, to Professor John P. 'Doc' Marshall of Tufts College (both men had an interest in Jumbo's corpse), dated two weeks *before* the train accident:

> Today I want to ask you a word about Jumbo. He was here lately and his keeper told my cousin (quietly) that he does not think he will live long, that it is now nearly a year since he has been able to lie down . . . I thought I would . . . ask you whether it is well understood that the skin of this interesting brute is to go to Tufts College.

And am I (if then alive) to have the mounting of it?
Both these things were told me by Mr. Barnum when
I last saw him.[6]

Whether or not Jumbo was terminally ill – thereby making
the Ontario train accident cruelly convenient – will never be
known. Nor whether Barnum may have set the whole thing
up – he was a world master at staging events and it would not
have been beyond him. Death from rheumatism, or some other
degenerative illness, at a youthful age, would be too banal, and
might provoke awkward questions from the American Society
for the Prevention of Cruelty to Animals – a perennial foe – as
to whether elephants could really thrive in the artificial world
of the circus, shuttled around the country on trains, and made
to do stressful tricks for the public night after night, poked day
and night with sharp sticks. Barnum was also over-extended at
this period and feared bankruptcy.

It is clear as daylight that, when it suited them, he and
Scott conspired to their mutual advantage – as, for example, in
the great show of Jumbo's 'grief-stricken' refusal to leave the
London Zoo. Scott had a mysterious set of acoustic commands
and semaphoric signals, and he could make Jumbo do
anything. But could he make him run headlong into a train?
Almost certainly yes.

A number of questions suggest themselves to the suspicious
mind. Why were Jumbo and Tom held back, and not loaded
first? Why did Jumbo run 'up' the line, *towards* the train, in
the close care of a keeper who could 'make him do anything'?
Why the change of time? Was the train really 'unscheduled'?
Canadian railways were meticulously run and timetabled.

Scepticism was not entirely irrational, and where Phineas
T. Barnum was concerned there were always good grounds

for it. As Saxon, the most reliable chronicler of the Prince of Humbugs, reports, 'Rumours have persisted to the present day of Jumbo's being afflicted with some chronic, perhaps fatal illness and of Barnum's complicity in his death.'[7]

Saxon is disposed to disbelieve the rumours. I'm in two minds.

Other more plausible newspaper ruminations on the death drew attention to Jumbo's known love of the bottle, particularly after a show. Scotty knew a post-performance snifter made his friend docile. They both liked a drop. Was Jumbo sozzled when the accident occurred? A bit unsteady on his legs? Too confused to understand what Scotty was shouting at him? We shall never know what the largest breathalyser in the world might have come up with.

Ever the showman, Barnum set out to make the disaster an 'event'. More importantly, a money-spinning event. Great in life, Jumbo should be even greater in death: the Ozymandias of Elephants. But first the fast-rotting remains had to be disposed of and curated. No time was wasted. Morgue refrigerators did not come jumbo-sized (interestingly, that phrase comes up regularly nowadays in discussion of the large cremating vessels needed for the increasingly corpulent American population).

The appointed taxidermist, Henry Ward, came to St Thomas post haste, along with a talented young taxidermist, Carl E. Akeley.[8] With the help of six local butchers (who had something more interesting than lamb chops to talk about for the rest of their lives) the carcass was quartered and disembogued. The odour of the already putrefying cadaver was, reportedly, overpowering. When Chunee died the services of local West End perfumiers was called on, but that wouldn't work in the open air. Noses were held. Three large tanks were hired from a local pork factory to boil the flesh and 'innards' down. It took, it is recorded, 'five cords of wood' to do the boiling. The rendered jelly was, of course, highly saleable.

Jumbo's legs were cut off at the knees, the easier to roll him over and get to the other side of his massive cadaver. One of the butchers, a man called Peters, was assigned to deal with the now eviscerated belly and do the 'inside work'. He knew what Jonah must have gone through inside the great fish, he later quipped. Butchers are a famously jolly profession, but some of the rubber-neckers were by now, it was reported, 'pretty white around the gills'.

The skin was expertly stripped off. It was so tough that one of the butchers recalled he and his fellows had to stop every few minutes and sharpen their blades on their whetstones. Taxidermy was a highly developed skill in North America. Hunters loved memorials of what they had killed. Jumbo, however, was bigger than any bison or grizzly. The hide alone weighed 1,538 lb and it was promised to Tufts College.

So, too, the skeleton was promised (eventually) to the Smithsonian. The bones were taken off to Ward's institution in New York for articulation and over the next six months what was left of Jumbo was dissected, analysed for its scientific interest and prepared for exhibition to the paying public and (after the payments dwindled) academic resting places. Slices of his stunted tusks were sold off to a variety of institutions or given to friends.

Peters removed the indigestible objects from Jumbo's stomach. They included an English bobby's whistle, many keys, rivets, wire (from his food, incompetently unbaled), nails, ladies' trinkets, and a 'hatful' of English pennies and a half-crown. Jumbo went to his grave, it is pleasing to recall, with English Victorian *mementi* in his stomach – carrying the head of the Queen to his death. All American coins had been excreted; the English policeman's whistle remains mysterious.

Barnum had enjoyed a long association with Tufts as a trustee and major donor, and the connection valuably raised his image as a great philanthropist. Tufts had been established in the neighbourhood of Bridgeport, his hometown, and the college was founded on congenial, Universalist, religious doctrines. It had an enterprising animal-biology department to whom Barnum had some years earlier promised Jumbo's hide for stuffing and display – when in the distant future it became available. The promise was called in.

At Barnum's instruction, the stuffed Jumbo should be considerably larger than life. They did it on statues – think of the Lincoln Memorial – so why not on his elephant? Wasn't the statue there enlarged? Jumbo's skull, smashed by the train's impact on his tusk, could be repaired but nothing could be done to enlarge the bones. The taxidermist's upholstery would have to do the trick. It did, and more. When it went on display *The New York Times* noted, wryly, that death had not prevented Jumbo from continuing to grow.

Cornell University took possession of Jumbo's heart for a bargain-price $40 and the press breathlessly reported it to be 'the largest heart in the world'. It came in at a reported 47 lb, still moist. Measurements established it to be 28 inches long and 24 inches wide, with walls of the artery 5/8 of an inch thick. About the size of a small pig. Professor Burt G. Wilder, Cornell's distinguished comparative anatomist, planned to display and dissect it for the edification of his students.

Wilder was legendary among students on the campus for his 'brains in jars', including his prize exhibit, the brain of the murderer Edward H. Rulloff. It is recorded as the 'second largest on record' and is still proudly on display, with the rest of the professor's brain collection, at the university. Rulloff, a particularly horrible murderer, is famous for his last words to the hangman, 'Hurry it up! I want to be in *Hell* in time for dinner'.

Like other recipients of Jumbo's various parts, Cornell had to wait for their prize. The heart was shipped to the university in around 1889. Despite the long wait the zoology department did not have in stock a glass jar large enough to hold an anatomical object 2 feet in diameter. The massive organ was temporarily stored in a barrel of alcohol (the ghostly Jumbo doubtless hiccupped happily) until a large enough specimen jar was procured from the college glazier, with hooks and loops in the rim for suspended display.

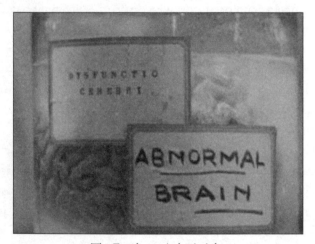

The Frankenstein brain joke

Thereafter things get hazy. As the years passed, interest in Jumbo's organ waned. It wasn't, to be honest, much to look at, and the jar and its contents went into dusty storage. Occasionally veterinarians would go into the vaults and take a peek. In the 1950s it was brought up, with other stored jars.

But that labelled, prominently, 'Jumbo's Heart' was mysteriously empty. How had it happened? One explanation was that the preservative fluid had evaporated over the years, desiccating the organ as it dried out. 'Dust thou art' etc. It was not found entirely plausible.

Mortuary expenses came to $1,650 – not, of course, picked up by Barnum, but by the increasingly impatient recipients of their promised Jumbo relics. The Civil War, and the American preference for shipping the bodies of slain warriors back to their loved ones (along with techniques of embalming to rival those of the ancient Egyptians), had made the country a world leader in the corporeal preservative arts.

Jumbo posed challenges, however, for the best morticians that even America could boast. The taxidermist Carl Akeley was commissioned to prepare the hide and the stuffed Jumbo for Tufts. He had been one of the first on the scene at St Thomas. Akeley was twenty-one years old and it was his first major commission. He rose to the challenge magnificently. The Jumbo job would make his name. Akeley went on to become a world-famous collector and curator of dead African mammals and is remembered to this day as 'the father of modern taxidermy'. Theodore Roosevelt, a doughty slayer of elephants, recruited him for his presidential safari in 1909. No other animal stuffer was as distinguished – but that was all in the future, after Jumbo.

Elephants would always be Akeley's *pièces de résistance*. He was renowned for his minute attention to wrinkles, texture, posture and minutely accurate zoological details, all of which produced wonderfully life-like results. He had begun stuffing animals aged 12 – wildlife which was shot or trapped in his native Wisconsin. The Jumbo pelt allowed him to hone and upsize his innovative techniques and take his craft, and his reputation, to new levels where it ceased to be craft and could legitimately be called art.

Before Akeley, taxidermy was a crude business of simply stuffing straw or cotton into skin, the bones (if they were bothered with) crudely sewn together. Anatomical upholstery. He, by contrast, had an artist's eye, deeply informed by the latest zoological science. He would begin with a base framework of wood and wire or even the skeleton itself (unavailable, given Barnum's crass division of the Jumbo spoils). Modelling clay would be used to create muscular contours and lines of tendon. Seams in the hide itself would be cunningly rendered invisible. The 'cement gun' and 'shotcrete' Akeley invented proved useful elsewhere in the conservation of old historically interesting buildings. If there was a Nobel Prize for animal stuffing, Carl Akeley would have had it on his mantelpiece. And over that mantelpiece would be an elephant skull (until late in life, when he underwent a change of heart, Akeley enjoyed killing animals as much as stuffing them).

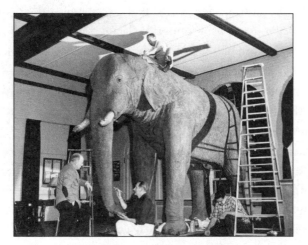

Carl Akeley's stuffed masterpiece

The promised recipients of the Jumbo skin and bones, Tufts and the Smithsonian, would have to wait awhile, their owner decreed. First for the remains to be prepared for display, then for Barnum to display those remains for commercial gain. Lots of it. He conceived for that purpose what he called a 'Double Jumbo' travelling exhibition – nicknamed 'the funeral tour'. To embellish the tour Barnum purchased Alice from London Zoo. The arrival of 'the widow of the late lamented Jumbo' on 16 April 1886 was, the New York press claimed, 'the talk of the town'. It was not, apparently, an easy voyage. As the *Reading Eagle* told its readers: 'There was a report that the stranded French steamer carrying her was waterlogged and Alice had been thrown overboard. This proved to be incorrect.'[9]

Alas, it was not death by water which would, in a few months, kill her. Mrs Jumbo was now the second most famous widow in the world. As the *Reading Eagle* went on to report (unironically): 'Alice will be the first widow on record to have the satisfaction of standing alongside her stuffed husband, deceased.'

Probably true. The other royal widow, Queen Victoria, would not have been amused at the thought of doing so. Madame Tussaud's had a wax Albert, not a stuffed one – one doubts whether the Queen ever saw it. She had, of course, decreed the erection of a truly jumbo-sized monument in Hyde Park for her deceased consort. And the monarch was reported to have discreetly visited the Regent's Park Zoo to 'bid her elephantine majesty, Alice, an adieu' – queens in black, both of them.

The New York Times (penned, clearly enough, by Barnum himself) reported that when Barnum and 'Tody' (Barnum's press agent, R.R. Hamilton) came on board, to welcome Alice, 'The recognition was instantaneous, and she seemed to read in their eyes the awful intelligence that her dear old Jumbo was no more. She burst into a flood of tears and throwing her trunk around Tody's neck seemed to whisper between sobs, "I know you were my husband's friend".'

She was then landed on shore by the 'great derrick "Ox"', which she suffered 'serenely'. She was, it was clear, a real 'lady'.

The encounter with the remains of 'her late lord and master' in Madison Square Garden was, the paper's readers were informed, another trauma for the widow:

> When Alice first saw the stuffed skin of Jumbo she seemed like one in a trance. Then she touched his skin with her trunk and again burst into a flood of tears. She knew at last that he was dead, and as she looked into his glassy eyes and fondled his stuffed forehead with her trunk she seemed to say: 'My poor old Jumbo, your Alice weeps for you'. She was gently led to the Madison Avenue end of the Garden where his skeleton stands, and chained with a bolt close to it. Then she wept as only a widow can weep and the trough, thoughtfully arranged for her tears, was soon filled to overflowing. Tomorrow she will be on show at the Garden.[10]

(At 25¢ a ticket, of course.)

When asked if she really recognised Jumbo, Scott replied, indignantly, 'Of course she did. She *told* me so.' He was, since his great friend's death, going melancholy mad. Barnum, to his credit, pensioned him and gave him a job looking after the circus's small animals.

Exactly a year after Jumbo's death, the two great skin-and-bone relics, along with fleshy Alice, were exhibited to the world at a gala event in New York. A 'gelatin snack', allegedly prepared from Jumbo's pulverised tusks, was on offer by way of refreshment. It's not recorded whether it was much relished by those daring enough to taste it. There was, for those who had been close to Jumbo, something obscurely cannibalistic about doing so, but 'ivory' shavings had been available as homeopathic medicine from the 1850s. They were boiled up to produce a thick jelly which – advertisements broadly hinted . . . were a sovereign remedy for male erectile dysfunction. Barnum had been selling shavings and clippings of Jumbo-tusk for some months, and quite a lot had been pirated at St Thomas. One hopes it added to human happiness.

One of the advantages of Jumbo being now dead was that he was more easily carted around America and the world. No more need for a 'Palace Car', or the gigantic metal-ribbed container which had brought him to the US. A plain wooden box would now serve. Jumbo could even be transported back to England, and indeed he was, in collaboration with that country's leading Sanger's Circus, a partner in the Barnum & Bailey consortium. This far-flung stop on the 'Funeral Tour' was rendered easier by a fire having broken out in the circus winter quarters, which conveniently incinerated Alice in 1886. Suttee, of a kind. It attracted relatively little notice. Jumbo, as ever, was the story. (Barnum was rumoured to have set the fire via some convenient arsonist. It was unlikely – but you never knew with him.)

The college and the museum chafed, awaiting their promised Jumbo relics, but Barnum was determined to squeeze every last cent out of his elephant property, before parting with it.

Despite the picture overleaf, the skeleton and mummy were never placed side by side or that close in the tent because of their embarrassing difference in size. But no one seems to have

P.T.BARNUM & CO'S GREATEST SHOW ON EARTH
& THE GREAT LONDON CIRCUS COMBINED WITH

SANGERS ROYAL BRITISH MENAGERIE & GRAND INTERNATIONAL SHOWS

Jumbo and Alice on their goodbye tour of the world

complained and the crowds flocked in. *The New York Times* archly reported, 'Jumbo Stuffed a Greater Attraction than Jumbo Alive.'

It was not until 1889 that the hide and bones were dispatched to their final destinations. William Burnip went to his final destination in the San Francisco earthquake of 1906 and a despondent Matthew Scott spent his final years in near destitution at the circus's winter quarters in Bridgeport. He wrote an incomplete, incoherent, ghost-written account of his relationship with Jumbo, which attracted no notice, and he died in the city almshouse, Barnum having gone to his reward some time ago and the pension evidently ceasing. Scott is reported to have passed his final days talking to an imaginary Jumbo, despondently. The better part of him had perished alongside his beloved friend on that awful September night. And only he knew exactly what had happened.

St Thomas retained a proprietary interest in what, alas, would forever be their best-known, if briefly resident, inhabitant. In 1977 a memorial plaque was solemnly unveiled and on

28 June 1985 a centenary statue was erected. A fine structure, by Winston Bronnum, it bestows on Jumbo the tusks he never, in his lifetime, had. The Prince of Humbugs would have approved of the fanciful dentures. The honour of unveiling the statue was awarded to the only surviving witness of the tragedy, Ruby Copeman; she was 105 years old.

Jumbo's memorial statue in St Thomas

Postscript

The memory of Jumbo was kept alive by the universality of the epithet. A Broadway musical, called *Jumbo*, was staged in 1935, based on his life and death. It ran for over 200 performances and there was nothing small about the venture, which was advertised as 'the most expensive play ever to be staged on Broadway'. It cost $340,000. The producer, Billy Rose (a legendary Broadway figure), put $35,000 of his own money into it and the Hippodrome Theater had to be rebuilt, to accommodate the spectacle and its animal performers. They included an elephant, of course, and 500 other animals, a revolving stage and trapezes.

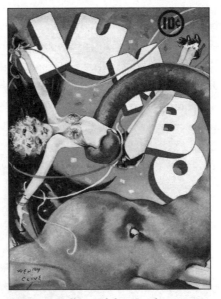

Hollywood does Jumbo

Jumbo the musical had a distinguished Rodgers and Hart score, performed in the theatre by Paul Whiteman and his orchestra, then the most popular band in America, fusing as it did dance music with jazz. The story loosely hinged on a circus constantly on the brink of financial collapse. The comic star of the piece was Jimmy the 'Schnoz' Durante, famous for his own Jumbo-sized proboscis. At the end of each performance, Durante lay down on the stage and allowed a live elephant to place its foot upon his head. It was reported that:

> The biggest laugh in the show always erupted when Durante's character was stopped by the sheriff in the process of trying to smuggle Jumbo out of the circus. 'Where are you going with that elephant?' demanded the lawman. Looking around innocently, Durante replied, 'What elephant?'[11]

Even after its jumbo-sized run the musical lost money and would be remembered principally as a warning not to attempt anything as lavish again. The musical resurfaced as the film *Billy Rose's Jumbo* in 1962. It starred Doris Day ('America's Sweetheart') and the thirty years older 'Schnoz' Durante, his hallmark feature if anything enlarged to truly elephantine length with age.

The Smithsonian never did get the promised skeleton. It went to the American Museum of Natural History in New York, where it was kept on display until 1977, when it was carted off to the Museum's stores, along with similarly cumbersome whale skeletons which were taking up too much room, but were too valuable to put into the garbage grinder.

Jumbo's final turn

The skeleton was most recently re-exhibited in 1993, a date established as the bicentenary of the circus in America. As always, visitors could not refrain from touching it 'for luck', and the lower bones glistened, as if French-polished, from all the tactile contact they had received. After the exhibition it was put back in storage, where, presumably, it still rests and patiently awaits the tricentenary.

Jumbo Goes to College

Tufts College finally got its hide, extravagantly stuffed, in 1889, Barnum having by then extracted every cent he could from displaying it around the world. As the college chronicle recalls:

> Jumbo (i.e. the stuffed simulacrum) arrived at the North Somerville station, via the main line of the Boston & Lowell Railroad, then continued on a private sidetrack of the Somerville Electric Light Company. After being unloaded at the junction of Highland and Willow Avenues, he was hauled to Tufts by a double team of horses. When that team proved unable to pull him up College Hill, more than 50 Tufts professors and students, aided by some local boys, completed the task.[1]

Barnum, as has been said, had been drawn to Tufts by its closeness to his Bridgeport home and its connection with his brand of evangelical religion. He was appointed a trustee, but never attended a single meeting and is recorded as only having come to the campus once, in 1886, when his Jumbo 'Funeral Tour' was getting on the road. But he put lots of money the college's way and, as the college history records:

As benefactors go Barnum was stellar: His interest in natural history led him to donate hundreds of choice specimens to the college as well as the funds to build and maintain the Barnum Museum of Natural History. (His initial 'secret' gift of more than $50,000 built the museum; another $30,000 or more came to Tufts through Barnum's will, following his death in 1891.)[2]

He did, characteristically, stipulate that the word 'Barnum' should be prominent on the outside of the building. The college swallowed any shame the connection between their Ivory Tower and the 'Greatest Show on Earth' might have engendered among the crustier trustees; $50,000 sweetens most things.

Jumbo was promptly adopted as the college's mascot – in line with the University of California's bear, Princeton's tiger and (my favourite) UC Santa Cruz's banana slug, and their battle chant, 'Go! Slugs! Go!'

Tufts' girls go wild for Jumbo

'Jumbos, Jumbos, Jumbos' is the loyal cry, to this day, at Tufts ball games, one is told. Live elephants are occasionally rented for big games from nearby zoos, and there is a thriving trade in memorabilia. College buildings are named after the great beast and the university website notes, obscurely, that 'Jumbo vendible tchotchkes' are available in the campus shop. The jumbo insignia is loyally etched on mugs, T-shirts, bumper stickers and innumerable knick-knacks. It is noticeable, however, that over the years the image has remained one to terrify the opposition on the field of (football) battle.

Somewhere in the heaven he firmly believed in (and was sure he was destined for) Phineas T. Barnum must be furious that he did not trademark the Jumbo image, as Walt Disney did with Dumbo.

Over the years after 1889 it became a ritual for Tufts students to ceremonially pull Jumbo's tail for good luck, before big games and exams, and put pennies in his trunk. The trunk bore the donations well, the tail, alas, had a harder time with the tugging and in 1952 it was yanked off. The original tail was carefully stored in the library's rare book vaults, along with all the vellum and calfskin, and a replacement was attached to Jumbo for future yanking.

The desecration proved, in a way, lucky. The Barnum Museum was burned down on 14 April 1975 when refrigeration wires short-circuited and Jumbo perished in the flames, along with the banner name the donor had insisted be placed over the entrance, to keep that name famous forever. Sic transit. What happened next is recounted, vividly, in the university chronicle:

Former athletic director Rocco J. 'Rocky' Carzo vividly recalls how Phyllis Byrne, the athletic department's administrative assistant, rushed into his office the morning of April 15 with the frightening news of the fire. She got a peanut butter jar and gave it to a guy named George Wilson, who was on the maintenance staff. Phyllis said to him, 'I want you to get me some of Jumbo's ashes up there. He's our mascot and we ought to save these ashes.' So [George] came back later with this jar filled with these ashes.[3]

It was a 14-oz (has it come to this?) Peter Pan Crunchy Peanut Butter jar. Empty, of course – peanut butter does not stick around long at Tufts. The jar, to this day, serves as the football team's good luck charm. Go, Jumbos! Whenever a director of athletics retires at Tufts, the sacred jar is passed on to his/her successor.

The tail survives and is as lovingly preserved as the Turin Shroud. Alongside a fire extinguisher, one trusts.

It would not, one suspects, please either Jumbo or Barnum to know that the team which bears the elephant name and mascot plays in the New England Small College Athletic Conference, inspired by a 14-oz peanut butter jar. It currently ranks ninth in the NESCAC rankings. Small!

Bigger Than Jumbo: The Death of Jingo

To fill the large hole left by Jumbo, the ZSL purchased Jingo, another fine African elephant. He was acquired, for £300, from the same dealer who had supplied the zoo with Jumbo's 'mate', Alice. Jingo arrived at the zoo in early July, three months after Jumbo's departure, and was installed in Jumbo's old den. He was small, and judging by a popular picture of him, only a few years old. The name, clearly, was meant to echo heart-warmingly. And, unlike 'Jumbo', it echoed the war song which has left us the word 'jingoism' ('belligerent patriotism', as the dictionaries will starchily inform you). The arrival of Jingo coincided with the outbreak of the 1882 Anglo-Egyptian war. It was a campaign of conquest in a region of North Africa not far from the ancient Nubia, where once African elephants had roamed in their vast herds. The war song was popular in the early 1880s in music halls and pubs. It opens:

> We don't want to fight but *by Jingo* if we do
> We've got the ships, we've got the men, we've got the money too.

Jingo was an unlikely war elephant but, in a way, that's what he was. Note the quasi-military uniform, the masterly hand. Compare it with the civilian sloppiness of Matthew Scott, who always looked as if he'd just rolled out of the Prince Albert pub in nearby Regent's Park Road, still the nearest watering hole to the zoo:

Jingo and his smart keeper

Compared with Jumbo, history has left little record of Jingo – wholly eclipsed as he was by his predecessor. He figures on postcards and was in adulthood finely tusked (always considered a bit of a risk with children around) and the zoo's lead elephant. He grew to a massive size, larger by at least a couple of inches than Jumbo in height. But he was leaner in the leg and shank and weighed in some 2 tons lighter than Jumbo.

Jingo dutifully carried many hundreds of thousands of children in the 'amiable monster' fashion pioneered by his noble predecessor. But troubles cropped up around 1901. Jingo was young – still in his early twenties. Ominous news stories – jokey, but worrying – began to appear. In September of 1901 (a period dominated by the death of the Queen) it emerged Jingo had for two years been sleeping standing up, leaning against the wall of his cell. Despite Sir Thomas Browne's ideas, this is not normal. In their natural habitat African elephants do not slumber leaning against trees (allowing the wily native to capture them by quietly cutting the tree down). Jingo's legs were weakening. Then, one night, evidently feeling too weak to stand, he finally lay down on the bed which his handlers prepared for him every night. The next morning his 'matutinal bun' (as the press archly called it) was brought and it was found that he could not raise himself on his legs to eat it.

The zoo director, a man called Thompson, arranged for ropes and pulleys to be brought. A rope was passed around the 'great beast's hind quarters' with a pulley to a beam above. Thirty men pulled lustily. The rope broke. The vast backside didn't move. It was the old story with elephants, immovable objects, resistible forces – nor was Jingo taking the operation well. Eventually he was raised sufficiently for him to regain his hind legs and then his forequarters. He was very grumpy and one of the handlers was buffeted badly.

At this point in his life Jingo's temper deteriorated. It wasn't, as with Jumbo, sex which was at the root of it; it was more like premature senility. He was old before his time and it was now judged wise to keep him from children and anyone other than his closest attendants – and even they were wise to be careful. He was closely penned up for two years, which did nothing for his temper and nothing for the zoo's investment in him. This was not an elephant rest home.

Then, exactly as had happened with Jumbo, a stroke of luck appeared in the form of a Yankee huckster, with more money than sense. Frank C. Bostock made the wholly reckless offer of $100,000 for 'the biggest elephant in the world', who also had 2-foot tusks. By now measurement proved that Jingo outstripped Jumbo by 2 inches, hoof to skull (one wonders if the

ZSL procured an elastic tape measure). The zoo was desperate to get rid of Jingo, who was eating them out of house and home, and earning nothing for his keep. Bostock did not take the minimal precaution of checking whether the beast's pins were up to supporting the biggest animal in the world. *Caveat emptor*. The American, as Barnum would say, had been suckered.

Bostock is an interestingly zany character.[1] He was actually born in Derbyshire, England, in 1866 and worked in small circuses in Britain before going to where the real action was, in the United States. His style, when he became a proprietor himself, was massed animals – composing 'pyramids' of them with himself placed in the middle. He loved what he called the 'great arena' concept, using animals dramatically and balletically. 'Imagine', ran the programme at the Pan-American Exposition of 1901, 'one man surrounded by twenty-five monster lions, sitting calmly in their midst reading a newspaper, while they group themselves about him as peacefully as kittens around a little child!'

The Bostock style was ultra-theatrical. And he himself was always at the centre and front of stage – 'the Animal King'. Often at the risk of his life, something that added to the event. Rajah, a Bengal tiger, came near to ripping his arm off in 1901, and left him scarred for life. But it was claw for claw. Bostock wrote a book on training wild animals in which he declared his philosophy to be:

> Wild animals are never to be trusted until they are dead. They may respect their trainer, his coolness and his determination, but they do not love him. I was born among wild beasts and have devoted every day of my life to them, and you may take my word for it that nothing is so treacherous as a wild animal.[2]

Frank C. Bostock, Animal King

Bostock loved stunts, and so did his thousands-strong audiences. He was the first to introduce the boxing kangaroo to America. In 1901 he dispatched a large crocodile over Niagara Falls and introduced an aroma of sexual mystique into his shows (something that strait-laced Barnum never would have done) with characters like Madame Morelli, the little Frenchwoman who lounged among jaguars and leopards, and Madame Aurora, the dancing bear trainer.

Bostock's circus toured but his home base was the Cyclotron theatre and gardens in Baltimore. The price of admission was 25¢ per adult and 15¢ per child. He owned, at his peak, 400 animals including pumas (Theodore Roosevelt had some hunter's questions about how they compared with leopards), polar bears, monkeys, an extensive menagerie of smaller animals and a wildly fluttering aviary of birds. And of course, an elephant – Big Liz – offering Jumbo-style rides.

It all came to grief on the night of 30 January 1901 when the Cyclotron caught fire and burned to the ground, illuminating the whole of East Baltimore. It was, in fact, *son et lumière*. All the animals perished and, as one newspaper graphically put it: 'Bostock's Animals Groan in Agony as They Roast'.

Unsurprisingly, he was denied permission to rebuild on the ashes of this animal barbecue and was lucky not to be ridden out of the town he had done so much to destroy on a rail. He had, however, been careful to insure (his canniness in this department often led to suspicions of fraud). He determined, having lost out in Baltimore, to move his business to Coney Island, where he built 'Bostock's Dreamland'. It was a large, electrically lit (then a crowd-drawing novelty), amusement park with an animal arena, rides and cabinets of curiosities, all dominated by a central tower higher than any building in New York City.

Bostock's Dreamland

It was for this new show, opening in summer 1904, that, like the patriarch of his profession, he wanted the 'largest elephant in the world'. And he found it exactly where Barnum had – London Zoo.

The usual 'wail' went up from the British newspapers at the loss of Jingo. But since he had not been on display in recent years, the lament was muted and short-lived compared with Jumbomania. A huge teakwood box had been prepared in America for Jingo's transport, 'heavily strapped with iron'. It was placed, with the door open, against Jingo's cell, with a heap of tempting fodder (hay, carrots, onions) placed inside at the far end. One could see it as the largest mousetrap in the world. But Jingo was canny – he suspected a trap and refused to move. The standoff, and hunger strike, lasted two days. It was dangerous for an elephant to go without food so long – and the worst preparation for a transatlantic voyage. As indeed it proved.

Jingo finally lumbered, surlily, into what would be his coffin. This was 3 March 1901. The doors were battened down. 'I guess that will hold him for a while,' gloated Thompson, the zoo director who (evidence suggests) hated the beast which had given the zoo such great trouble. But the huge box was not, it emerged, huge enough and it cramped poor Jingo like a straitjacket. This too was bad.

Jingo was transported to nearby Camden Goods Yard, then on to Liverpool, by Great Western rail, the box resting on a flatbed truck. It couldn't get through some tunnels, which had to be dismantled, brick by brick. On 5 March, he was loaded on board the White Star steamship *Georgic*, where he was stowed, in his over-tight crate on the airless lower deck aft. Bostock had hired four keepers – there was no Matthew Scott or mahout to soothe Jingo as there had been for Jumbo, and no passengers feeding him on sweetmeats and champagne. He was, effectively, in solitary confinement.

One of the keepers later recorded that 'from the time of sailing from Liverpool he lost interest in life'. It was reported that 'For sixty hours the mammoth beast trumpeted without cessation'.[3] His cries roused a cargo of leopards and tigers also being transported on board. It was animal cacophony; the relentless noise drove the crew near to madness. On the fifth day Jingo's condition became so hysterical that his keepers gave him gallons of whisky soaked in biscuits. Jingo became more savage than ever under the influence of the alcohol, the discomfort of a stormy crossing and what seems to have been terminal baffled fury. At 9 a.m. on 12 March the trumpeting stopped. He was dead.

The captain of the *Georgic*, at the end of his tether in this ark of madness, was insistent that he was not going to carry any decomposing elephants on board. The four men who acted as keepers, their employment now terminated, asked if they could flay the animal and have the hide. The captain firmly refused – he did not want butchery on board any more than he wanted putrefying pachyderm. Burial at sea, immediately, was ordered. The magnificent 2-foot tusks were cut off. It was all that Mr Bostock was going to get for his $100,000 purchase, other than the insurance money (as usual, it was suspected he might come out ahead).

For the obsequies, a special derrick and four winches were erected on deck. Sixteen men were required to do the hauling, and the corpse was thrown overboard, taking the port railing with it. There was a 'tremendous splash'. The captain did not, as ritual required with seaboard deaths, read any prayer, although he may privately have thanked God. He was evidently glad to be rid of the damned thing. The vessel was now almost exactly halfway across the Atlantic.

'Jingo was booked', as *The New York Times* archly put it, 'for transfer to a submarine menagerie'. But, it transpired, he wasn't. On 24 April, a month and a half later, under the headline 'Jingo a Floating Island', it was reported that the British steamer *Colorado* had sighted the body of Jingo, 700 miles from where it had been cast into the waves. It was a sad end to a very sad elephant tale. Only Milton's lines are appropriate:

> Thus Satan talking to his neerest Mate
> With Head up-lift above the wave, and Eyes
> That sparkling blaz'd, his other Parts besides
> Prone on the Flood, extended long and large
> Lay floating many a rood, in bulk as huge
> As whom the Fables name of monstrous size,
> Titanian, or Earth-born, that warr'd on Jove,
> Briarios or Typhon, whom the Den
> By ancient Tarsus held, or that Sea-beast
>   Leviathan[4]

Bigger and Better Than Jumbo:
The White Elephant

The ZSL had decided to replace Jumbo with Jumbo II – the spectacularly ill-fated Jingo – but that was not Barnum's style. He went for something bigger and better – if not in size then in 'mystique'. Barnum and his principal rival Forepaugh had so many elephants, and had put them on show in so many places, that the public was in danger of becoming blasé with more of the same.

It would, the Prince of Hokum decided, have to be the white elephant, the beast that was 'sacred' in Siam (present-day Thailand) – a country with many glamorous associations. The King of Siam, intending the highest respect, had sent a tuft of white elephant hair to Queen Victoria, who was probably rather mystified. White elephants were not merely royal mascots, they were religious icons: Buddha was supposed to inhabit their pale bodies.[1]

Barnum, a religious man by nature, had for some time been toying with the idea of an Indian yogi – beds of nails, stopped heartbeats, forty days without food and all that. But a naked native was intrinsically unglamorous and verging on the freakish kind of exhibit he was resolutely trying to put behind him. And, anyway, his scouts in India had been unable to find a yogi who seemed genuine – even by the showman's flexible standards. It was, Barnum said, frustratedly, like trying to buy 'Santy Claus'.

White elephants would be perfect for his purposes. In zoological fact they are simply albinos – no more uncommon than albinos of any species. They are also known as 'pink elephants'; their hides are often mottled pink, and their eyes are that colour – not pretty. They are, nonetheless, regarded as supremely holy in Siam and are cared for by a cadre of priests. They are never taken into captivity in that country and never put to work. They cost a fortune to keep up and give nothing in return except, hopefully, divine favour. Proverbially they are gifts which you give someone whom you want to bankrupt. Barnum, of course, had no intention of respecting the sacredness of his white elephant, when he got his specimen. Its idle life would be over. It would work as hard as had his famous Siamese twins, the conjoined Chang and Eng Bunker, in making him money. He might, though, hire some likely looking priests to add to the spectacle. That was as far as he was prepared to go with the holiness stuff. But first he had to get his white elephant.

Barnum's quest led to one of the more comical episodes in American circus history, the 'War of the White Elephant'. His agent in Bangkok, J.B. Gaylord, was charged to find the desired beast and hang the cost. Gaylord's first effort went well enough but then fanatic Siamese priests (it was plausibly suspected) contrived to poison the animal on the eve of its being shipped to America. Better death than sacrilege was their view of the matter. White elephants belonged in Buddhist temples, not circus tents. 'Bring skin, tusks and bones enough to stuff,' cabled Barnum, unwilling to write off all his investment.

In late 1883, Gaylord succeeded, not in Siam but Burma. Huge bribes were required before the deal was clinched and Barnum later claimed that $250,000 was eventually expended. In *The Times* he released a bulletin letting it be known the purchase price alone was $40,000. It probably wasn't but he almost certainly paid more than the $10,000 Jumbo cost. The Burmese King Thibaw was hard up at the time and Barnum's dollars induced him to override any religious scruples to part with the sacred and (hopefully) glistening white animal called Toung Taloung – something to amaze American eyes.

Toung Taloung broke his journey from Rangoon to New York with a three-month stay, from January to March 1884, in the ZSL. The stopover was convenient to all parties. The exotic visitor – landed with the usual Barnum promotional song and dance – would swell the London institution's coffers (these were traditionally dead months) with a useful rake-off for Barnum.

Toung Taloung would be, *The Times* grandly promised on 22 December, 'the first and only genuine white elephant ever imported to England'. Unfortunately the only genuinely white thing about the great white elephant was its tusks and the lies Barnum was spreading about. When reporters actually viewed Toung Taloung with their own eyes the British paper of record changed its tune radically. It had been hoaxed; the whole British nation had been hoaxed. 'At first glance,' it told its readers on 17 January:

> The beast . . . looked very much like any other elephant, except that it had been lying in dust. He is 15 years old. A more careful examination, however, showed it to be of lighter complexion, though it seems to be a stretch of language to call it 'white'. It has a mottled appearance,

but it may be that when the animal has had a good scrubbing he will approach much nearer than he does at present to what a 'white elephant' ought to be.

The Pears' Soap publicity department was quick to pick up the 'good scrubbing' tip. While Toung Taloung was still in residence in Jumbo's old stall at the ZSL it rushed out 'screaming' advertisements: 'THE REAL SECRET OF THE WHITE ELEPHANT—PEARS' SOAP. Matchless for the Complexion'.

Pears is quick off the mark

The Spectator, unwilling to forgive Barnum for the 'theft' of Jumbo, was particularly hard on the so-called white elephant in its issue of 19 January:

The public fancies that white elephant is white, and will hold that a slate-coloured brute with pink patches, not eight feet high, and not otherwise remarkable, is not the animal it is looking for . . . but Toung is neither big nor beautiful, nor anything else, except possibly 'sacred' among a people who are less known in England than any race in Asia. Mr Barnum should give some sharp Yankee chemist a few thousand dollars to invent a new bleaching process, and then show his elephant in the colours which the populace expect.

In the zoo itself attendance spiked with sightseers whose disappointment was universal. Dark comments were made about elephantine leprosy. It wasn't helped by Barnum staging a phoney ceremony of Buddhist 'priests' venerating the sacred animal. They were no more priests than Toung Taloung was Snow White. Christians and genuine Buddhists were appalled. How low would Barnum sink? As low as he had to, it seemed.

In his jaunty chronicle of the Great Showman's humbuggery, Neil Harris quotes one of the cockney-smart handlers at the ZSL: 'White, sir? – Well, sir, not *werry* white, exactly; but, so I am given to understand – *werry* sacred'.[2]

On the animal's arrival in the US Barnum rushed down to the dock in a cab, shouting over his shoulder instructions that the President should be informed. But in the US the reception was much the same as it had been in England – baffled disappointment. Where was this wonderful 'white' elephant? This one was gray with pink blotches. Barnum was forced into the not entirely satisfactory justification that 'there is no such thing as a really pure white elephant . . . this is as white as God makes 'em'. It might fly in the royal court of Siam, but it didn't in

THE BURMESE WHITE ELEPHANT, "TOUNG TALOUNG"

A 'white' elephant?

Madison Square Garden. Even the suckers were unimpressed by the white elephant that wasn't white.

Things got a lot worse. Barnum's great enemy, Adam Forepaugh, was getting his own white elephant. He had noted the public disapproval in London at the lack of anything that could be called white about Barnum's animal. All's fair in love and circus wars. Before his specimen, the Light of Asia, left Liverpool, Forepaugh made arrangements to whitewash the beast. He hadn't been fool enough to show it off in England; he merely painted it for its arrival in the US. He also stole a march by getting it there a good week before the shabby Toung Taloung.

Forepaugh's elephant really was white. 'Too white for Barnum,' Forepaugh's brazen advertisements proclaimed. His was the real thing. The 'highest scientific authority' had vouched for it. Barnum's beast was 'a rank fraud'.

Forepaugh attracted the punters while Barnum was left feebly arguing that you couldn't expect his elephant to be white because God didn't make white elephants. It was game set and match to Forepaugh, who had out-humbugged

Forepaugh's whiter elephant

the Prince of Humbugs. It didn't happen often but it had happened now.

The war of the white elephants ended in carnage. The Light of Asia died in less than a year, poisoned by the fortnightly painting inflicted on it. 'Died? He was already dyed,' cracked Barnum, when he heard the news. But he did not laugh long. In November 1887 Toung Taloung was killed in the same fire that killed 'Mrs Jumbo', Alice, in the circus's Bridgeport winter quarters. As with Jumbo, Barnum confected a pretty death legend. Toung had forced his way back into the burning building, choosing suicide; or call it male suttee. Perhaps he was just fed up with being made fun of.

Mark Twain (a staunch admirer of Barnum – he loved virtuosic fakery) got in on the act with a short story, *The Stolen*

White Elephant (1882). A white elephant, dispatched as a gift from the King of Siam to Queen Victoria, goes missing in New Jersey, where he stopped for some medical treatment. The police, led by the sharp Inspector Blunt, are quickly on to it. Who has snaffled the white elephant? Given the date only one name pops up. Who, in America, was so desperate to get one that he was prepared to pay $40,000 for a white elephant? Sly references to Jumbo and Barnum throughout dissolve any lingering doubt as to whodunit. The Prince of Hokum had, we assume, done it again.

One mustn't give the story away. Enough to quote the following when the white elephant's 'deliverer' (handler) reports his loss to a pettifogging clerk in the missing person's department, who insists on treating the missing elephant as if it were a missing person:

He took a pen and some paper. 'Now – name of the elephant?'

'Hassan Ben Ali Ben Selim Abdallah Mohammed Mois Alhammal Jamsetjejeebhoy Dhuleep Sultan Ebu Bhudpoor.'

'Very well. Given name?'

'Jumbo.'

'Very well. Place of birth?'

'The capital city of Siam.'

'Parents living?'

'No – dead.'

'Had they any other issue besides this one?'

'None. He was an only child.'

Apart from little flashes like this it's not vintage Twain, but it must have been mustard sharp in 1882 and ever sharper in 1887, when the white elephant war was everywhere being bruited in the press.

Postscript

There's another odd little surfacing of the mysterious beast in Ernest Hemingway's enigmatic (very) short story, *Hills Like White Elephants* (1927). A man and a woman are waiting in a station bar for a train in rural Spain. Sporadic words are exchanged, which inform the reader not at all. They seem to be lovers and, the reader infers, she is pregnant. As they sip their drinks, she regards the landscape and the distant hills:

'They look like white elephants,' she said.
'I've never seen one,' the man drank his beer.
'No, you wouldn't have.'
'I might have,' the man said. 'Just because you say I wouldn't have doesn't prove anything.'
The girl looked at the bead curtain. 'They've painted something on it,' she said. 'What does it say?'
'Anis del Toro. It's a drink.'
'Could we try it?'

I've never made sense of the white elephants' reference and a lot of commentary I've read on the subject makes nonsense, in my view. Perhaps one should force any interpretation and just enjoy the narrative sounds and sonorous Hemingway-esque silences. But the conjunction of 'white elephant' and 'paint' strikes an echo, if one knows anything about the 'war' between Barnum and Forepaugh.

Hemingway, as it happened, had seen lots of elephants and shot quite a few. His elephant gun is famed and much written about. It was a double-barrelled .577-calibre Nitro Express and weighed 16 lb. The monster was made in London in 1913, by the firm of Westley Richards. Unlucky the elephant, of whatever colours, that found itself at the other end of those massive barrels.

During the Second World War Hemingway served the US coastguard by scouting for German U-boats in the Gulf of Mexico. His boat was unarmed but he brought his trusty .577 with him, confident he could sink any submarine he came across. He had better luck with elephants.

Gray Elephants, Pink Elephants and Blue Elephants

'I am an alcoholic.' I've said it innumerable times at meetings and I hope to say it, sober, many times more. Was Jumbo a fellow alcoholic? I like to fancy he was. It's one of the things which has given me a sense of intimacy with the great animal.

Jumbo was the only animal in Barnum's circus (or, before that, the London Zoo) reported to have a love of the bottle. The great pachyderm – about to amaze and charm the children of the new world – had a bout of stage fright and steeled his nerves for disembarkation in New York harbour with an appropriate bottle of port, dextrously transported from trunk to mouth and glugged it down as fast as a yard of ale in a college fraternity drinking game. I used to do something similar in my early days as a university lecturer before taking the lectern.

Jumbo's habitual boozing was entirely contrary to the wishes of Barnum, who was an evangelistic abstainer and the author of grandiloquent temperance tracts. He must have been the unjolliest of dinner guests, and probably the most garrulous. It was his proud boast that abstention was the law of his animal kingdom. 'Pure water,' he proclaimed, 'is the natural drink for man and beast. My lions, tigers, and even the great Jumbo himself drink nothing stronger than water.'[1]

It was, of course, so much Barnum humbuggery. Just because alcohol doesn't cross your lips doesn't mean that fibs can't traverse in the opposite direction. Jumbo, we are told, 'according to several witnesses was in the habit of drinking daily a keg of beer'.[2] On his trip over to New York, he was publicly given plentiful draughts of champagne by revelling fellow passengers, who were amazed by what he could do with a bottle.

Barnum, who could not but witness the drink-fuelled high jinks, sourly observed, without irony, apparently: 'that animal's growth has been stunted by beer'. (He was always uneasy that the paying public would, when they actually saw him in the 11-foot and 6-ton flesh, realise that Jumbo was magnitudes smaller than the advertising posters and would cry foul, as an embarrassing number of them had done about his Fejee Mermaid.) But, disapproving though he was, he did not put a stop to Jumbo's 'habit'. It kept him docile. And Barnum did not want any more of those musth shenanigans which had so alarmed the English.

The classic overindulgence of the 'solitary drinker' seems to have been Jumbo's style. As is often the case with those who drink alone, one could easily suppose that he lapsed into alcoholism, or that, at the very least, the condition of an elephantine 'problem drinker'. Solitary drinkers, of course, can drink with other solitary drinkers and still merit the term that identifies them. Matthew Scott had long been in the habit of taking a nightly bottle of whisky into Jumbo's den at Regent's Park for the two of them to get the wrinkles of the day out of their necks. They made merry and, Chambers records, 'as the pair fell under the influence of alcohol Scott would break into song, to which his elephant would provide a very loud trumpeting accompaniment'.[3] Apparently it caused Bartlett sleepless nights. I'm inclined to give credence to the view that Jumbo may well have been sozzled on the night he was killed. Why else would you run a hundred yards into the path of a thundering train, with everyone shouting at you to get off the tracks?

Speaking as an alcoholic, I can vouch for the fact one does not, legless, see pink elephants. DTs (alas, I can also vouch for those as well) are not amusing. It's toads in my case. But LSD is something else. It's long been folklore that the Disney operation (even Uncle Walt himself) were into psychedelic drugs. One commentator on the Web notes that the Disney team seem, knowingly, to have confused alcoholic dementia with 'taking a shitload of acid'. In the LSD mania of the 1960s, trippers loved to watch Disney movies, elevating their highs to stratospheric levels, up there with Telstar. Sex, drugs, rock 'n' roll and Disney. Many tabs of acid carried a pink Dumbo insignia. Walt himself was addicted to nothing worse than cigarettes, one is assured.

The 'Pink Elephants on Parade' sequence has traditionally disturbed moralists in America. The 'Christian Answers' website, while approving generally of the film, has severe reservations about the parade. Its spokesman (one for whom the eighteenth amendment was never revoked) lays down the official Prohibition line:

> Dumbo and Timothy accidentally get drunk because the clowns dropped a bottle of liquor into a watering bucket; we share the pair's hallucinations through the song 'Pink Elephants on Parade', which may be the first 'psychedelic' music video ever made. When my daughter was younger, I skipped that scene entirely; now I let her watch the fancy animation, but mute the sound. The scene even makes me uncomfortable.[4]

It made the high-ups in the Disney office uncomfortable as well. They protested that the sequence had been designed to discourage teenage drinking. It was unconvincing. Any kid with an ounce of spirit would want to dip their trunk into that bucket and 'see the elephants'. The Dumbo ride at Disneyland in Anaheim, California, originally had pink elephants. A last-minute instruction from Walt himself, we are told, changed it to dull gray, to kill any overt allusion to the film's 'tipsy parade'. It may also be that they wanted to extirpate any suggestion that Dumbo and Tim were rather too buddy. Whatever one's reaction to the drunk-as-a-skunk-with-a-trunk sequence, pink elephants have become proverbial.

Disney popularised it but he did not invent the pink elephant. It was Jack London, in his 'alcoholic memoir', *John Barleycorn* (1913), who is first recorded as putting it into print. One suspects it was saloon slang long before that. London uses the phrase as part of his acute anatomy of the different kinds of drunk:

> There are, broadly speaking, two types of drinkers. There is the man whom we all know, stupid, unimaginative, whose brain is bitten numbly by numb maggots; who walks generously with wide-spread, tentative legs, falls frequently in the gutter, and who sees, in the extremity of his ecstasy, blue mice and pink elephants. He is the type that gives rise to the jokes in the funny papers.
>
> The other type of drinker has imagination, vision. Even when most pleasantly jingled, he walks straight and naturally, never staggers nor falls, and knows just where he is and what he is doing. It is not his body but his brain that is drunken.[5]

Elephants' love of drink has always been proverbially confirmed by the elephants themselves when they can get near the stuff. One of Old Bet's tricks was, when on show at taverns, to uncork as many bottles of beer as were offered her and glug them down. But are elephants in the wild, who lack access to the amenities of civilisation, teetotal? Legend, and regular tabloid newspaper stories, would have it they are not.

One of the perennial myths about *Loxodonta Africana*, the tribe of Jumbo, is that they like to get themselves tiddly on the fruit of the marula tree. The mango-like, sugary fruit of the tree is used by natives in the manufacture of a liqueur, Amarula, which I have never tasted (and hope I never will) but am told is palatable. But how do elephants actually get their Amarula hooch? Drinkers, as I have observed, are careful to preserve their 'stash'. Reputedly elephants get their booze by eating rotting, or rotten windfall on the ground – food which, did it not pack a kick, would be wholly distasteful. It's further reputed that these highly intelligent beasts, who can put two and two together, are in the habit of rocking the trees, to bring down the fruit, which they then leave on the ground until it's, so to speak, drinkable.

Alas, an article in the 2006 issue of the journal *Physiological and Biochemical Zoology* by the biologist Steve Morris pours cold water on this legend. It doesn't happen, his research reveals. 'People just want to believe in drunken elephants,' he says. It's true that elephants push over marula trees, but it's to get the fresh fruit, not to stock their booze cabinet. And if fresh fruit does fall on the ground, it's so delicious that every animal in the area, not just elephants, rushes to gobble it up. Elephants, testifies another expert, 'regularly visit and revisit the same marula trees, checking the fruits and the bark for palatability and devour the fruits when they are ripe.' Ripe, not rotten.

The elephant's belly and intestines, of course, are as large as any metal 'still' and its pipework. Could the necessary fermentation of the fruit take place internally alongside the normal processes of digestion? Is the elephant a four-legged walking brewery – the slang-proverbial 'piss tank'? Unfortunately for this theory the vast amounts of vegetable food the elephant eats pass through its system at astonishing speed. Don't stand behind one, as the old joke says.

As regards the walking piss-tank thesis, science instructs that there simply isn't time enough for the necessary internal fermentation to happen. Boa constrictors (which take up to a month in digestion, legend has it) perhaps could, although there are no records of boozed-up monsters of the Amazon. The internal fermentation thesis is further disproved by the same spoilsport Dr Morris's calculation that it would require the fermented juice of some 1,400 marula fruits (around a quarter of a ton), properly prepared, to get an elephant enjoyably drunk. Since drunkenness has a relationship with body mass, the elephant probably has that enviable thing for alcoholics, 'a good head'.

Despite the efforts of Dr Morris and his ilk, the public wants desperately to believe in the drunken elephant and wilfully insists on doing so. Newspapers regularly run stories of the 'Trunk and disorderly' kind. There have probably been several between my writing this and your reading it. The following kind of thing, for example, to choose one of many, turned up by an 'elephant + drunken' search. It's from *Metro*, 6 November 2012, and is lifted, as many such stories are, from *The Hindustan Times*:

The trunk and disorderly mammals ransacked a shop, three houses and ruined crops in the eastern village of Dumurkota, India.

Police say the gang of over-the-limit tuskers downed more than 500 litres of moonshine alcohol, managing to drink the place dry in a matter of minutes.

The unruly mob demolished dozens of houses in their desperate hunt for more booze after hoovering up the hard stuff in record time.

Local police officer Asish Samanat said the drunken elephants were more 'aggressive' than usual after their mammoth drinking session.

'Unfortunately these animals live in close proximity to man and they recognised the smell of the drink,' he explained.

'They were like any other drunk – aggressive and unreasonable but much, much bigger.'

Police and villagers eventually restored order by herding the elephants over a local river back to their normal migration route.

Officer Samanat added: 'They'll have one heck of a hangover.'

The drinks industry has, sensibly enough, exploited the traditional link between its product and the world's favourite mammal, and Jumbo does for the beer can what he does for the airliner: he makes it cosy and 'safe'. Carlsberg has a strong-selling line called 'Elephant Beer'. It's very potent, I'm told, and tasty. In 2009 the firm proudly described its tipple in press releases for the fiftieth anniversary of the beer's arrival in the drinking holes of the world:

Elephant Beer was launched in a time where Danish design, architecture and crafts achieved great interna-tional success. Carlsberg has a long tradition of producing promotional posters reflected by the changing times, and as a result poster artist Kjeld Nielsen was asked to develop an icon that could be used in advertising. He came up with a small blue elephant that almost looked like something out of a children's book. To the international audience this may seem somewhat misleading, considering that the beer definitely is not intended for children. But to fully grasp the geniality of Nielsen's design, one needs to understand the Danish sense of humour and subtle irony. The blue elephant soon became a much-loved symbol and was used extensively for more than a decade. Today the Elephant Beer's mascot is even considered a design icon by many artists and graphic designers. Kjeld Nielsen's work is regarded as some of the most original promotional materials in Carlsberg's history. On the occasion of the 50-year anniversary new enamel signs with Nielsen's blue elephant have been produced.

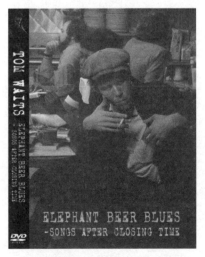

Tom Waits enjoying an Elephant

Tom Waits, the singer (composer of the immortal ditty, 'The Piano Has Been Drinking') appeared sloshed on Danish TV in 1976, knocking back bottles of Elephant Beer, to which he is, apparently, partial. Waits composed a song specially for the occasion: 'Elephant Beer Blues'. He followed it up with an album.

Airborne Jumbos

I first saw the Disney film *Dumbo* as a child, when my life was anything but Technicolor. It was some time after the film was made – around 1947. It was the age of austerity and bitter winters – a world which was not even black and white, but gray and gray. 'Flicks' (where worlds were more colourful) were one of the few pleasures available to a nine-year-old in Colchester at that shrivelled time. As I've said, my home town was dimly aware of its Roman heritage. At the time it had five cinemas, all of which nostalgically harked back to that noble Camulodunum era: the Empire (known unofficially as the 'fleapit'), the Playhouse, the Regal, the Hippodrome and the Headgate (alluding to the Roman Wall).

I saw the film at the Empire, with my mother. I remember walking back with her and buying fish and chips for supper and eating them in the street. My mother was unimpressed, as I recall, and eager to get out for some adult evening entertainment, and I was left alone in my bedroom to think over the film and other things big in the world of a child. It was cold. These details remain with me because the film, specifically the little elephant's Quasimodo sufferings, made a huge impression. I too had comically big ears ('lugs'), and was mocked for them at school. The film spoke to me.

His big flapping ears, zoologically, indicate that Dumbo is an African elephant. His mother, oddly, isn't judging by her lesser 'auricular appendages' (as Barnum liked to call them). But is she his mother? One of the oddest features of the film is that Dumbo is, apparently, the product of a virgin birth. He is delivered by a stork (complaining, bitterly, about the weight) as the circus train rumbles across the country. His mother names the 'little fella' Jumbo Jr. No Jumbo Sr is ever seen, or alluded to. In a world like mine, where most of the men during the war had been away from home (like my uncles) or dead (like my father), this also spoke to me. No male elephant is seen in the film, other than the juvenile Jumbo Jr, who is cruelly bullied and nicknamed 'Dumbo'. No one is sure where the name 'Jumbo' comes from. Every English speaker knows what 'Dumbo' means and it is not difficult to work out where the obnoxious name originates. It means 'stupid' and it was first applied to those hordes of non-English immigrants who flooded into America at the turn of the twentieth century. When asked a question (initially by the immigration officer), they were silent – 'dumb'. Not, that is, lacking organs of speech, but without any command of English. They looked stupid and dazed. It's significant that in a film with a lot of talking (the dialogue is razor-sharp in places – particularly in the African-American 'crow' scenes) Dumbo, the central character, says not a word.

The film's action opens with the big top being erected (the female crew of elephants do the necessary hauling). They are a peculiarly bitchy crew. Mrs Jumbo, by contrast, is a *mater dolorosa* throughout. When the circus opens for business a big-eared lout mocks Dumbo for his grotesquely even larger ears, and pulls his tail. It maddens Mrs Jumbo who, in the cause of protecting her infant, goes 'mad'. She spanks the little swine who has been cruel to Dumbo and her reaction is zoologically correct. All white hunters concur that the most dangerous of elephants is a cow protecting her calf over the two years of its maternal care and tutelage. Panic ensues. 'Mad elephant!' Enter the ringmaster with his whip. We have now moved well beyond spanking. Mrs Jumbo is locked up – imprisoned – and Dumbo is even more sadistically treated by being made to top a pyramid, formed of the circus's other elephants (this, incidentally, seems to be a hit at Frank C. Bostock's style of circus, not Barnum's). Dumbo is frightened of heights. He is mercilessly mocked and teased by clowns – representatives of humanity at its most inhumane. Or, one might think, Barnumism at its most Barnumist.

With his mother locked up, Dumbo finds a new friend, Timothy Q. Mouse (Disney had a fondness for little rodents – it's also a sly in-joke about elephants being frightened of mice). Timothy suggests that Dumbo can gain the respect of the world with a diving stunt, jumping off a burning building into a small tub of water, but it goes disastrously wrong. The big top is pulled down, panicking the audience. Dumbo is, from now on, a clown: something to be laughed at. The other bitch-crew elephants are merciless and jubilant.

One should remember that, in addition to his wildly anthropomorphical cartoons with animal protagonists, Disney was a pioneer in 'nature' photography – the kind of thing we associate with David Attenborough – and the studio had a zoological research department. It's relevant to quote the following:

> African elephant society is highly complex and arranged around family units composed of groups of closely related females and their calves. Each family unit

contains around ten individuals, led by an old female known as the 'matriarch'. Family units often join up with other bands of females to form 'kinship groups' or 'bond groups', and larger herds may number well over a hundred individuals. The male elephant leaves its natal group at puberty and tends to form much more fluid alliances with other males.[1]

Or male mice, in this case.

Dumbo is taken by Timothy to see his mother, in her cage. On the way back, a tearful Dumbo has an attack of hiccups. Timothy gives him some water from a bucket. Unknown to them, a bottle of champagne (one recalls Jumbo's fondness for the tipple) has been poured into it. It tastes oddly good and they soon find themselves stinking drunk. Dumbo hallucinates pink elephants before they both black out. They come round and find themselves mysteriously in the upper branches of a tree in the company of some cheerful black crows. One, it emerges, is actually called 'Jim Crow' – the generic, and socio-culturally heavily loaded, term for the former practice of segregating African-Americans. Dumbo, of course, (viz the ears) is a *Loxodonta Africana* – a 'brother'.

How did he and Timothy end up in a tree? He can fly, it emerges. Those big ears are as effective as a bird's wings. Is it a bird, is it a plane? No, it's an elephant. The crows break into jive song and dance. (Check it out on YouTube – it's universally 'liked'. Someone appends the note, 'PLZ NO COMMENTS ABOUT RACISM CUZ ITS NOT!!').

The two friends return to the circus. Now, when he does his jumping from a building trick, Dumbo flies like a bird. He dive-bombs his former tormentors. But they can torment him no more – he is a star. He is reunited with his mother, who is released from her prison. Like the original Jumbo, from now on they have their own 'Palace Car' on the train – the happiest of endings.

Except that it wasn't. *Dumbo* was released in the last week of October 1941 – a few weeks before the 'Day of Infamy', 7 December, when Pearl Harbor was dive-bombed. The film's climax, with Dumbo's sneak attack on the circus, was no longer funny. It had been planned by Disney to recoup recent losses on hugely ambitious 'art' projects, like *Fantasia* (1940). *Dumbo*, to coin a phrase, bombed.

It's a pity. The film is largely the work of one of the most gifted of Disney's animators, Vladimir 'Bill' Tytla (it was he who had come up with Grumpy in *Snow White and the Seven Dwarfs* and the chilling 'Night on Bald Mountain' in *Fantasia*). The first half of the film – up to the hallucinogenic pink elephant episode – is brutal and terrifying to many children (me, certainly). Thereafter it is pure 'compensation fantasy' – the imaginary revenges on the cruel world which children console themselves with. The film is, in short, a most brilliant variation on the Jumbo theme. See it, with the innocent wondering eye of childhood, or the thoughtful eye of adulthood. Or just for nostalgia.

My own childhood coincided with the last days of the music hall and the travelling circus. They've now disappeared, alas, but they were then a cultural link with the Victorian period whose rich literature would be a main interest in my professional life. These exhibitions featured, among other attractions (not least 'performing' elephants), the 'human cannonball'.

A bulky man, dressed usually in a bathing suit of the old type (male breasts were no more to be visible than the other kind) was solemnly stuffed into the mouth of a vast artillery piece to be fired through the air. Breath was held. Would the human missile come out in shrapnel – a kind of meaty grape shot? There would be a dull phut, stage smoke, and out he would plop, 50 yards or so into the safety net. One breathed again. A man had flown – fast as a bullet. Wonders never ceased.

As the crows in *Dumbo* put it, 'I think I seen 'bout everything, when I see an *elephant* fly'. I live, nowadays, not far from the Heathrow incoming passenger plane flight path, and, from the large window in front of my writing desk, if I lift my eyes from the screen I may well see thin aluminium tubes, travelling at the speed of a bullet, but, due to parallax or something, seeming to hover in the distant air like mayflies. They can and do carry a cargo of up to 400 souls.

Since the introduction of the wide-bodied jet, capable of carrying those hundreds of people and their impedimenta, passenger traffic through the atmosphere has increased exponentially. More of us 'fly' every year. Travelling in a plane remains, however, inherently terrifying. One of the ways in which the terror is calmed is the epithet cunningly applied to these aerial monsters: '*jumbo* jets'. It works as well as '*Prozac* Plane' would – but subliminally and more subtly.

It's also more complex. 'Jumbo jet' is one of those terms that the critic Jacques Derrida calls 'pharmakons' (the Greek origin word can mean poison/medicine).[2] They mean, simultaneously, two contrary things. For example, 'drug dealer' and 'drug store'; or 'Coke' you drink (it refreshes) or 'coke' you snort (it kills). Or even the much pondered over 'jumbo shrimp' which means, simultaneously, something very small and very large.

When coupled with 'jet' the word 'jumbo' acknowledges reference to something frighteningly big and dangerous (whose pulse, even that of the 'frequent flyer', does not quicken a little on take-off – who would not tremble in the face of a charging elephant?), but something at the same time comfortingly safe. A 'cobra jet' would not serve the same linguistic-therapeutic purpose. The military do, of course, often choose names for their planes which signal martial threat – 'Spitfire', for example, or 'Raptor' (the 'Sopwith Camel' has, I confess, always stumped me).

'Jumbo' has just the opposite effect. The epithet recalls all those little children, crowded onto the howdah, in Regent's Park. But 'Jumbo the Children's Friend' is also the beast which came close to bringing down the Roman Empire. A terrible weapon of war, it contains within itself mighty power. It could kill those children as easily as a housewife swats a fly.

Our lives get riskier all the time in ways we do not care to dwell on, for our own peace of mind. In the spoof film *Airplane*, after the pilot and all the crew are plunged into eructating incapacity by the fish supper, the passengers (those who wisely chose chicken) are asked over the address system 'can anyone fly an airliner'? Only one acutely ill-equipped fellow, of the hundreds on board, can make a stab at it.

If the same question were asked on a double-decker bus in London, half the passengers would leap to the wheel. In Mr Pickwick's horse-drawn carriage, it would be every male – they'd look forward to the challenge of taking the reins with relish. Stagecoach drivers in the nineteenth century invariably made a bit on the side letting male passengers take the whip and reins. Now we are just packages of meat, hurtling through the thin frigid atmosphere at 550mph, no more capable of taking charge of our destiny than a piece of Gucci luggage, but the word 'Jumbo' soothes. It serves to make the terrifying unterrifying. Look at the caption on another Barnum poster: We are not talking gerbils. 'The Children's Giant Pet' is a

JUMBO

Fly Jumbo fly safe

'monster'. Cartoons of the jumbo jet habitually use the same trick and render it as a children's toy.

It was a stroke of genius, whoever at Boeing came up with the name. 'Airbus' is another clever name, but it doesn't have quite the same soothe-factor. And soothing is in order for any passenger (or whoever has seen the first film in the *Final Destination* series) who thinks flying is intrinsically unnatural and hazardous – as unnatural as an elephant that flies. And, if one thinks further about it, the comforting jumbo jet has an extremely dangerous stablemate and progenitor, one that has it in its power to destroy the planet. I refer to Boeing's B-52 Stratofortress, the most powerful and enduring piece of weaponry in the great American aerial arsenal – and the plane from which the jumbo jet was engendered.

The Stratofortress came into the service in the 1950s, when passenger planes were still, most of them, propeller driven. It descends, ancestrally, from the wartime B-17 Flying Fortress through the B-29 and B-52 Superfortresses. All of those agents of mass destruction I recall seeing in flight over

196

my air-spotting childhood, CND-badge-wearing adolescence, and uniltateral-disarmament-favouring adult head. They all carried sufficient munitions, of course, to blast me and all around me to oblivion. Only the CND badge (made of indestructible ceramic, one was told) would survive. And some molluscs, deep in the protective mud of the River Mersey.

The B-52 can carry up to 70,000 lb of bombs, including the most destructive nuclear weapons humanity has yet come up with. Strategic Air Command (motto, 'Peace is our Profession' – they are very ironic) keeps some in the air, ready to strike like coiled, hooded cobras, at all times. The B-52 has been up there, over our heads, for sixty years and present estimates are that it will stay in active service until the 2040s. Probably versions of its kindred jumbo jet will last as long. These are, ironically, a less endangered species than the African elephant.

Those who fly the machine, or have professional contact with it, nickname the Stratofortress 'BUFF'. The acronym stands for 'Big Ugly Fat Fucker'. Picture the scene at Heathrow, Kennedy or Reagan when the tannoy announces: 'Will passengers booked on United Flight 30 to Washington please board their Big Ugly Fat Fucker now'.

Topsy

Elephants, it has been frequently observed, have what looks like a metaphysical interest in death and dying. Their lifespan is similar to that of humankind – around sixty-five years in the wild. They die, in their natural habitat, when their sixth set of teeth give out. When one of their herd dies, they will often go to examine the corpse.

They have large brains; larger than ours, and they seem to be trying to work out what it means. Better dentistry would have helped their evolutionary chances, they perhaps think. Their propensity, like the poet Thomas Gray, to meditate in elephant graveyards, usually by water holes, is one of the ways in which hunters trap them, leaving a cadaver to lie in the wild for its fellows to come and mourn over. The habit may well be what inspired the unknown author of the *Arabian Nights* to invent the fable of the Elephant Graveyard, where Sinbad finds the 500 tusks which will make him a free man.

We on our part are fascinated by the deaths of elephants and they have, of course, been killed many ways. Only one, as far as I am aware, has met its end by the electric chair. It remains one of the gothic horrors of American history.

The elephant named Topsy was born around 1875, a small-eared Asian breed. She was so named, presumably, in honour of the little girl in *Uncle Tom's Cabin* who 'just grow'd and grow'd'. Elephants, unlike other mammals, do grow continuously through life, although the rate slows down in later years. By 1903, Topsy was 10 feet high, close on 20 feet in length, and 3 tons in weight. Big, but by no means Jumbo big. Topsy was, like Jumbo, a public performer. She had belonged for many years to Barnum's great rival, Adam Forepaugh.

Forepaugh's prize specimen, Bolivar (Sri Lankan and tuskless), was as tall and heavy as Jumbo – according to the advertisements which proudly proclaimed him 'The Largest and Heaviest Elephant in the World', but he was an evil beast of vicious temper, unlike the gentle giant of Barnum's show. 'Elephant Bill', having known thousands of the beasts, tells us that 'savage elephants are as rare as really savage men'.[1] Bolivar was one of those rare specimens. He had killed two keepers before being chained up in the Philadelphia Zoological Gardens for the last 18 years of his life, incarceration which reportedly did nothing for his temper. He died in 1908 at the early age of forty (ish). He was famous for not sleeping for sixteen of those last years. Death must have been a blessed relief.

The fact that few elephants in circus or zoo captivity ever reach their 'three score years and five' span is argument that evolution hasn't designed them for zoos and circuses. Bolivar's stuffed body and skeleton were preserved, side by side, in the Academy of Natural Sciences of Drexel University in Philadelphia for thirty years, until the public lost interest. They are now somewhere in the cellars. Or not. Elephant remains have an odd habit of disappearing.

The propensity of Forepaugh's elephants to kill people makes one wonder if his ménage was crueller than Barnum's. Eric Scigliano, for example, quotes one of Forepaugh's circus trainers:

Bolivar on display

They're the trickiest beasts that live. They know more than the rest of the animals put together. They'll fool you for a long time, by allowing you to think they love you, when they are just waiting for a chance to put you out of business . . . I hate them, though I'm a trainer. I rule them by brutality and fear, not by kindness.[2]

Forepaugh's business wound down at the end of the century and what was left was taken over by his son, Adam Jr, a much less talented showman. Topsy was sold on to the firm of Thompson & Dundy in 1902 for their soon-to-be-opened 22-acre Luna Park, Coney Island – a forerunner of Disneyland. Among other attractions, this proto-theme park was constructing roller coaster 'rides' to the moon, a ferris wheel, a 'Canals of Venice' boating section and an 'infant incubator' with premature babies on display (something picked up for the plot of the HBO miniseries, *Boardwalk Empire*).

They also planned a wild animal park where camels and elephants would roam free. The partners went for broke, paying for the construction of this wonderland by the boardwalk. When it eventually opened, they had only $12 left between them, scarcely enough to make change for the first twelve customers.

Welcome to Luna Park

Luna Park was scheduled to open on 16 May 1903. But her new Coney Island arrangements, and possibly all the banging of the construction work, did not suit Topsy at all. What sketchy accounts there are suggest she was considerably less equable by nature than Jumbo, and there were other good reasons, which would soon emerge, why Thompson & Dundy had acquired her on the cheap.

There is an imperfect record and some patent falsification about what happened, but the resourceful Scigliano seems to have dug out a reliable account. In the spring of 1902, while she was still touring with the Forepaugh circus in nearby Brooklyn, a drunken hanger on, J.F. Blount (reportedly in a more than usually inebriated state), was injudicious enough to offer Topsy a lighted cigar. Topsy's handler warned him to back off. Blount replied, airily, 'Don't worry about me, brother, I know what I'm doing.' Famous last words. The lighted end of the cigar touched Topsy's tongue. Infuriated, she wrapped her trunk round Blount, lifted him high in the air and dashed him to the ground. He died instantly. *The New York Times*, which evidently got the story from a spectator, reported the next day it wasn't a cigar – the luckless Blount threw sand in the elephant's face. Whichever, the elephant was provoked. No immediate punitive action was taken against her beyond the usual whipping and sledgehammering, one suspects.

It was alleged to be Topsy's third homicide. She had, the press claimed, killed two handlers a year or so ago in Texas, although the details are blurry. Her handler, Fred Ault, nick-named 'Whitey', maintained Topsy was an 'amiable' beast – more so than most elephants, he said. Her previous 'kills' are, frankly, dubious and they were quite likely invented.

What could her new owners, Fred Thompson and Skip Dundy, do with their elephant? Their theme park was nearing completion and Topsy was used for some labouring and heaving. She also gave a few children's rides, in the newly laid out petting zoo. More trouble then occurred. Whitey, of whom Topsy was apparently very fond, had a weakness for drink. What it led to was reported in *The New York Times*, on 6 December 1902, under the eye-catching headline: 'ELEPHANT TERRORIZES CONEY ISLAND POLICE'.

It opened 'Coney Islanders were badly scared yesterday'. In fact they were vastly entertained with that rarest of things on

the Island, a show that didn't cost you 25¢. It was all the fault
of 'Whitey':

> At noon Ault, who was inebriated, left Luna Park astride
> the animal's neck. They went lumbering along Surf
> Avenue, the motion causing the mahout to become more
> dizzy. A crowd gathered and fell in behind. At every
> corner its numbers were augmented. After traversing
> nearly half a mile the animal suddenly stopped and Ault
> slid off. He began prodding the animal's trunk in an
> angry manner. Policeman Conlin arrested him where-
> upon Ault said he would turn the elephant loose upon
> the crowd. Drawing his revolver the policeman ordered
> him to walk on ahead and threatened to shoot him if
> he turned the animal loose upon the people. Arrived at
> the police station on West Eighth Street Ault refused to
> tie the elephant which, mounting the five broad granite
> steps leading to the station, she tried to enter. Topsy
> became wedged in the door, however, and set up a
> terrific trumpeting. The crowd scattered in terror while
> the policemen in the station house were not less alarmed
> and some of them sought refuge upstairs and in the cells.
>
> Sgt Levis begged Ault to drive the animal back
> and the keeper finally did. Then for fifteen minutes he
> kept the policemen busy obeying his orders to drive the
> crowd away and fetch dainties for Topsy. They could do
> nothing with the man and were afraid to lock him up
> because of the elephant. Finally Frederick Thompson,
> one of the proprietors of Luna Park, appeared on the
> scene and he induced Ault, with the permission of the
> police, to take the animal back to the park where, it
> appears, Topsy is sometimes employed to haul heavy

articles around the pleasure grounds. Mr Thompson
also gave Ault bail to answer a charge of disorderly
conduct.

A few weeks ago the Society for the Prevention of
Cruelty to Animals prosecuted Ault for wounding the
elephant near the eye with a pitchfork.

Evidently a stormy relationship.[3]
Topsy's days were numbered. And not only in the petting
zoo. If a little girl offered her as much as a peanut, it was
suggested, Topsy might splat her. Particularly if the drunken
Ault was in charge.

The partners came up with a brilliant idea, worthy of
Barnum himself but much nastier than anything he would
dream up. Topsy should be sentenced to death and 'executed'
(not 'put down', 'euthanised' or 'destroyed', but 'executed') as a
mass murderer. Details of her homicides were scanty, but there
was no appeal and the sentence should be carried out publicly
– a twentieth-century version of what were, in the nineteenth
century, called 'hang fairs'. The crowds would come, for a
certainty, even if it was winter. It was not every day you saw an
elephant topped. It would publicise the new park wonderfully.

But how should the execution be carried out? It was a period
in which America was deeply curious about modes of execution as, indeed, it still is. For the greatest and most progressive
country on God's earth it was felt that something appropriate
to the modern age, to replace the old-world barbarism of the
rope, axe, guillotine and firing squad, should be devised.

Simplest, of course, would be what mahouts are reported
as doing when their beloved beasts need to be put down: sit
astride the beast's neck and drive a large metal stake into the
brain with a hammer. Whitey – the only person who could

have done it without risk of becoming victim number four – was disinclined. He claimed to love her too much. Or, more likely, he recalled Mr Blount's squelched remains. Elephants are no fools and they could soon work out what a hammer and stake were for.

Hanging by the neck was proposed. But, given the size of the gibbet required, the possibility of the head snapping off and, most importantly, the protests of the American Society for the Prevention of Cruelty to Animals, the idea was reluctantly put aside. It's a good thing it was. It would certainly have been spectacular but it would even more have been cruel, unusual and very gruesome. No one could recall an elephant being hanged by the neck until it was dead. Fifteen years later, the experiment would be tried. It would go on to be one of the legendary events in American elephant lore – the 'Big Mary' execution. It's worth digressing a paragraph or two to describe it.

Big Mary (nicknamed 'Murderous Mary') was the big attraction in the small-time Sparks Circus. 'Big' means 5 tons. As was routine, the circus advertised her as 'the largest animal on earth' – bigger than even Jumbo (which she wasn't). In Tennessee, where the circus was touring, an abysmally inexperienced handler called 'Red', hired for the day, annoyed Mary while she was being paraded down the public highway. Joan Vannorsdall Schroeder, a Tennessee historian, quotes eyewitness testimony from a nineteen-year-old witness of what happened:

> There was a big ditch at that time, run up through Center Street . . . And they'd sent these boys to ride the elephants . . . There was, oh, I don't know now, seven or eight elephants . . . and they went down to water them and on the way back each boy had a little stick-like, that was a spear or a hook in the end of it . . . And this big

old elephant reach over to get her a watermelon rind,
about half a watermelon somebody eat and just laid
it down there; 'n he did, the boy give him a jerk. He
pulled him away from 'em, and he just blowed real big,
and when he did, he took him right around the waist
. . . and throwed him against the side of the drink stand
and he just knocked the whole side out of it. I guess it
killed him, but when he hit the ground the elephant just
walked over and set his foot on his head . . . and blood
and brains and stuff just squirted all over the street.[4]

The carnage was witnessed by a crowd of passers-by (some
allegedly blood-spattered with Red's gore). Their first reaction
was the traditional one in that southern part of the world: they
pulled out their firearms and blasted away. To quote Schroeder
again:

Guns, of course, were the first course of action. Just after
Red Eldridge's death, blacksmith Hench Cox fired his
32-20 five times at Mary; the story goes that the bullets
hardly phased her. 'Kill the elephant. Let's kill him,' the
crowd began chanting. Later, Sheriff Gallahan 'knocked
chips out of her hide a little' with his .45, according
to witness Bud Jones. But the circus manager stated,
'There ain't gun enough in this country that he could be
killed'; another approach would have to be attempted.

Someone suggested tearing her apart with two railway
engines. Too messy, it was decided. And expensive. Locomotive
hire didn't come cheap.

The local community of Erwin, lynching being traditional
in that part of the world (some 3,000 took place between 1885

and 1930), next demanded a good old-fashioned hanging. That seemed the sensible course. It was arranged to be carried out in the nearby Erwin train marshalling yard, using a flat-truck mounted mechanical crane. A huge crowd of 2,500 people assembled on a drizzly September morning to see the murderous pachyderm get her just desserts.

All the town's children were present. One recalled: 'We kids hung back because we were scared to death, but still we wanted to see it.' See it they would. No entrance fee was charged for what was an event worthy of Caligula's colosseum. The circus had been informed that if Mary weren't hanged all other towns in the region would boycott their show. The owner, Charlie Sparks, reluctantly went along with it. He had four other elephants and, whatever else, it was publicity.

The hanging was a debacle. Elephants just weren't anatomically engineered for that kind of treatment. It began badly when the crane started pulling at Mary's neck before one of her feet had been released from the rail holding it. Snapping bone and ligaments were audible round the yard. Then that was put right and she was hoisted up. On the first 'drop' the hawser around Mary's neck snapped and she fell to the ground, breaking her hip. She dragged herself into a sitting position, in agonising pain.

Breaking strains had been miscalculated. A stronger chain was attached and she was lifted again. She was, duly, hanged until she died, and was allowed to dangle for half an hour before her body was taken down and buried in a grave dug by a steam excavator, near where she had swung. Postcards (with faked photos) were printed of the event. There is to this day, apparently, a Hanging Elephant Antique Shop in Erwin which sells commemorative T-shirts.

Schroeder finishes her account with a grisly coda:

There is a final irony clinging to the story of Murderous Mary, one that firmly places Mary's murder in a time and place. In an article published in the March 1971 issue of the Tennessee Folklore Society Bulletin, author Thomas Burton reports that some local residents recall 'two Negro keepers' being hung alongside Mary, and that others remember Mary's corpse being burned on a pile of crossties. 'This belief,' Burton writes, 'may stem from a fusion of the hanging with another incident that occurred in Erwin, the burning on a pile of crossties of a Negro who allegedly abducted a white girl.'

Mary's grisly end

All this was in the future, although it confirmed the rightness of the ASPCA's prohibition on hanging unwanted elephants. And it probably stood as a warning for any circus owners intrepid enough to venture into East Tennessee.

Back to Coney Island. With hanging discarded as a viable option, cyanide-laced carrots were the next idea for disposing of Topsy. It was a version of the hemlock prescribed to ancient Greeks. But, humane as it was, elephants cannot be forcibly fed and they inspect their food fastidiously. The quantity of cyanide required to destroy 3 tons of flesh (half a pound at least, it was estimated) might make even the crunchiest carrots somewhat less than unappetising and elephants, zoologists tell us, have smell sensors in their trunks that would shame a bloodhound. Nor would it make much of a public spectacle, watching an elephant deciding whether or not she wanted an odd-smelling root vegetable, and spectacle was what was wanted for the launch of Luna Park.

The third option was the newfangled electric chair – with the necessary modifications. It so happened that there was a so-called 'current war' raging at the time between America's two great 'electricians', Thomas Edison and George Westinghouse as to the merits of Alternating (AC) or Direct (DC) currents. With the vast new market for electricity, millions of dollars hinged on which of the two supplies would work best in the homes, workplaces and infrastructure of America. Edison had innumerable patents and royalties to protect as they were his main source of income – and they were all DC. He also knew the advertising pull of the elephant. He had called one of his early generators 'the Jumbo'.

Edison wanted a definitive demonstration that DC was safe and that AC (the Westinghouse method) was lethal. His protégé and former employee, Harold P. Brown, 'father of the electric chair', had been supplying AC electrical devices for the disposal of the condemned-to-die since 1890. It was called 'riding the lightning'. Edison called it being 'Westinghoused'.

DC, Edison liked to boast, would not jolt a kitten. What would you rather have in your house? Edison, as it happened, enjoyed giving animals fatal jolts 'in the cause of science' and to impress on watchers the dangers of AC with the smell of burning flesh and animal screams. Stray dogs and cats (and yes, kittens too) were his most easily procured victims, although he also electrocuted (with the deadly AC, of course) cows, horses, gorillas and an orang-utan. All publicly.

Would Mr Edison, asked Thompson and Dundy, 'do' Topsy? He leapt at the opportunity. It would be his biggest and best demonstration – a veritably jumbo-sized proof of his case and a killing (literally) blow in the war of the currents. If AC could kill an elephant, what might it not do to your child, or husband, or hoovering housemaid? Edison had a nearby power station which could be easily modified to supply the 6,600 volts of AC which, it was calculated, would be required for 3-ton Topsy. The show was scheduled for 4 January 1903. Despite the New York winter cold, 1,500 paying spectators turned up.

Topsy, a dutiful beast when people weren't dropping lighted cigarettes on her tongue, obediently put her hooves in specially designed wooden sandals, lined with copper wiring. She did it, wrote one commentator, with the delicacy of a dancer. She was chained down and secured with harbour hawsers, lest she run amok. A long wire was hooked up to Edison's electric light plant, where technicians waited to throw the switch. Bulbs would dull all over the region commemorating the execution.

Edison, a pioneer of the movie camera and moving picture technology, filmed what happened next. It was not for historical purposes; the movie, *Electrocuting an Elephant*, would be released in a month or two in nickelodeons all over the country.

Topsy's grisly end

The film made money and, more importantly, it made the Edisonian point that AC kills.

Just to be safe – no elephant had been electrocuted before – Topsy was fed the cyanide-laced carrots moments before the charge paralysed her. It was a belt-and-braces measure and proved unnecessary. Smoke billowed up from her feet. It caused, newspapers reported, 'an unpleasant smell to mingle with the scent of roasted peanuts, sold at two cents a bag'. Topsy groaned and struggled as she burned and her organs failed. In a minute or two it was all over: she had been well and truly Westinghoused. It was, said *The New York Times*, 'a rather inglorious affair'.

The execution was witnessed by millions of Americans, and still is. Edison's film is available nowadays on YouTube with 'likes' and 'dislikes' running evenly (put me down as 'dislike'). Fred Thompson, alleged to be a lover of elephants, preserved two of the elephant's feet and part of her hide for an office chair. It is not recorded whether he made an ashtray out of one of her toenails.

Luna Park was a huge success after its electrifying launch party, but Fred and Skip, honoured today as pioneers of the entertainment industry, drank and womanised themselves into bankruptcy in a few years. Luna Park, under different ownership, burned down in 1946 – 'Topsy's revenge', wags called it. On the hundredth anniversary a memorial was raised to Topsy in the Coney Island Museum on the boardwalk, described by the unimpressed BBC as 'the faded holiday resort famous for its freak shows, fair rides and Russian mafiosi'.[5] And, of course, electrocuted elephants.

And, final irony, America eventually chose to go with AC and Westinghouse. Topsy had smoked and quivered in vain.

But Sometimes the Hoof is on the Other Foot

Elephants which have been 'executed', or otherwise subjected to cruel and unusual death, is a morbid subject. Even more morbid, however, is the chronicle of elephants themselves used as executioners. Legends of the practice have clustered around the chronicles of ancient potentates such as the Mughal emperor, Akbar the Great. The most influential account of elephants as executioners in colonial history was published in Robert Knox's informative *An Historical Relation of the Island Ceylon in the East Indies* (1681). It is accompanied by a grisly illustration. As Knox describes:

> The King makes use of elephants for Executioners; they will run their Teeth through the body, and then tear it in pieces, and throw it limb from limb. They have sharp Iron with a socket with three edges, which they put on their Teeth at such times; for the Elephants that are kept have all the ends of their Teeth cut to make them grow the better, and they do grow out again.[1]

The elephant executioner can, one is told, protract the agony by slowly pressing down, as quickly or slowly as commanded.

An Execution by an Eliphant.

Ceylonese execution by elephant

The atrocity was publicised by the bestselling Sir Walter Scott, in his novel *The Surgeon's Daughter* (1831). The story is about an adventurer who persuades a fair Scottish maiden to elope with him to India, where he plans to sell her to an Indian prince. The swine is foiled and condemned to death by elephant. Scott – who had himself never been to India – realised his tale needed 'a small seasoning of curry powder' and got it from his friend, the old Indian hand Colonel James Ferguson.

It was Ferguson who told Scott about execution by elephant. The Wizard of the North was interested in execution and at around the same period paid for a window to watch the hanging of the notorious body snatchers Burke and Hare. This is how the more exotic death of Richard Middlemas is described in *The Surgeon's Daughter*:

'Hold, Feringi,' said Hyder. 'Thou hast received all that was promised thee by the bounty of Tippoo. Accept now what is the fruit of the justice of Hyder.'

As he spoke, he signed with his finger, and the driver of the elephant instantly conveyed to the animal the pleasure of the Nawaub. Curling his long trunk around the neck of the ill-fated European, the monster suddenly threw the wretch prostrate before him, and stamping his huge shapeless foot upon his breast, put an end at once to his life and to his crimes. The cry which the victim uttered was mimicked by the roar of the monster, and a sound like an hysterical laugh mingling with a scream, which rung from under the veil of the Begum. The elephant once more raised his trunk aloft, and gaped fearfully.

Plenty of curry powder here.

The horrible thrill of execution by elephant was popularised later in the century by Louis Rousselet, who put into print an account of his 1868 expedition to central India. Rousselet commissioned a woodcut illustration of the brutal affair, which was widely recycled (most influentially in *Harper's Weekly*).

This is how Rousselet expands on the above. In an attempted revolt in the region a local locksmith was found guilty of helping Waghur prisoners to escape: 'and condemned to the punishment of death by elephant':

This punishment is one of the most frightful that can possibly be imagined. The culprit, bound hand and foot, is fastened by a long cord, passed round his waist, to the elephant's hind leg. The latter is urged into a rapid

Indian execution by elephant

trot in the streets, and every step gives the cord a violent
jerk, which makes the body of the condemned wretch
bound on the pavement. The only hope that remains for
the unhappy man is to be killed by one of these shocks;
if not, after traversing the city, he is released, and, by
a refinement of cruelty, a glass of water is given him.
Then his head is placed upon a stone, and the elephant
executioner crushes it beneath his enormous foot.[2]

In the period after the Indian Mutiny such things were,
allegedly, winked at by the British authorities who generally,
to use the least appropriate image, took pains to stamp the
practice out.

It's one of the curiosities of literature that the most critically
acclaimed novel about elephants does not introduce a single

elephant into the narrative. Like Berilia, Tubul, Great T'Phon and Jerakeen, the foundational four in Terry Pratchett's *Discworld*, they are *there* but never seen. The novel, of course, is *Heart of Darkness* (1899).

The biographical seed for the story was Joseph Conrad's (then a mariner) being commissioned in 1890 to skipper a decrepit steamer up the Congo River to an inland station, run by a manager called 'Klein' (renamed, not very obscuringly, 'Kurtz' in *Heart of Darkness*) to see what was going on with him.[3] For a few months Conrad – a man of inherent decency, if not immune from the racial and ecological prejudices of his age and class – was an employee of the most iniquitous colonial agency that Europe should, forever, be ashamed of, the Société Anonyme Belge pour le Commerce du Haut-Congo. Otherwise, and unofficially, the most efficient killers of elephants in recorded history.

The so-called Congo Free State (a bitter jest of a name) had been founded in 1885 by Belgium, one of the minor European imperial powers. 'Free' meant free to plunder. King Leopold farmed the million square miles his country had purloined to whatever firm would cough up most to the royal coffers. What those firms chose to do thereafter with their colonial leasehold was entirely up to them. Among the property on offer were the 'human cattle', to be used as slave labour and abused as the whim took their white owners.

The result was what has been called 'the first genocide of the modern era'. What is now the Democratic Republic of Congo has never recovered. Belgium has survived its crimes very well, and now has another little empire to mismanage, the EU. The 1890 river voyage had a profound influence on Conrad: 'Before the Congo I was just a mere animal,' he later said.[4] It took eight years for the 'horror' (a key word in the novel) to settle sufficiently in his mind to write *Heart of Darkness*: first as a three-part serial in *Blackwood's Magazine* then, a couple of years later, as a novella-length book.

The story is simple. Marlow (Conrad's series hero-narrator, a version of himself), now in his mature years, entertains some friends, as the sun sinks over the yardarm, on his yacht, the *Nellie*, bobbing sedately in the mouth of the Thames. In a momentary lull in conversation, he says, musingly, 'this also has been one of the dark places of the earth.' He is thinking of the Romans and ancient Britain. Behind every empire, we apprehend, lies crime.

Inspired by the observation, Marlow goes on to spin a yarn about a command he had in his early thirties. He was recruited in Brussels (a 'whitened sepulchre' of a city – as white, we will later gather, as ivory) to go on a mission in Africa (the heart-shaped continent) up the Congo to an inner station that has apparently gone crazy in the process of harvesting vast amounts of elephant ivory, by every unscrupulous means. The voyage is one which takes Marlow into the dark truth of things – empire, human nature and, ultimately, himself.

Kurtz, as Marlow is told in the downriver headquarters of the firm, 'is a very remarkable person. [He] sends in as much ivory as all the others put together'.[5] His remarkable ivorian achievement is elaborated. Marlow is told in 'tones of jealousy and admiration'. He has 'collected, bartered, swindled, or stolen more ivory than all the other agents together'. When Marlow – at the risk of his life and vessels – gets to the station he witnesses Kurtz's 'remarkable' achievement with his own eyes: 'Ivory? I should think so. Heaps of it, stacks of it. The old mud shanty was bursting with it. You would think there was not a single tusk left either above or below the ground in the whole country'.

Kurtz does not himself hunt the elephants. He bribes the natives to do the dirty work with trinkets, little luxuries from his store and tiny sums of money.

'White Gold' in the Heart of Darkness

Kurtz gives Marlow an incomplete pamphlet which he began writing when, years ago, he first embarked for the Congo, seeing himself as an emissary of civilisation – a bearer of sweetness and light. The deeper he penetrated into the jungle the more gloomy he became until, finally, he flipped into terminal madness. The pamphlet was never completed. It tails off with the postscript, 'exterminate all the brutes'.

It has always been assumed by critical commentators that Kurtz means 'exterminate all the blacks'. Certainly a lot of that is going on (his station is embellished with any number of skulls on sticks). But the 'brutes' in question could as well be African Forest elephants. He is brought back in Marlow's boat, at death's door. But almost his last words are a bitter allusion to the fact that it is not he who is being rescued, it is the ivory. 'Save me! – save the ivory, you mean,' he grumpily observes. The boat is loaded to the gunwhales with the stuff. Marlow is, unwillingly, complicit in elephanticide.

What is remarkable is that we see many things looming in the dark of Conrad's novel. One thing we do not see is an actual elephant – even though the whole novel centres on the beast. If *Loxodonta Africana* were tuskless, Kurtz would presumably have taken orders and gone into the dark continent as a missionary, harmlessly thumping the Bible.

There is only one mention of the word 'elephant' in the whole of the novel's text. It occurs in the description of Kurtz's native mistress:

> She walked with measured steps, draped in striped and fringed cloths, treading the earth proudly, with a slight jingle and flash of barbarous ornaments. She carried her head high; her hair was done in the shape of a helmet; she had brass leggings to the knee, brass wire gauntlets to the elbow, a crimson spot on her tawny cheek, innumerable necklaces of glass beads on her neck; bizarre things, charms, gifts of itch-men, that hung about her, glittered and trembled at every step. She must have had the value of several elephant tusks upon her. She was savage and superb, wild-eyed and magnificent; there was something ominous and stately in her deliberate progress.

Tellingly it is not the animal itself, but the value of the tusks in the European market place, which is cited to describe the ostentation of her adornments. In the wild Kurtz's lady would no more think of wearing raw ivory than Queen Victoria would wear a bone necklace made of that evening's roast chicken. And how much were the elephants of the Congo worth to *Société Anonyme Belge pour le Commerce du Haut-Congo* in the markets of the West? It is estimated 50,000 at least were 'harvested' for their 'white gold'. Conrad called it 'the vilest scramble for loot that ever disfigured the history of human conscience.'[6] He, for a short while, was part of that looting.

Why was what Kurtz was supplying so valuable to his employers – worth the genocide of a people and the extinction of a species? The answer is simple. Balls. Or, to be more precise, billiard balls and pool halls.

Historically billiards began as a royal game, a kind of indoor French aristos' croquet, played on a manicured lawn. Marie Antoinette is reported to have been a player and Mary Queen of Scots had a billiard table (supposedly her beheaded body was covered with its baize). One of billiards' attractions was that it could be played by women. Hence the following exchange in Shakespeare's *Antony and Cleopatra* in which the Queen of Egypt finds herself bored:

Cleopatra: Give me some music; music, moody food
Of us that trade in love.
Attendants: The music, ho!
[Enter MARDIAN]
Cleopatra: Let it alone; let's to billiards: come, Charmian.
Charmian: My arm is sore; best play with Mardian.
Cleopatra: As well a woman with an eunuch play'd
As with a woman. Come, you'll play with me, sir?
Mardian: As well as I can, madam.[7]

Bawdy as ever, Cleopatra slyly alludes to the fact that one of the things poor Mardian doesn't have is balls.

Billiards requires a number of skilfully tooled and costly materials if the game is to be played with any degree

Ladies at play

of pleasure. One of the necessary materials is baize – textile woven smooth and napless enough to offer no frictional resistance, and tough enough to be stretched skin-tight. It is dyed green so that the white and red balls stand out chromatically, but also in remembrance of the croquet grass. A perfectly flat slate surface is needed, to keep the course of the balls across the baize 'true'. Slate is very heavy, which makes the table, on its four stout legs, impossible to shake or tilt (unlike its remote descendant, the pinball machine). Seasoned wood 'cues' (from the French word 'queue', long object) – absolutely straight and cunningly tapered – with ferrule and leather tips (chalked) are similarly necessary, as are indoor, shaded, spotlights, and 'racks' for the cue and the score.

All this was too complex and too expensive for the working man in the period before the industrial revolution came up with its cornucopia of 'cheap luxuries' for the masses. The lower classes had up to this point to make do with 'bowling greens', decommissioned cannonballs, and the Mediterranean peoples' *boules* (effectively throwing stones at stones in the street).

All this changed in the nineteenth century with factory production of billiard apparatus and the discovery, by American saloon keepers, that customers could be attracted into their establishments by pool tables – pool being a game which, unlike billiards, did not have interminable 'breaks', extending a simple game for hours if the players were at all good at the art of the cannon. Pool was fast, easily learned, engrossing and a game which would keep the toper under their roofs for hours on end. Newly constructed pool rooms and billiard halls became the lair of the pool sharks, hustlers and the proverbial site of a 'misspent youth'.

English pubs, which had existed for centuries on small plots of land, did not have room for more than one or two tables (the backward pull of the cue to make a shot was infuriating to uninvolved drinkers). Dartboards were preferred. America, with its wide open spaces, was something else. Saloons and 'pool halls' the size of barns could be constructed – even in the largest cities.

For the pool table itself, baize, slate and wood could be acquired locally or from conveniently nearby places. The balls were something else. Only the dark continent could supply them to the required quality. The earliest record of an import of 'ivery' from Africa was for the Duke of Norfolk's 'billiard room' in 1588. It's nice to correlate it with Sir Francis Drake playing bowls on Plymouth Hoe, the same year, and finishing his game before settling the Spanish Armada's hash.

As the centuries passed every country house of any distinction would have its billiard room where, after supper, cigars and brandy would accompany the gentle clunk of ivory on ivory. Meanwhile, in another part of the building, the ladies – their hair combed to perfection and held in place with ivory combs – would be listening to the drawing room's grand piano.

Its white keys, unlike the billiard balls, supplied by soft ivory, from the maintained domestic herds of India. A standard keyboard used a pound and a half of ivory – half an elephant.

Billiard balls, of a sufficient quality to make the game really worthwhile, could only really be manufactured from hard, African ivory, courtesy of Mr Kurtz and co. Clay, wood, or animal-bone balls were wholly inferior; alligator teeth and whalebone proved a sad second best. It was a costly business. One tusk produced, on average, three balls of the necessary two-or-so-inch diameter. Many proved imperfect and had to be discarded.

The game of billiards required only three balls – white, spot and red. The fifteen multicoloured balls required for a game of pool would, therefore, necessitate the slaughter of at least five elephants. A good-sized pool room in one of the great American cities could boast as many as a dozen tables and would entail the slaughter of a whole herd. Don't call it a pool room, call it the elephant's graveyard.

Ivory from a live elephant, not exhumed tusks from some naturally dead beast, was required. Sinbad's elephants' graveyard was useless. Once harvested, the ivory itself required to be meticulously 'seasoned' for a couple of years, like timber, to harden and get the kinks out of it. On the living animal it is relatively soft and at its centre pulpy. Like the human tooth, it has nerves which makes it impossible to harvest leaving the elephant alive. Like the rhino horn you have to kill to cut.

Creating the perfect sphericality the billiard ball requires was an intricate process, requiring machinery and craft expertise. A whole American town, Ivoryton, established itself in Connecticut around its great factory, producing billiard balls (and, latterly, piano keys). At its zenith, in the pool mania of the late nineteenth and early twentieth centuries, some 90 per cent of the country's tusk imports (some of them, co-nominally, from West Africa's Ivory Coast) found their way to Ivoryton, to roll out as billiard and pool palls to every corner of the continent. Ivoryton could as aptly have been called Kurtzville.

In the early years of the twentieth century salvation came to Jumbo's brethren in that resonant word 'plastic'. Synthetic processes and the American laboratory brought some relief for the wild African herds. The respite was short. The twenty-first century ushered in even more dire threats to Jumbo's kind. The rising superpowers, Japan and China, had a traditional passion for ivory. As their wealth built up they sucked in vast amounts from Africa.

The new war on the elephant began soon after the Second World War. Japan's economic miracle, and the wealth it generated for the population at large, led to mass production of ivory hankos (name seals) – in solid, hard African ivory. Traditionally they had been accessories only for the wealthy, aristocratic and imperial. Now they were as universal as the automobile. Demand for hankos soon outstripped legal supply. And plastic would not serve.

That demand coincided, as the decades passed, with the massive spread of – what else? – the AK47, and civil unrest in Africa that made continent-wide legal control virtually impossible. Poachers no longer needed skill and their targets were walking barn doors. Rebels, funding their bloody little wars with poached ivory, were responsible.

Ivory fetched around $1,500 a pound if you could find some way of getting it to Hong Kong and thence to China. Ways were found; they always are. An African elephant tusk can weigh up to 80 lbs. The maths are lethal. As one official reported:

China and Japan are two key markets leading to more
and more deaths of more elephants and remember that
elephants are a social animal and there is evidence that
the poachers will kill one animal, wait for the elephants
to come and investigate and possibly mourn the death
of that animal and then kill the ones that come and
investigate.[8]

The value of poached ivory had soared to levels that made
it attractive to poachers with high-end slaughtering technol-
ogies. As the primatologist Jane Goodall noted ruefully in
December 2012: 'Tanzania has lost half its elephants in the last
three years. Ugandan military planes have been seen over the
Democratic Republic of the Congo shooting elephants from
the air. Armed militia are now shooting the elephants.'[9]

In Sudan, where Jumbo himself had been born, the
elephant population had been slaughterously reduced in a few
years from 130,000 to 5,000 – a level probably below viability.
Chad's elephants had declined, over the same period, from
40,000 to 2,000: the end of the line.

The New York Times, on 17 March 2013, reported that
central Africa's elephant population had declined by over 60
per cent between 2002 and 2011. Within a few decades, the
elephant would be a thing of the zoological past – as extinct
as its hairy-mammoth ancestor. A couple of days earlier, *The
Los Angeles Times* ran a similarly despairing editorial begin-
ning: 'Check off another majestic animal species your kids will
probably never get to see: the forest elephant of Cameroon.
Smaller than savanna elephants and with straighter tusks,
the intelligent behemoths are being cut down by poachers at
a horrifying pace.'

The World Wildlife Fund had given the species ten years to total extinction. No plastic was in prospect to save Jumbo's species this time round. But, no matter, there was always the Dumbo ride at Anaheim.

Biblical Jumboism

One hunts in vain for any hoof print of the elephant in the book of books – which is strange. That other most gigantic mammal, the whale, makes some memorable entries. A proto-Moby Dick gulps down Jonah, for example – in one of the most exotic (and faith-straining) episodes in the Old Testament. The credibility factor as regards Jonah's ingurgitation centres on: (1) whether the whale's gullet could gape wide enough to do it; (2) whether the prophet could survive three days in the oxygenless, acidic belly of the whale before being vomited out, as we are to understand, in perfect health, on dry land to prophesy with even greater confidence than before; (3) whether God would bother with such a nonsensical demonstration of His powers.

More interesting is one of the funnier wisecracks in the Bible when, in the Book of Job, it is asked of the reader:

'Cans't thou draw out Leviathan with an hook?'

How interesting it would be to find, in the same extended riff, 'cans't thou bring down Jumbo with a pea-shooter?' There is, as has been said, no mention of Jumbo's ancestors in the Bible. The term 'behemoth', in the same section of the Book of Job as that in which ('thar she blows!') Leviathan and the bent pin is scoffed at, is sometimes interpreted as elephantine. But the consensus is that the behemoth is just a big ugly monster.

William Blake's *Behemoth and
Leviathan*

Ivory is mentioned several times in the Old Testament
and once in the New Testament. It's odd that the Israelites
did not come across at least some spoor of the pachyderm
while enslaved in ancient Egypt, around 1400 BC (as it is
guessed), and have it stored for future reference in their folk
memory.

Elephants are assumed to have been extinct in northern
Africa at the period of the Israelite enslavement, but the
Israelites' captors loved ivory from predynastic times onwards.
Egyptians during the First Dynasty (about 3200 BC) knew
enough about elephants to have devised one hieroglyph
symbol for wild elephants, another for trained elephants and
were trading regionally in elephants a millennium before they
were trading in Israelite slaves. Pharaohs, like the Roman
Caesars, the Persians and Hannibal, trained elephants as
weapons of war. They must, surely, have been known about by
Israelite slaves. A golden elephant, for example, would have

served even better than a golden calf to enrage Moses when he descended with his tablets.

Did Jumbo's unwieldy ancestors, to go back a few books in the Bible, make it on to the ark? Some reassurance is given on the invaluable Christian Answers website, where it is hypothesised, given the measurements offered in the Bible (300 by 50 by 30 'cubits'), that Noah's vessel could have comfortably accommodated as many as 50,000 animal species and their fodder. The Website's answering service instructs us to: 'Remember there are really only a few very large animals, such as the dinosaur or the elephant, and these could be represented by young ones.'

Exactly the solution adopted by Casanova for Jumbo. Fully grown elephants require some hundreds of pounds of food a day. And, of course, excrete the same massive quantity. Of the eight members of the Noah family on board the ark, it would have been the shortest of straws to have been the one given the big shovel. The complacent conclusion of the website is that: 'It is evident, when all the facts are examined that there is no scientific evidence that the biblical account of Noah's ark is a myth or fable.'

It happened; just as it is written in Genesis, and we may be confident the biggest passengers were safely on board. Of course, it is not clear where Noah could have come by his pair of elephants. If, as suggested, God Himself drove them to the embarkation point, it would have taken many months for them to arrive across some very elephant-hostile territories from Nubia – their nearest habitat. But, apparently, He, and His nautical servant did ensure that one day, millennia hence, Jumbo would come into being and would not expire, with the luckless sauropod dinosaurs, in the deluge.

There is a final conundrum. If the elephant is unmentioned in the Bible, and thus not covered directly in the elaborate dietary rules laid down in Deuteronomy, is the meat kosher? Could an orthodox believer eat a Jumboburger if it were literally that? It is a question which has knitted brows on the internet. The 'best answer', as supplied by Yahoo, is as follows:

> No – elephants are NOT Kosher as the laws of kashrut state that for an animal to be Kosher it has to have BOTH of cloven hooves and chew the cud. Since elephants do not have both these traits, they are not kosher.
>
> There is another practical matter that would prevent them from being kosher even if they did possess both these traits. For the meat of an animal to be kosher, it has to be killed in a specific way – by cutting across the carotid, jugular and windpipe in an unbroken motion. To do this to an elephant without getting crushed in the process is impossible, let alone having a knife sharp enough to cut through elephant skin with enough ease to do this![1]

Jumbo's kind – persecuted as they have been through the ages by gun, arrow, spear and trap – are safe, at least, from the cleansing rabbinical knife: assuming, that is, any rabbi were intrepid enough to scale a ladder and do the ritual necessity.

Big Game, Big Men

Barnum acquired Jumbo towards the end of his extraordinary career, in what for other men would be their declining years. But not for him. It was a period at which the showman formerly known, and happy to be known, as the Prince of Humbugs, had reimagined himself as 'the friend of children' and, at the same time, the creator of things so large that human beings would see him as quasi-divine. Elephants, and mastery over them, fed into this late-life megalomania.

He called his post-1880 three-ring, railroad circus (as did Cecil B. DeMille, who monumentalised it in his 1952 movie) 'The Greatest Show on Earth'. A show, that is, whose three rings would rival what God had created in the first seven days. In his last years, the Jumbo years, Barnum was, in a sense, building his pyramid. He wanted, in his last years (he had by now lived a very long time), to be remembered as a great man and a great friend of humanity – not a huckster who treated his fellow human beings as suckers and palmed off on them such hoaxes as the Feejee Mermaid.

Jumbo was in the centre of the self-aggrandising mix. Elephants do, observably, elicit in some white men a condition which one could call 'elephantiasis of the ego'. Typically it strikes in mid-to-late life. It's all too easy to draw conclusions about why, at that drooping time of life it happens. It's clearly what impels Ulysses, in Tennyson's poem, having done and seen more than ten men, to take to the seas again:

> It little profits that an idle king,
> By this still hearth, among these barren crags,
> Matched with an agèd wife, I mete and dole
> Unequal laws unto a savage race,
> That hoard, and sleep, and feed, and know not me.
> I cannot rest from travel: I will drink
> Life to the lees.

Assuming he was thirty when he went off to Troy, spent ten years there and ten years coming back, Homer's hero is now, as Tennyson picks him up, seventy-odd. It's the awful sense of being that age, one suspects, which impels him to go out for more adventure instead of warming his slippered feet by the fire in Ithaca, his ever-faithful hound Argos (who must himself be in his twenties) by his side.

Three weeks after being deposed as President, Theodore Roosevelt, in March 1909, the most outdoor of leaders his country has ever known (and, bless him, the founder of its magnificent national parks) resolved go off on 'safari', a relatively new travel concept. He was fifty-two. Not old, quite: the male-menopause years. He had ridden Jumbo as a child and admiration for the largest elephant on God's soil, one would like to think, had entered his soul on that never-to-be-forgotten day in Regent's Park.

Now, he resolved, was time to kill a few elephants for the good of his soul. It might compensate for no longer being by office the most powerful man on earth to bag, unofficially, a few of the biggest creatures on earth. And it would prove to himself that catastrophically poor eyesight (so bad, it was said, he could not recognise his own sons from further than a few feet away) and impaired hearing (one ear was permanently gone, the other dulled to near deafness by, among other things, the bangs of his personal artillery) were not 'disabilities' if the will were strong enough. Slaughtering elephants would prove something important. To him and to the world. Lesser men in his condition splurge on a BMW.

On what would be a year-long safari through the dark continent, he was accompanied by his son Kermit, himself a 'white hunter' of some repute, and 250 native porters, guides, handlers and a photographer. He evidently forewent the manicurist and court jester. He made two smart deals before embarking. One was with *Scribner's Magazine* which offered him $50,000 for a series of articles, later to be a book. The other was with the Smithsonian Institution to take delivery of the more scientifically significant trophies and evidence of new species for their collections in Washington. Paying the cost, of course, of Roosevelt's getting them.

Before leaving he recruited two 'mighty hunters', both Englishmen, to make arrangements for him in Africa. It was not all hunting and shooting. Roosevelt had cultivated an expertise in the investigation of flora. He routinely slit open the bellies of herbivores he had killed to examine their contents, and what information about dietary habits the undigested food revealed. He liked to disembogue what he had killed and butcher it himself, and he feasted on his 'kill'. It was his right, having proved his mastery, and, in a way, sacramental.

The safari took him, and his small army of helpers, from East Africa to the Belgian Congo – Kurtz's jungle territory. The book, which gathers his safari notes, experiences and reflections, opens, grandiloquently, with the Roosevelt hall-mark megaphonics:

'I SPEAK of Africa and golden joys'; the joy of wandering through lonely lands; the joy of hunting the mighty and terrible lords of the wilderness, the cunning, the wary, and the grim.

In these greatest of the world's great hunting-grounds there are mountain-peaks whose snows are dazzling under the equatorial sun; swamps where the slime oozes and bubbles and festers in the steaming heat; lakes like seas; skies that burn above deserts where the iron desolation is shrouded from view by the wavering mockery of the mirage; vast grassy plains where palms and thorn-trees fringe the dwindling streams; mighty rivers rushing out of the heart of the continent through the sadness of endless marshes; forests of gorgeous beauty, where death broods in the dark and silent depths.[1]

The ex-President brought a fair amount of death with him. The two Roosevelts bagged between them more than five hundred animals, including seventeen lions, eleven elephants and twenty rhinos. After killing his first bull elephant, Theodore dined on elephant trunk soup and arranged for two of the finer carcases of the four elephants he had shot that day to be shipped back to America for the Smithsonian.

When he wasn't blasting them with his mighty Fox No. 12 shotgun ('no better gun was ever made') Roosevelt thought deeply about elephants. The species, whose blood he was splattering all over Africa, induced in him some very sage conclusions overlaid with what one could call stylistic

Roosevelt with his kill

elephantiasis (to use the word again) – a kind of trumpeting eloquence. His elephant musings warrant quoting at length, but skip the following if it bangs the inner ear too hard.

No other animal, not the lion himself, is so constant a theme of talk, and a subject of such unflagging interest round the camp-fires of African hunters and in the native villages of the African wilderness, as the elephant. Indeed, the elephant has always profoundly impressed the imagination of mankind. It is, not only to hunters, but to naturalists, and to all people who possess any curiosity about wild creatures and the wild life of nature, the most interesting of all animals. Its huge bulk, its singular form, the value of its ivory, its great intelligence – in which it is only matched, if at all, by the highest apes, and possibly by one or two of the highest carnivores — and its varied habits, all combine to give it an interest such as attaches to no other living creature below the rank of man.[2]

At the heart of Roosevelt's book is the contention that only the hunter knows the elephant. The Smithsonian has its specimens, its research papers, its men in white coats. But it does not 'know' the elephant as intimately as the man in buckskin who shoots it, disembowels it, and eats it. It sets up an odd contradiction. One must destroy in order to love and, more importantly, to preserve. The contradiction was manifest in a little ceremony which took place at the White House, a few months earlier. It was something to warm the heart of the National Rifle Association.

Mr. E. N. Buxton took the lead in the matter when he heard that I intended making a trip after big game in Africa. I received the rifle at the White House, while I was President. Inside the case was the:

list of zoologists and sportsmen who are donors of a double elephant rifle to the Hon. Theodore Roosevelt, President U.S.A. in recognition of his services on behalf of the preservation of species by means of national parks and forest reserves, and by other means.[3]

Does the elephant gun preserve? Or exterminate? The elephant today, facing a hail of bullets from poachers' AK47s, might believe the second.

Nonetheless the record shows that Roosevelt did more to preserve wildlife and wilderness with his National Parks Acts than any President before or since. He was a conservationist with a mighty gun. Conservation does not come naturally to America. I spent a quarter of a century working in California, under a state flag fluttering over the institution which employed me with a magnificent golden bear on it.

The last surviving golden bear was shot by a hunter in 1922. The flag symbolises something rather sinister if one thinks about it. 'Ask not for whom the elephant gun booms, it booms for thee'.

Roosevelt in unpresidential garb

Great white hunters are a noble species (if one forgives the slaughter) but they are typically handier with the elephant gun than the pen. Roosevelt was, among much else, a gifted writer. His description of actually killing an elephant in the Congo (Kurtz's territory) is among the most vivid put on paper:

> We continually heard them breaking branches, and making rumbling or squeaking sounds . . . we followed faster in the big footprints of the bull we had selected. Suddenly, in an open glade, Kongoni crouched and beckoned to me, and through a bush I caught a glimpse of the tusker. But at that instant he either heard us,

saw us, or caught a whiff of our wind, and without a moment's hesitation he himself assumed the offensive. With his huge ears cocked at right angles to his head, and his trunk hanging down, he charged full tilt at us, coming steadily, silently, and at a great pace, his feet swishing through the long grass; and a formidable monster he looked. At forty yards I fired the right barrel of the Holland into his head, and, though I missed the brain, the shock dazed him and brought him to an instant halt. Immediately Kermit put a bullet from the Winchester into his head; as he wheeled I gave him the second barrel between the neck and shoulder, through his ear; and Kermit gave him three more shots before he slewed round and disappeared. There were not many minutes of daylight left, and we followed hard on his trail, Kongoni leading. At first there was only an occasional gout of dark blood, but soon we found splashes of red froth from the lungs; then we came to where he had fallen, and then we heard him crashing among the branches in thick jungle to the right. In we went after him, through the gathering gloom, Kongoni leading and I close behind, with the rifle ready for instant action; for, though his strength was evidently fast failing, he was also evidently in a savage temper, anxious to wreak his vengeance before he died. On we went, following the bloody trail through dim, cavernous windings in the dark, vine-covered jungle; we heard him smash the branches but a few yards ahead, and fall and rise; and, stealing forward, Kermit and I slipped up to within a dozen feet of him as he stood on the other side of some small twisted trees hung with a mat of creepers. I put a bullet into his heart; Kermit fired. Each of us fired again on the instant; the mighty bull threw up his trunk, crashed over backward, and lay dead on his side among the bushes. A fine sight he was, a sight to gladden any hunter's heart, as he lay in the twilight, a giant in death.[4]

Not to overload this book with quotation, but it is tempting to align the above with George Orwell's famous description of killing an elephant during his time as a colonial policeman in Burma. Orwell, then Lt Eric Blair, ranks as the saddest white hunter on record. The essay ponders the paradox of colonial impunity. Orwell did not want to kill the beast – which in a momentary spasm of musth had trampled a man to death, before calming down again. But the 'subject people', the Burmese crowd, behind him willed him to do it. It was they, the subjugated, who had the power to pull the trigger and kill the elephant. This is how Orwell describes the kill, symbolising the impotence within the power of the British Empire:

There was only one alternative. I shoved the cartridges into the magazine and lay down on the road to get a better aim. The crowd grew very still, and a deep, low, happy sigh, as of people who see the theatre curtain go up at last, breathed from innumerable throats. They were going to have their bit of fun after all. The rifle was a beautiful German thing with cross-hair sights. I did not then know that in shooting an elephant one would shoot to cut an imaginary bar running from ear-hole to ear-hole. I ought, therefore, as the elephant was sideways on, to have aimed straight at his ear-hole, actually I aimed several inches in front of this, thinking the brain would be further forward.

When I pulled the trigger I did not hear the bang or

feel the kick – one never does when a shot goes home – but I heard the devilish roar of glee that went up from the crowd. In that instant, in too short a time, one would have thought, even for the bullet to get there, a mysterious, terrible change had come over the elephant. He neither stirred nor fell, but every line of his body had altered. He looked suddenly stricken, shrunken, immensely old, as though the frightful impact of the bullet had paralysed him without knocking him down. At last, after what seemed a long time – it might have been five seconds, I dare say – he sagged flabbily to his knees. His mouth slobbered. An enormous senility seemed to have settled upon him. One could have imagined him thousands of years old. I fired again into the same spot. At the second shot he did not collapse but climbed with desperate slowness to his feet and stood weakly upright, with legs sagging and head drooping. I fired a third time. That was the shot that did for him. You could see the agony of it jolt his whole body and knock the last remnant of strength from his legs. But in falling he seemed for a moment to rise, for as his hind legs collapsed beneath him he seemed to tower upward like a huge rock toppling, his trunk reaching skyward like a tree. He trumpeted, for the first and only time. And then down he came, his belly towards me, with a crash that seemed to shake the ground even where I lay.[5]

Orwell's biographers have sought in vain for documentary evidence that he did, actually, kill an elephant. It would certainly have been recorded and, just as certainly, there would have been some court of enquiry. Perhaps it's fiction. But so beautifully is it written that one is drawn to echo his wife Sonia

Orwell's furious riposte to a sceptical biographer: 'Of course he shot a fucking elephant. He said he did. Why do you always doubt his fucking word?'

Jumbo Dung and Jumbo Sex

Civilisation is often described as the distance man puts between his nose and his excrement. But not all excrement (as every dog owner who also owns a cat and a parrot will testify) is the same. Nor possessed of the same noisomeness to the human nose. The human nose, lamentably, is the most neglected of our sense organs. As a dog owner, I have noted (dutiful plastic bag in hand) that dogs are only interested in dog excrement, in which they seem to find as much information as I find on the front page of my morning paper. No other creature's droppings are of interest. They use their nose intelligently and discriminatingly, unlike us. But they have to contort themselves by bending down for examination (as do I to pick up the damn stuff). The elephant can reach its nose to the top branches of a tree, or root in the dust, without moving its head or its body.

Orwell in his essay on Swift and the English language notes the eighteenth-century author's near lunatic distaste for human excrement, expressed in such poems as 'The Lady's Dressing Room'. The narrative is that of the lover, Strephon, peeping like Shakespeare's Iachimo into the dressing room of his beloved, Celia, as she disrobes. He sees more than he bargains for, and is a lover no more:

> Thus finishing his grand Survey,
> Disgusted *Strephon* stole away
> Repeating in his amorous Fits,
> Oh! *Celia, Celia, Celia* shits!

The biological fact of human excretion smeared, for Swift, the whole human condition. The first thing that happens to Gulliver, on his fourth voyage, is that he finds himself in a terra incognita inhabited by Yahoos ('noble savages' – humans in a state of nature). They climb up trees and 'discharge their excrements' on the stranger's head by way of welcome to Yahooland. They have not put any distance whatsoever between themselves and their excrement and are deeply uncivilised.

Gulliver then moves on to reside with the Houyhnhnms (horses) whom he finds rational, clean and in every way preferable to Yahoo-humans: not least in their excremental functions and the nature of that stuff. Orwell speculates, plausibly, that Swift felt that 'horseshit', to borrow a favourite American term, liberally sprinkled over their conversations, is the least offensive of animal droppings. One could even get to like it. Or, at least, live with it as the Victorians did (there were a million horses using the streets of London in Jumbo's time, dropping incontinently their waste matter).

Had he lived at a period, a century and a half later, when he could have visited London Zoo, or otherwise come in contact with elephants, it might have been Jumbo, rather than the Houyhnhnms, that Swift/Gulliver found the most tolerable (least shitty) of animal kind. A pretty fantasy, Gulliver's fifth visit to Jumboland.

Elephant dung is, all witnesses confirm, relatively inoffensive – even less offensive than horseshit. There is, of course, a lot of it produced on a daily basis. Zoologists inform us that an elephant will consume up to 300 kilograms every day, spending more than half the day in pursuit of vegetation. However, it does not digest much of this volume, excreting approximately 60% of it in a relatively untouched form. This aids with seed dispersal and the distribution of plant species, as these beasts travel several kilometres during any given day.[1]

In Africa elephants and their 'dung piles' are an invaluable ecological dynamic in the growth and decay of forest vegetation. 'Recent studies,' one is told, 'have shown that ninety different tree species depend on hungry elephants in order to prosper. Without elephants, Africa would look vastly different'.[2] The Mongongo tree, possessed of a delicate velvety fruit and a rock-hard nut, is, apparently, particularly dependent on elephant throughput for its dissemination.

Eco-websites stress this beautifully cyclical fact. Elephants excrete new life from their rear end; they shit creation. For farmers, in the few places left on earth where elephants roam free, it is a different matter. Voluminous and fast as their intake is, elephants are highly discriminating eaters. They crave a wide range of foodstuffs, for the various minerals and vitamins their vast bodies and complex nervous systems require. Forests and grasslands supply the necessary nutrients – but so, more irresistibly temptingly, do crop fields, which have the same attraction for wild Jumbos as the smells wafting to the street from the kitchens of the Ritz to a hungry passer-by.

What fence can keep an elephant out in its eagerness to convert hard-raised crops, necessary for the farmer's survival, into massive steaming dung piles? Helpful to the Mongongo tree they may be, but what good are those piles to a farmer with a family to feed? The elephant is, for subsistence farmers, a 5-ton locust. It's war. The angry farmer is as much an enemy of the elephant as the poacher with his AK-47 or elephanticidal Kurtz himself.

Elephant excrement doesn't offend even the most morbidly Swiftian nose because it goes through so fast it hardly stops long enough to become excrement (60 per cent of it never does, coming out much as it went in, only wetter and softer). And because it goes through these 'huge eating machines' at such velocity it is not compacted. Put crudely, there is no such thing as an elephant turd. What exists is the excremental equivalent of the proverbial shit shower. It inspired a famous 'urban legend' which was picked up by gullible tabloid papers around the world and became 'newspaper fact':

PADERBORN, GERMANY – Overzealous zookeeper Friedrich Riesfeldt fed his constipated elephant Stefan 22 doses of animal laxative and more than a bushel of berries, figs and prunes before the plugged-up pachyderm finally let fly – and suffocated the keeper under 200 pounds of poop. Investigators say ill-fated Friedrich, 46, was attempting to give the ailing elephant an olive-oil enema when the relieved beast unloaded on him like a dump truck full of mud.

'The sheer force of the elephant's unexpected defecation knocked Mr. Riesfeldt to the ground, where he struck his head on a rock and lay unconscious as the elephant continued to evacuate his bowels on top of him,' said flabbergasted Paderborn police detective Erik Dern. 'With no one there to help him, he lay under all that dung for at least an hour before a watchman came along, and during that time he suffocated. It seems to be just one of those freak accidents that happen sometimes – a billion-to-one shot, at least.'[3]

Mr Riesfeldt's demise won the Darwin Society's Urban Legend award in 1998 and red faces in some press rooms worldwide. It's nicely told (the prunes are a good touch) but a moment's thought – not something one always finds in the tabloid press – raises suspicion. The usual calculation is that there is 1 lb of elephant excrement for every 5 lb of vegetation eaten, most of it being water. The amount the elephant would have had to eat to bury its keeper Mr Riesfeldt is – well, do the maths.

What, curiosity impels one to ask, happened to Jumbo's dung piles? In London they were probably sold, or donated, for fertiliser to the adjoining Regent's Park, where they could be lavishly re-piled, without grossly offending any cockney nostrils, on flower beds and other plant displays for which the park has for 200 years been justly famous. I'm sorry to recall that a promising 'bog garden', on the south side of the park, for which I had great hopes, failed to survive a few years ago. A bog garden would have been a good destination for elephant dung. The garden, just down from the St Andrew's gate entrance, was, for three years (1999–2002) surrounded, oddly enough, by massive sculptures of elephants by an artist called Ronald Rae, for example (see overleaf).

While in this reminiscential vein, I'm old enough to remember that whenever carthorses (dray animals, used for coal and milk vehicles) dropped dung, as they seemed to every few yards, the housewife occupants of the terraced artisan cottage street where I lived as a child would rush out, dustpan and brush in hand, to scoop it up. 'For the roses', it was explained. Plenty of roses in Regent's Park. No passing elephants, alas, since Claudius's day, in Colchester. The town does, though, have one of the country's most famous rose shows.

Ronald Rae's elephant mother

It was the Victorians who, under the superintendence of Joseph Bazalgette (are those tusks?) laid our wonderful underground sewage system (creating plenty of 'distance' from the fastidious nose for civilisation), and that strangely oxymoronic thing, the 'sewage farm'. They overdid it at times, however, and were so fond of dumping multiple excrements on arable soil that they created a uniquely Victorian condition – 'sewage sick fields'.

Other, and more creative, uses have been found for elephant dung in modern times. It has, for example, become a favoured substance on the artist's palette. The Leonardo of elephant dung is the 'outlaw' and 'trash' artist David Hammons, who took Greenwich Village by storm in the 1980s. The aim was to outrage – which was royally achieved. But what Hammons demonstrated with his sculptures was that elephant dung is one

Joseph Bazalgette and his tusk-like
moustache

of the few animal excrements an artist can work with. Urine, from whatever source, as in Serrano's enraging 'Piss Christ', could not be *worked*. All you could do was dump things in it, like a cocktail swizzle stick or olive (a crucifix or a rosary, perhaps) and hope to offend. You could, by contrast, convert elephant dung into aesthetic turds, as the potter converts clay into ceramic.

Hammons blazed a trail (one could playfully adapt that metaphor – 'dropped a spoor'?), which has been profitably, and more newsworthily, followed by the British Turner Prize-winning artist Chris Ofili. Ofili starts from a different, less antagonistic, place than did Hammons. His aim is not to *épater* (literally 'spatter') the *bourgeoisie*, but to create works of art in a spirit of reverence. Ofili's is politically correct, eco-OK, holy even, elephant shit-art. His philosophy of creation is more in line with the forest nourishment which the elephant supplies to the hungry soil in the forests and grasslands of its natural habitat. It's recycling, not spatter. Other artists carve on ivory, craftsmen make whips out of elephant hide (they were a favourite with the overseers in Conrad's *Heart of Darkness*), chefs make elephant trunk soup (which the American President Theodore Roosevelt particularly relished). All these require that the beast be dead. Excrement art requires the beast to be alive, and eating heartily, and still producing the raw material of art. The material must be warm from the body. Old elephant excrement is useless. Geologists find it petrified, often in large solid lumps, but it is of no more than curiosity value.

Ofili was born in 1968 in Manchester to Nigerian parents. Nigeria is reported to have lost its last indigenous elephant in 2005, a fact which will not have escaped its gifted son. In 1992, Ofili won a scholarship which he used to travel to Zimbabwe. He went on safari, and followed trails of elephant droppings. He never, however, saw an elephant. He became fascinated by the possibility of using the dung as a stipple effect on canvas, or creating tensions between its naturalness and the conventionally artificial (and increasingly chemical) materials of art. Ofili has said that he was influenced by the fact that Zimbabwean natives venerate elephant dung and make artworks out of it – which has been disputed by Zimbabweans. But, whether true or not, it enabled him to create a kind of foundational myth for his art which is not intended to affront.

But affront it inevitably did. 'Chrysophilia' (the beautiful interlayings of wood and ivory) had descended to coprophilia (a sexual excremental fetish) complained the art critic Brian Sewell with a barrage of eloquent abuse against Ofili. Ofili's 'Holy Virgin Mary', which portrayed a black Madonna, a collage of other demotic African-American and pornographic images, and a fine finishing spray of elephant dung, led to prosecutions instituted by the then New York mayor, Rudy Giuliani, who did not share the Zimbabwean reverence for the substance. Heroin on the streets of the city was a problem. This was sacrilege, by God.

Ofili had packed some elephant dung in his luggage on the return trip from Zimbabwe ('Do you have anything to declare, Sir...'). On his return he began creating such works as 'Painting with Shit on It'. When asked where he gets his elephant materials from nowadays the answer is 'London Zoo'. Jumbo droppings, *de nos jours*. His agent adds: 'Ofili always uses dung from a particular group of elephants there, like he was collaborating with them.' One of the art galleries specialising in his work, however, adds, nervously, in its brochure: 'Chris Ofili's work often incorporates elephant dung, not straight out the elephant, but chemically treated to avoid putrefaction, odour and flies.'[4] Nothing in it, however, to stop attracting shitloads of money. Straight out of the customer.

Another reverent use of elephant dung is that developed by a Mr Wanchai in Thailand who, noting the fibrousness of the material in the piles he passed daily, began experimenting with it for the manufacture of paper. An elephant supplies enough to make over a hundred sheets of high-quality note-paper a day, one is told. And the elephant is a kind of combine harvester. It ingests the fibrous material, soaks and breaks it down, and drops it neatly, heaped, but not damagingly over-digested, ready for the mill. Elephant Dung Paper is now a thriving niche industry. Mr Wanchai is rich. His business serves the conservation cause nobly, although Mrs Wanchai is reported to be irritated by the hundredweights of the stuff stinking out her house.

Myths about the elephant's gastric prowess abound. More

importantly, they can make jumbo-bucks for those propagating them. In 2012 a hotel chain in the Maldives received a lot of worldwide publicity by selling, at $1,100 (£687) per kilo, what it called 'Black Ivory Coffee'. The *Daily Mail* (7 December 2012) called it less romantically 'coffee harvested from elephant poo'. This is how they described it:

> It works by coffee beans being digested and 'naturally refined' by Thai elephants. Research indicates that during digestion, the enzymes of the elephant break down coffee protein. As protein is one of the main factors responsible for the bitterness in coffee, less protein means there is almost no bitterness to the coffee.

'This tastes like crap!' – the coffee drinker will say, *approvingly*.

Barnum had some hopes that the virginal Jumbo could procreate and set up a pairing with an Asian cow, Hebe. She was named, promisingly, after the goddess of youth. The cross-species pairing did not, apparently, work. Details are scarce. But in Barnum's circus Jumbo seems not to have given any signs of the recurrent outbreaks of male sexuality which so worried Victorian England. It's odd, since he was the most closely observed and written about elephant in the history of the world. Was he, one wonders, gelded? That was the sovereign remedy for wayward male animals, as with virtually the whole dog population of the UK today and much of the horse population in the US in the nineteenth century.

Probably not, it seems. The elephant gelder follows a difficult profession and was not yet in existence. There's a relevant account which I'll quote in full, not merely for its information content (which is high) but because the author, Robert M. Miller, is such a fine tale-teller; and it's a gripping tale he tells. Dr Miller, doctor of veterinary medicine, also has the distinction of being a pioneer elephant castrator. It's not a densely populated area of the animal medicine business. His account of what it involves is racily titled: 'Mind Over Miller: An Elephant-Size Job' and was first published in the *Journal of Veterinary Medicine* (1 April 2006) – not a location one normally searches for racy articles:

> I helped castrate a 9,000-lb bull elephant once. The owner of Circus Vargas called me because he had a highly trained bull elephant that was becoming unruly with age, and he wanted me to castrate it. I told Mr. Vargas that I would perform the operation provided that Dr. Murray Fowler of the University of California School of Veterinary Medicine was available to be the chief surgeon. At the time, Dr. Fowler was the only person who had castrated a male elephant and had it survive.
>
> I telephoned Dr. Fowler, and he readily agreed to help. He said, enthusiastically, that he had created a new instrument for the task – a three-and-a-half-foot-long écraseur that could remove testicles from deep in the belly of a full-grown elephant – and he was eager to try it out.
>
> I then assembled the rest of the surgical team. My partner, Dr. Jim Peddie, would be the second surgeon, and another partner, Dr. Bob Kind, who was six-and-a-half-feet tall and had long arms, would be the third surgeon. I would be the anesthetist, and for the task, I planned to use a combination of xylazine and etorphine.

We agreed to meet at 9 on a Monday morning on the circus lot in Northridge, Calif.

At 5 a.m. that Monday, Dr. Fowler went to the Sacramento airport. He carried his long, steel écraseur, which was autoclaved and wrapped. At the time, airport X-ray machines were not yet in use, but a series of hijackings had created the need for the first airport security stations. As Dr. Fowler went through security with his carryon luggage, the security officer asked him to unwrap his package.

'I can't,' he explained. 'It's a sterilized surgical instrument.'

The officer lifted the submachine-gun-size package and asked, 'What kind of surgical instrument?'

Dr. Fowler, who was dressed in a field jacket, blue jeans, and work boots, said, 'It's for castrating elephants. I'm on my way to Los Angeles to castrate an elephant.'

The security officer reacted to this in a completely unreasonable manner, and Dr. Fowler nearly missed his flight before it was determined he was a professor and not a terrorist.

Castrating male animals is one of the most common procedures in veterinary practice, but this case was a bit unusual. If you are ever asked to castrate an elephant, I recommend that you consider referring the case to Dr. Fowler.

Miller is also a cartoonist and more of his wit and wisdom can be found on www.robertmmiller.com. Well worth a visit to the lair of elephant castrator.

The question remains, of course. How did Barnum keep Jumbo 'suppressed', where the best zoological brains in London had failed? My guess is judiciously administered alcohol. Jumbo-size swigs.

Jumbo Exiled

Bridgeport was Barnum's town. He had erected four fine mansions for himself there (one of which is now the site of the town's university) and, as mayor, brought clean water, higher morality (he instigated ruthless raids on brothels and bars), and a good hospital to the town. His circus money flowed philanthropically through many channels into the place he loved and served and made a better place. He is memorialised in statues and named institutional buildings (notably the town's Barnum Museum). Jumbo, of course, was an honoured visitor – and for much of the year a resident. The Barnum circus winter quarters were located in one of Bridgeport's open spaces. It was where elephants were trained and the local population, particularly youngsters, got a free circus treat.

Alas, the Prince of Humbugs (aka the Mayor of Bridgeport) is no longer the town's favourite son. Every fall since 1880 it was the annual routine of the circus which bears his name (Ringling Bros, and Barnum & Bailey, in modern times) to pitch their great tents in Bridgeport at the Arena at Harbor Yard. In 2010 the *Connecticut Post*, Bridgeport's hometown newspaper, came out with an editorial in response to the pictures being circulated on the Web chronicling, it was alleged, programmatic cruelty by the circus – especially in its treatment of elephants. It was a highly critical editorial.

There had, since 2006, been annual protests and arrests outside the Arena. The protests have grown year by year. A vexed local administration took their right to arrest obstructive protestors to the state supreme court in 2012, and the judges found in their favour. But the protests go on, bigger every year, and it seems only a matter of time before Barnum's circus is banned from Barnum's town. The show must not go on.

For the Queen's Diamond Jubilee in June 2012, the Palace gave permission to the ZSL to release a charming picture from 1938 (my year of birth, as it happens – which adds to the charm for me). It showed the future monarch delightedly riding one of the London Zoo elephants – a tradition which went back to the offspring of Queen Victoria.

The future queen rides in style

Even the elephant looks proud. The press release added that 'the Royal Patron of ZSL London Zoo has visited regularly since she was small'. She rarely laughs as much as she is doing on that glorious day, one suspects.

Our monarch, thank the heavens, has lasted longer (alas) than the elephant ride: another of the relics of the empire blown away by the winds of change. No picture of Prince Charles has been released, but he will be the last heir apparent to have ridden the London howdah, a line of royal succession which goes back to Jumbo.

Elephant rides were suspended in 1960 – the age of austerity. They have never been restored. It gets worse (or, arguably, better if you are an elephant). Over the next four decades 'seeing the elephant', that great thrill for children and adults alike, and feeding the elephant, were continued, but with ever more vigilant superintendence. There were some very awkward moments. The Casson 'elephant house' led to accidents. The animals kept falling in the dry moat – sometimes, as with 'Dicksie' a twenty-nine-year-old African bush elephant in 1967, fatally. Casson's structure had served the zoo as a bomb shelter during the war but it was clearly not fit for elephant purpose.

Meanwhile, growing enlightenment about the natural world – thanks to TV, largely, and pre-eminently David Attenborough – fostered a feeling that zoos were somehow intrinsically wrong and circus exotic animal shows even more wrong. Attenborough had begun, in the 1950s, with programmes based in the zoo. But, over the years, the zoology he promulgated – educationally to millions – became more and more based on the idea that animal and animal habitat are inseparable. The hugely successful *Life on Earth* series confirmed a sense that animals did not belong behind bars. At the sharp end of this new zoological enlightenment were the increasingly aggressive 'animal rights' activists. The issue was creating angry splits in the RSPCA.

The 'elephant in the zoo' issue went critical in October 2001. One of the ZSL's three animals, Mya, a 4-ton Burmese elephant, killed her keeper, Jim Robson. In what looked like a damage limitation exercise it was first given out that Mya had 'rolled on' the unfortunate Mr Robson, crushing him fatally. At the inquest grislier details were reported – lip-smackingly – by the press. 'In front of dozens of shocked visitors', the Westminster Court coroner was told:

> The 20-year-old female elephant pushed over keeper James Robson, then wrapped her trunk around his legs to hold him down before stamping on his head. As Mr Robson screamed for help, two other elephants tried to save him from Mya, the court was told. But 45-year-old Mr Robson – a zookeeper for 26 years who virtually lived with the animals – was pronounced dead two hours later with massive head injuries. Experts later said Mya may have picked on him because she had recognised his 'introverted nature' and turned savage.
>
> Unmarried Mr Robson, of Hampstead, had been playing with Mya and two other female Asian elephants, Geetha and Azizah, in their Regent's Park enclosure. American Jerry Finley told the court Mr Robson was conducting a show involving the elephants moving enormous logs round their paddock at the time of the attack. He said: 'I picked up my son so he could watch what was going on. But then the elephant wrapped his trunk against the guy's legs and pushed him to the ground. The keeper started screaming for help.'

'I made my son turn round so that he could not see what was happening. The elephant held the keeper down on the ground and then he stamped on his head...I believe it was an attempt to kill the man. Its actions were continuous, it never stopped attacking once it started.' Mr Finley added: 'The other elephants tried positioning themselves between the attacking elephant and the man.'

During the inquest executives at London Zoo – which nearly went bankrupt in 1990 – denied cost-cutting measures had led to Mr Robson's death.

The Coroner Dr Paul Knapman noted: 'It has been said that cost-cutting may have played a part in a shortage of handlers and lack of safety at the zoo', while recording a verdict of accidental death.[1]

Call it Bartlett's nightmare. It was exactly the kind of thing which was bound to happen if keepers forgot their place and, like that damned Matthew Scott, got into too 'introverted' a relationship with elephants in their care. And it raised, said the *London Evening Standard*, choosing its words carefully, 'serious questions over the future of Victorian-era animal attractions. Many of London Zoo's buildings date from a period when animal welfare was less of a consideration than spectators' convenience and are listed, making modernising or expanding them difficult.'

There had been elephants at London Zoo since pre-Victorian 1831 and, since the heyday of Jumbo, they had been, along with the penguins (a particular favourite of the young Princess Elizabeth, one was told) a crowd-drawing attraction. But the penguins had pecked no keeper to death.

Mya had been at the zoo for thirteen years, and had been

brought over with two others from Burma, aged seven. Killing elephants was a horrible business, even if they themselves were killers. Bartlett's elephant gun was no longer an option. Mya was forgiven her trespass and consigned with the zoo's other two London elephants, Dilberta and Layang-Layang (names had become more ethnically correct over the years – no more imperial jingoism) to the ZSL wild animal park at Whipsnade. Virginia McKenna, founder of the Born Free Foundation, which had fought to have the animals moved to Whipsnade, welcomed the move. 'At last,' she said, 'we have a positive step towards the phasing out of elephants in city zoos.'[2] The ZSL management announced, somewhat unconvincingly, that the relocation was part of a 'long-term plan'.

The Whipsnade – 'zoo-ark' – defence was that elephants were an endangered species (only 30,000 Asian elephants left) and that if they had a future, it was in 'parks'. The RSPCA's spokesperson, Ann Grain, pushed the issue with the uncompromising statement that a 'closed environment cannot provide for the elephant's natural needs'. The Society, she said, did not even support the Whipsnade solution: 'We believe wild animals should be maintained in their natural habitat.'[3] Elephants were not indigenous to Bedfordshire.

Ominously, the RSPCA had commissioned experts at Oxford University to carry out a study on the welfare of elephants in zoos. The whole public zoo concept looked as if it were going the way of the Royal Menagerie, into the dustbin of history.

Epilogue: Elephant Miscellany

The Elephant is Earth's largest surviving land animal. It has the largest brain, at a full-grown weight of 11–12 lb eleven and twelve pounds, three times heavier than its human equivalent. The size of its organ is held to account for the elephant's sophisticated social behaviour, its varied vocalisations and 'calls', which some believe comprise a language, and its ability to learn and carry out useful labour and entertaining 'tricks'. Alexander Pope, in his *An Essay on Man*, compliments the elephant as 'half reasn'ing'.

*

According to 'Elephant Bill' (J.H. Williams) the elephant in captivity 'never knows its name, as a dog does'. That must be the fault of the missing half.

*

According to Sillar and Meyler: 'The Romans were the first to display elephants in circuses in Europe and it is recorded by Pliny and others that Metellius in 251 BC brought to Rome elephants which he had captured from the Carthaginians at the Battle of Palermo. From then on elephants often appeared in Triumphs held in Rome. Their first appearance as combatants fighting to the death in a circus was when they were introduced by the consuls Cornelius Scipio Nasica and C. Lentulus in about 131 BC.[1] Let's hope Ganesha, the Indian elephant god, prepared a fittingly painful afterlife for these pioneer ring-masters – poking each other with swords in a gladiatorial arena for eternity while thousands of elephants sit round applauding.

*

According to Jonathan Swift, 'elephants are always drawn smaller than life, but fleas always larger'.

*

There is uncertainty as to whether African and Asian elephants are two variants of the same species, or two quite different species. Scientific opinion, supported by DNA evidence, seems to be moving towards the second theory. Cross-breeding of the two types in captivity has not been successful.

*

Pliny, whose pioneering work on *Natural History* (AD 77) is observed to be remarkably accurate, nonetheless propagated the still widely credited myth that elephants are 'unable to swim, in consequence of their bulk'. The opposite is true. Elephants can indeed swim, on the surface of water and under-neath it, using their trunks as a snorkel. Their survival, while dozens of other varieties of proboscidea have gone under in the great evolutionary struggle, is plausibly credited to the fact that like the hippopotamus (Earth's third largest land animal) they are amphibious and can stay under water, breathing through their trunk, longer than any other land animal. Their internal organs are also protected (unlike humans') from extremes of water pressure. To paraphrase Disney, 'I think I seen 'bout everythin' when I see an elephant swim'.

*

If you think the elephant preposterous
You've probably never seen a rhinosteros.
Ogden Nash. Rhinos, it is reported, cannot swim.

*

According to 'Elephant Bill' (J.H. Williams), 'savage elephants are as rare as really wicked men.'[2]

*

From earliest Roman times the elephant's ability to respond intelligently to music – dancing, and occasionally trumpeting tunefully – was noted, and exploited for public performance. Research has discovered that elephants, along with primates, are the only land mammals capable of non-instinctual vocalisation learning and mimicry. 'Elephants have learned how to chirp, purr, hum, croak and whistle. One elephant reportedly learned to imitate the sound of a truck engine – and another is said to imitate the commands of his human keeper.' Some have suggested they occasionally do this in a spirit of mockery.

*

Unlike other mammals elephants continue to grow throughout the whole of their lives. With females the growth slows down after twenty-five years and males after fifty years. By these dates, in natural habitats, the animals will weigh around 6,000 lb and 11,000 lb respectively.

*

That the 'elephant never forgets' is proverbial and is wittily commemorated in Dorothy Parker's verse:

> Prince, a precept I'd leave for you
> Coined in Eden, existing yet:
> Skirt the parlor, and shun the zoo –
> Women and elephants *never forget*.

The elephant's 'never forgetting' has had, over the millennia, a valuable survival benefit since they are, in the wild, nomadic, but must remain within some 50 miles of a known watering supply (hole, spring or river). Paths and grazing trails must be remembered. Herds of elephants will, legend has it, knock down houses that obstruct their traditionally remembered paths.

*

Elephants in zoos breed poorly or not at all. People would probably be similarly disinclined to mate if the urge came but once a year and strangers were looking at them. Their admirable modesty augurs ill for their survival. Breeding elephants in captivity has proved feasible but generally impractical.

*

Female elephants are called 'cows', male elephants 'bulls' and young elephants 'calves'. None of the terms (borrowed as they are from domestic cattle) strikes one as appropriate.

*

John Donne celebrates the elephant in the thirty-ninth stanza of his poem *The Progress of the Soul* (the verse is knotty, but his point – a typically witty one – is that all creation kneels before God, even the kneeless elephant):

> Nature's great master-peece, an Elephant,
> The onely harmlesse great thing; the giant
> Of beasts; who thought, no more had gone, to make one
>   wise
> But to be just, and thankfull, loth to offend,
> (Yet nature hath given him no knees to bend)
> Himselfe he up-props, on himselfe relies,
> And foe to none, suspects no enemies,
> Still sleeping stood; vex't not his fantasie
> Blacke dreames, like and unbent bow, carelessly
> His sinewy Proboscis did remisly lie.

Donne is right on one count. Elephants are, in general, 'harmless' since in the wild no other four-legged animal is large or savage enough, or stupid enough, to visit harm on them. But Donne is wrong on three other counts. Elephants do indeed have knees – and other joints. As Bill Watterson explains in his treatise on animal and insect knees:

> What looks like the elephant's front knees are actually its wrists. There's a popular internet factoid which states that the elephant is the only animal which has four knees. But it doesn't; it has two knees at the back, and elbows and wrists at the front, exactly like other quadrupeds. Elephants, horses, dogs and all other quadruped mammals have two knees and two elbows. Almost all mammals have basically the same skeletal structure because we are descended from common ancestors.[3]

Elephants can, indeed, kneel. It's one of the ways humans find it more easy to get on their backs. Nor, as Donne assumes, do elephants sleep standing up. As Emily Rothwell, of San Diego Zoo, reports:

> I am frequently asked how elephants sleep, and you may be surprised to hear that they do sleep lying down. The popular assumption is that elephants always sleep standing up, which can be true for a quick cat nap. However, elephants lie down on the ground when they sleep soundly for a few hours each night. There are even records of elephants snoring while deep in sleep! I have also seen at least one of our adult females, Swazi, kicking her feet while sleeping, much like dogs do when they are dreaming.[4]

Nor is the elephant trunk 'sinewy'. It is entirely muscular. But who ever read John Donne for the zoology?

*

Elephants are strict herbivores. They live, on average, as long as the longest-lived humans – an excellent advertisement for the health benefits of a vegetarian high-cellulose diet.

*

Despite its huge physical bulk, the elephant eye is not much larger than its human equivalent. They are reputed to have relatively poor sight – keenest at dawn or dusk, the most dangerous periods of the daily cycle. The small eyes, as with human physiognomy, are popularly thought to correlate with cunning, slyness, and roguishness – which is probably something of a slander on the species (and small-eyed humans, come to that). Their eyes, situated on the sides of their heads, are less efficient than ours for binocular and stereoscopic vision but more useful for all-round defence.

*

Some two-thirds of elephant calls and 'voicings' are inaudible (being 'infrasonic') to the human ear, although elephants communicate to each other (silently, as far as any human is concerned) across distances as great as 5 miles. Their vocal repertoire falls into four categories: 'rumbling' (used as sexual invitation, or warning, or an expression of mild pleasure); 'trumpeting' – blowing through the nostrils, indicating excitement, the furthest carrying of elephant vocalisations; 'squealing', used exclusively by juveniles in distress; and 'screaming', used by adults in distress, or as a threat. Forest elephants vocalise at levels as low as 14 Hertz below, one is told, what even the keenest-hearing human can pick up. Pick up 'consciously', one should add. Exposure to infrasound, in the ranges elephants habitually employ, is reported to have a profoundly unsettling effect on humans. Often it is associated with the supposed experience of paranormal phenomena. Countries with the highest number of 'authenticated' ghost sightings, it is reported, are those countries with the highest elephant populations. Weird.

*

It was Pliny, in his *Natural History*, who recorded that 'the elephant hates the mouse above all other creatures'. But small rodents no more run (suffocatingly) into elephants' trunks than earwigs have any inclination to explore human ears. Elephants, in the wild, are not observed to be frightened of mice. They do, however, Dr Todd Palmer of the Mpala Research Centre in Kenya has discovered, profoundly dislike ants, and will avoid plants, trees and places visibly swarming with them.[5]

*

A grown elephant consumes around 5 per cent of its body weight every day (some 300 lb) and drinks up to 50 gallons of water.

*

The elephant's tusks are actually teeth. They are elongated second upper incisors which grow as the elephant itself grows throughout life. Both sexes have tusks (but not all Asian elephants, particularly females). Elephants have one set of tusks through life and six sets of teeth proper. Tusks are used as tools and, by males, for fighting. As with human hands, elephants are right, or left, tusked.

*

Elephants have twenty-four teeth within their mouths. Unlike human beings, who have two sets during a lifetime, elephants will have six. Each new set pushes forward from the rear of the jaw, displacing the worn-out teeth. After the sixth set wears out the elephant will starve to death. Wanted: elephant orthodontist.

*

Elephants can be born, and grow to maturity, tuskless. The fact that they are, in this condition, worthless to modern poachers and (if lucky) left alone means that by (un)natural selection and breeding patterns, their numbers, where the species survives, are swelling.

*

The elephant trunk is, organically, a fusion of upper lip and nose. It is estimated to have thousands of intricately interacting muscles and is entirely muscular. It has no bones or cartilage. In a mature animal the trunk is around 6 feet long, weighs 300 lb or more, and has prehensile 'fingers' on top and bottom of the tip for holding small objects, and has two 'nostrils' at the tip. Elephants' sense of smell is acute, and they can detect water as far as 12 miles away, it is reported. Seventy per cent of what the animal breathes is inhaled through the trunk, the remainder by mouth. The trunk is not used to drink, although it can hold up to 2 gallons of water to be conveyed to the mouth or sprayed over the body. Socially, elephants rub trunks, as Inuit are reputed to rub noses by way of greeting, or as signs of affection. The trunk is also used to slap or caress. Elephants are very tactile, and the trunk is the only means they have, apart from flank rubbing and sexual intercourse, for tactility. Scientists speculate that the multitasking trunk may have first evolved for snorkelling in deep water, at a period when the elephant was amphibious.

*

With the aid of their trunks, principally, elephants are tool-using animals. They are recorded as picking up logs and rocks to throw at enemies, and they pluck tree branches for use as fly swatters.

*

In addition to their upper and lower eyelids, elephants have a third eyelid, or 'nictitating membrane' which moves across the eye to keep it moist and protect it. This too may date back to pre-historic periods when elephantidae were more aquatic than now.

*

Curiosity about the elephant penis can be satisfied on any number of websites, most mirthful, using the respectable or unrespectable terminology. Enough to say that, as with the brain, the size is impressive.

*

Elephants possess the largest skull in the animal world. It has evolved to carry the combined apparatus of the tusks, teeth, brain, and trunk. The skull comprises a quarter of the elephant's total body weight. It is too large, as trophy-loving big-game hunters must have lamented, to hang on a wall. They have to make do with the elephant foot umbrella holders and tusk-legged coffee tables.

*

The Swahili for 'elephant' is 'tembo', which may explain Jumbo's name – although its origin will probably always remain a matter of linguistic dispute.

*

The patterns on an elephant's foot are, one is told, as unique to the animal as a human's fingerprint. The underside of the foot is cushioned, or padded, which means they can walk, where the ground is firm, virtually noiselessly.

*

In the catastrophic Asian tsunami of 2004 it was noted that many elephants felt the vibrations, picked up, presciently, by sensor cells in their feet. It is further speculated that they can communicate through these hypersensitive parts of their body, by a kind of pedal Morse code.

*

Elephants, unlike horses and dogs, have only one basic 'gait' – an amble. Their normal walking speed is around 4mph. When obliged to, they can move at around 25mph. Excellent swimmers, they can make a water speed of 1mph and, in good condition, if they had any reason for doing so, would probably be able to swim the English Channel. On the other hand, being unable to jump, leap or scramble on their columnar legs, they cannot cross a ditch of as little as 7 feet wide.

*

Elephants are classified as 'pachyderms'. Their skin, or hide, is, at around an inch, exceptionally thick in places where protection is most useful. But even at its thickest their skin is sensitive enough to register a fly landing on it. The skin is paper thin inside the ears, mouth and anus.

*

Elephant skin is characteristically wrinkled – they all look old, from childhood onwards. But unlike the wrinkles on the aged human face and body, those on the elephant serve a useful purpose at all periods of life. The wrinkles retain liquid and caked mud, serving to cool the body.

*

Elephants have huge ears (especially in Africa, where they can droop 8 feet – Asian elephant ears are around half the size). The ears serve not merely for listening, but thermoregulation – physiological aircon. They can be flapped and their blanket size, and the quantities of blood pumped through them, allows the release of excessive body heat. The ears can also, one is told, be used for signalling, semaphorically, moods and emotional states. Spread ears are said to indicate threat. Like wire-walkers' poles, ears are said sometimes to be used to aid balance over tricky surfaces (such as the trails over the Alps in which Hannibal famously took his war elephants). Although there is some disagreement as to how acute their hearing is, hunters are wise to be wary approaching their prey. Elephants can hear low-frequency sounds (which the human may not be aware of making) better than any animal ever tested. The ears of African elephants, it has been noted, resemble the geographical shape of the African continent.

*

The most sanitary of animals, where they can elephants like to bathe in water daily.

*

Elephant pregnancy lasts twenty-two months – the longest of any land mammal. The lengthy gestation means that the baby elephant is physically mature, stands some 3 feet tall, weighs up to 200 lb, and can walk in a few hours after birth, which ensures that the herd is not impeded in its nomadic peregrinations and rhythms. Left to themselves elephants spend an average of sixteen hours a day feeding and four to five hours sleeping – both activities coordinated with the herd. Elephants are observed to be protective of fellow cows giving birth.

*

Genetically elephants are very ancient and much evolved, to the despair of Creationists who picture them in Eden. The family to which they belong is estimated to have emerged 16 million years ago. African and Asian elephants, and mammoths, separated as species, some 8 million years ago. Asian elephant DNA reveals a closer genetic link with mammoths than their African counterparts. Savannah and forest elephants in Africa diverged, instinctually, some 2 million years ago. The once numerous proboscidea are reduced, in current times, to one surviving variety – elephants. Their closest living relatives are hyrax, sea cows and golden moles. The last are described as small, solitary burrowers with shiny pale brown fur, who live on a diet of termites. The link is not obvious to those without expertise in genetic biology.

*

Piano keys were routinely made with ivory from the late nineteenth century until the turn of the twentieth. A standard keyboard required at least 1½ lb of ivory. Beneath almost every instrument was a dead elephant – slaughtered, in most cases, to make music.

*

Elephant social organisation is complex and highly gendered. Wild herds (which can extend from a dozen to hundreds in number) are hierarchical and matriarchal. The leader is typically a large old cow. She will be, among other responsibilities, the repository of the herd's stored knowledge of such things as terrain, pathways and food and water resources. There are complex social and 'clan' bonds within a large herd. The herds are mainly composed of cows and their calves. Bulls, male elephants, once adolescent, split off to live solitarily, or transiently bonded existences with other males. They return to the herd in musth as visitors to mate.

*

A study of wild African elephants in 2012 discovered that senior matriarchs build up over the decades of their lives a store of 'social memory', enabling them to recognise on sight known visitors: 'They signal whether an outsider is a friend or foe to the rest of the herd, allowing family members to focus on feeding and breeding when there is no danger'. Mother, as always, knows best.

*

Elephants live, roughly speaking, about as long as human beings. Other than poachers the main threats to their enjoying the biblical three score and ten are drought, constriction and removal of their natural habitats by humans, predation when young by lions and tigers, farmers protecting their crops against invasion, accidental slips and falls (elephants cannot clamber), males fighting when in musth (and females under the assault of a 15,000-lb would-be lover), and the same degenerative diseases of humans: cardiovascular decay, arthritis and strokes.

*

Elephants have long eyelashes, but relatively hairless bodies. An exception is the tail, which can be up to 4 feet long, 20 lb in weight, and tipped with wiry hair up to 3 feet extra in length. Elephants use their tails as precisely targeting fly swats.

*

The trunk-to-tail convoy, common for moving captive elephants and a favourite element in circus displays, is also a feature of elephants in the wild. Particularly young elephants hold on to their mothers' tails, as safety lines, on land and in water.

*

Only one novel about elephants has ever made top spot on *The New York Times* bestseller list: *Water for Elephants*, by Sara Gruen, in 2006. Gruen makes a heart-warming appeal for kindness to elephants and mounts a protest in her novel against their exploitation in modern circuses. The year 2006 saw an unprecedented rise in elephant poaching in Africa, supplying booming India and China with decorative and ornamental ivory.

*

The era of the 'great white hunter' is long gone. There would be considerable competition as to who was the greatest of them, but a strong contender, as regards the African elephant, would be James 'Jim' Sutherland (no relative – other than through wispy strands of DNA). Sutherland came to Africa intending to be a professional boxer, before discovering a more promising career in harvesting ivory ('white gold'). It is recorded that despite the fact that Sutherland's arrival in the hunting fields came at a time when Africa's elephant population was already in serious decline, and that he was twice involved in military service – in 1905–6 and 1914–18 – his career kills, counting bulls only, were estimated to total over a thousand elephants.

Jim died where he had done much of his killing, in the southern Sudan. Friends clubbed together to erect a bronze tablet to his memory, under a palm tree:

'To the Memory of that great elephant Hunter – JIM SUTHERLAND'.[6]

*

Sutherland would have been wise to hope that the deity welcoming him to his eternal afterlife was not Ganesha, the Indian God, who might have a thousand scores to settle. Ganesha has an elephant head and is revered, Hindu theology records, as 'the remover of obstacles'.

*

Salman Rushdie (although Muslim by birth) is a great admirer of Ganesha. Saleem, the massive-nosed and flap-eared hero of his most famous novel, *Midnight's Children*, often compares himself with the deity who is, as Rushdie points out, 'the patron saint of literature'.

*

The largest elephant on record weighed a little short of 11 tons and stood at 13 feet – considerably larger than Jumbo. Not a fact to please Phineas T. Barnum.

*

Elephants are observed to grieve, clustering mournfully around the body of dead herd members, sometimes fondling the bodily remains. This grieving, it is plausibly suggested, gave rise to the myth of the 'elephants' graveyard' – a place where elephants go to die together. It is immortally popularised in the seventh and final voyage of Sinbad the Sailor who returns, enriched by his plunder from the ivory Eldorado.

*

In January 2011 a team of Japanese scientists under Akira Iritani predicted they would successfully clone a woolly mammoth in the following five years. The project aimed to use mammoth DNA extracted from preserved corpses dug up in Siberia and insert it into African elephant eggs that had had their DNA removed. This exercise in 'de-extinction' may be a close-run thing. According to the PBS TV programme *Battle for the Elephants* (shown in 2013) it will be fewer than ten years before poachers have wholly eliminated African elephants from the wild. One 'de-extinguished' animal, an extinguished species. Well done, *Homo sapiens*!

*

Elephants, according to 'Elephant Bill', can never be domesticated – merely 'trained' and are forever unhappy 'captives'.

*

The poet who has penned the most sensitive poems to and about the elephant is Indian born-and-raised Rudyard Kipling. The most moving of his verses is 'The Captive's Dream':

> I will remember what I was
> I am sick of rope and chain.
> I will remember my old strength
> And all of my forest affairs.
> I will not sell my back to man
> For a bundle of sugar-cane.
> I will go out to my own kind
> And the wood-folk in their lairs.

I will go out until the day.
Until the morning break,
Out to the winds' untainted kiss,
The water's clean caress.
I will forget my ankle-ring
And snap my picket-stake.
I will revisit my lost loves
And playmates, masterless.

Dream on.

Notes

Where possible, I have cited easily available web-accessible sources and locations.

The following are book references, abbreviated to surname, in the notes which follow:

Bartlett, A.D. Bartlett. *Wild Animals in Captivity* (Chapman & Hall, London, 1899)

Chambers, Paul. *Jumbo: The Greatest Elephant in the World* (André Deutsch, London, 2007)

Harding, Les. *Elephant Story: Jumbo and P. T. Barnum under the Big Top* (McFarland & Co, New York, 1999)

Kistler, John M. *War Elephants* (Bison Books, London, 2007)

Meredith, Martin. *Africa's Elephant: A Biography* (Sceptre, London, 2002)

Nance, Susan. *Entertaining Elephants* (John Hopkins University Press, Baltimore, 2013)

Saxon, A.H. *P. T. Barnum: The Legend and the Man* (Columbia University Press, New York, 1989)

Scigliano, Eric. *Love, War and Circuses: The Age-Old Relationship between Elephants and Humans* (Bloomsbury, London, 2004)

Scott, Matthew. *Autobiography of Matthew Scott* (Bridgeport, 1885; reprint Kessinger, Montana, 2009)

Sillar, F.C., and Meyler, R.M. *Elephants* (Studio, London, 1968)

Williams, J.H. *Elephant Bill* (Hart-Davis, London 1953)

BLAZING THE TRAIL FOR JUMBO

1. The arguments of Dr Morris, a leading 'young creationist' (the world's youth, not his) can be found on www.icr.org/article/1208.
2. *The New York Times*, 31 May 1904.
3. This passage, along with other interesting zoological facts and elephant lore, can be found at http://www.krugerpark.co.za/africa_elephant.html.
4. Paris, Richard. 'Matthew Paris and Henry III's Elephant', www.academia.edu/755238/matthew_paris_and_henry_IIIs_elephant
5. See Sillar and Meyler, p. 141.

6. My account of the life, career, and death of Chunee draws on Altick, R.D.'s *The Shows of London* (Cambridge University Press, Massachusetts, 1978).
7. Goddard, Henry. *Memoirs of a Bow Street Runner* (Museum Press, USA, 1956), cited in www.victorianlondon.org/entertainment/crossmenagerie.htm
8. Birchall, Diana. *Did Jane Austen Ever See an Elephant?* (13 October 2010) http://austenauthors.net/did-jane-austen-ever-see-an-elephant.
9. Altick, p. 313.
10. *London Society*, Vol 6 (1864), reproduced by Hughes, K., and Hinshaw, V. onelondonone.blogspot.co.uk/2011/06/darker-side-of-19th-century-london.html. For 'the march of mind' in this part of London at this period, see Ashton, R. *Victorian Bloomsbury* (Yale University Press, Connecticut, 2012).
11. Bartlett, pp. 44–45.
12. See Ketabgian, Tamara Siroone. '"Melancholy Mad Elephants": Affect and the Animal Machine in *Hard Times*', *Victorian Studies*, Summer 2003, pp. 649-676.

THE MANY LIVES OF JUMBO

1. Kistler, p. 235.
2. Uncited quotations which follow are from Baker's *True Tales for my Grandsons* (Macmillan, London, 1883; reprinted BiblioBazaar, South Carolina, 2009) and my general account of Jumbo's early life is greatly indebted to Chambers, pp. 10–19.
3. Baker, S.W., *Wild Beasts and their Ways* (London, 1890), p. 19.
4. Baker, S.W. *The Nile Tributaries of Abyssinia and the Sword Hunters of the Hamran Arabs* (London, 1867; reprint Arc Manor, Maryland, 2009), p. 166.
5. Ibid p. 238.
6. Ibid p. 238.

THE MIDDLE PASSAGE AND MIDDLE MEN

1. See the latest web advertisement, www.hearstcastle.org/history-behind-hearst-castle/the-castle/the-zoo.
2. My account of Jumbo's journey from Africa to Europe draws on Chambers's third chapter, 'Crossing the Desert'.
3. The story of Miss Baba is authoritatively recounted in www.feuerwehr-nieder-rossla.de/miss_baba.
4. Lorenz, Konrad. *King Solomon's Ring* (London, 1949; reprint Routledge, London, 2013).
5. Meredith, pp. 162–3.

JUMBEAU

1. Baratay, Eric, and Hardouin-Fougier, Elisabeth, *Zoo: A History of Zoological Gardens in the West* (Reaktion Books, London, 2003), reproduced in aboutzoos.info/zoos/zoo-database/europe-zoo-database/170-paris-la-menagerie-du-jardin-des-plantes.
2. A concise history of London Zoo is offered by Barrington-Johnson, J., in *Zoo: The Story of London Zoo* (Robert Hale, London, 2005).
3. Owen, Richard, *The Life of Richard Owen* (London, 1894; reprint Ulan Press, London, 2011) p. 296.
4. Bartlett, p. 44.

5. Scott, p44; Chambers, p. 52; Bartlett, p. 55.
6. Scott ibid.
7. Bartlett pp. 45–6.
8. Chambers, pp. 67–9.
9. Bartlett, pp. 46–7
10. Williams, Chapter 6, 'The Training Camp'.
11. The *Independent*, 27 August 2004.

THE BATTLE FOR JUMBO'S SOUL

1. The fullest account of the Bartlett–Scott feud, and their backgrounds, is given in Chambers, Chapters 4–13. Particularly illuminating is the work Chambers has done in the ZSL archives. I draw on it gratefully in the pages which follow.
2. The story is collected in Emma Donoghue's *Astray* (Picador, London, 2012).
3. Bartlett, p. 51.
4. Payne, Katy. *Silent Thunder: The Hidden Voice of Elephants* (W&N, London, 1998).
5. Bartlett, p. 1.
6. Ibid p. 3.

THE NAME'S JUMBO

1. Williams, p. 61.

EVOLUTION OR INTELLIGENT DESIGN?

1. Meredith, pp. 134–5.
2. 'The Tale of the Trunk', www.pbs.org/wnet/nature/elephants/trunk.html.
3. Kistler, p. 7.

JUMBO: THE GREATEST 'SHOW' OF LONDON

1. Stanley Holloway introduced the 'Lion and Albert' monologue, delivered in a rich Lancashire accent, to music hall audiences in the 1930s. It became a popular 78rpm record.
2. March Tappan, Eva. *The World's Story: A History of the World in Story, Song and Art* (Boston, 1914; reprint Read Books, 2013); *Vol. II: India, Persia, Mesopotamia, and Palestine*, pp. 184–190. Reproduced in www.fordham.edu/halsall/india/1877empressvictoria.asp.

JUMBO'S LUCKY ESCAPE

1. Labouchère, Henry. *Diary of the Besieged Resident in Paris* (Evans & Co, London, 1871), p. 220.
2. Baxter, John. *The Perfect Meal: In Search of the Lost Tastes of France* (HarperPerennial, London, 2013), Chapter 11, 'First Catch your Elephant'.

JUMBO'S PRIVATE LIFE

1. Robert Knox, *An Historical Relation of the Island Ceylon, in the East-Indies* (London, 1681), p. 23.
2. http://curiouscox.wordpress.com/2012/06/23/green-penis-syndrome-in-african-elephants.
3. Baker, S.W. *Wild Beasts and their Ways* (Macmillan, London, 1890), p. 20.
4. Chambers, p. 114, and Chapter 13, 'Friction in the Elephant House'.

Notes

ENTER THE GREATEST SHOWMAN ON EARTH

1. Saxon, p. 291.

JUMBOMANIA

1. Harding, p. 43. Harding's Chapter 6, 'Jumbo, Don't Go', gives an excellent account of the hysterical British press reaction to Jumbo's export.
2. Ibid.
3. Boulenger, E.G. *An Introduction to Animal Behaviour* (Discovery, India, 2003) p. 133.
4. Harding, pp. 45–46.
5. Harding, p. 48
6. Saxon, p. 293.

FAREWELL TO ENGLAND

1. Chambers, p. 157
2. The following account of Jumbo's landfall in the US is taken, largely, from *The New York Times*, which took a headline interest in the story.
3. Steve Brodie did his jump, allegedly, on 23 July 1886. *The New York Times* credited the event, and gave it maximum publicity. The consensus of opinion now is that Brodie faked his 277-foot leap into the East River.

YANKEE DOODLE JUMBO

1. Tavel Clarke, Michael. *These Days of Large Things: The Culture of Size in America, 1865-1930* (The University of Michigan Press, Michigan, 2007), p. 4.
2. Nance, p. 140.
3. Nance, pp. 132–3.
4. See PETA's website: www.commondreams.org/headline/2012/07/12-0

THE DEATH AND AFTERLIVES OF JUMBO

1. Susan Wilson, in www.tufts.edu/alumni/magazine/spring2002/jumbo.html. Tufts College's interest in Jumbo is explained later.
2. Ibid.
3. Saxon, p. 298.
4. Ibid, p. 299.
5. Goodwin, George G. 'The Crowninshield Elephant' (October 1951), reproduced here: http://www.naturalhistorymag.com/editors_pick/1928_05-06_pick.html.
6. Susan Wilson, op cit.
7. Saxon, p. 298.
8. For Akeley's distinguished role in the preservation of Jumbo, see Jones, Jeanette E. *In Search of Brightest Africa: Reimagining the Dark Continent in American Culture, 1884–1936* (University of Georgia Press, Georgia, 2011), pp. 136–38.
9. The account of Alice's arrival in the US is taken from the papers cited (the *Reading Eagle* and *The New York Times*) 16–25 April 1886.
10. Ibid.
11. Wilmeth, Don B. *The Cambridge Guide to American Theatre* (Cambridge University Press, Massachusetts 2007), p. 40.

JUMBO

JUMBO GOES TO COLLEGE

1. Susan Wilson, op cit.
2. Ibid.
3. Ibid.

BIGGER THAN JUMBO: THE DEATH OF JINGO

1. The most useful introduction to the life of Bostock is that prepared for the University of Sheffield's 'National Fairground Archive', which offers portals to key primary sources. See www.nfa.dept.shef.ac.uk/jungle/index1a.html.
2. Bostock, *The Training of Wild Animals* (London, 1903; reprint Rough Draft, Oregon, 2009), p. 76.
3. www.elephant.se/database2.php?elephant_id=3762. The account of Jingo's last voyage and death which follows is taken from the *Boston Evening Transcript*, 18 March 1903, reproduced here http://news.google.com/newspapers?nid=2249&dat=19030318&id=DY4-AAAA-IBAJ&sjid=6lkMAAAAIBAJ&pg=4035,2400597; http://paperspast.natlib.govt.nz/cgi-bin/paperspast?a=d&d=NZH19030502.2.100.19, and *The New York Times*, as dated in the text.
4. Milton, John. *Paradise Lost* (Peter Parker, London, 1667), I.192–201.

BIGGER AND BETTER THAN JUMBO: THE WHITE ELEPHANT

1. The following account of Barnum's acquisition of a white elephant, and the subsequent 'war of the white elephant' with Adam Forepaugh is taken from the following sources: www.elephant.se/database2.php?elephant_id=3864; Sarah Amato, 'The White Elephant in London: An Episode of Trickery, Racism and Advertising', http://muse.jhu.edu/journals/journal_of_social_history pp. 31–66; and Saxon, pp. 303–307.
2. Harris, Neil. *Humbug: The Art of P. T. Barnum* (Little Brown, London, 1973), p. 267.

GRAY ELEPHANTS, PINK ELEPHANTS AND BLUE ELEPHANTS

1. Saxon, p. 64.
2. Ibid, p. 295.
3. Chambers, p. 107.
4. Willis, Brett. http://christiananswers.net/spotlight/movies/pre2000/dumbo.
5. London, Jack. *John Barleycorn* (The Century Company, USA, 1913; reprint Oxford University Press, 1989, ed. Sutherland, J.) p. 6.

AIRBORNE JUMBOS

1. www.arkive.org/african-elephant/loxodonta-africana/image-G133573.
2. Derrida, Jacques. 'Plato's Pharmacy' in *Dissemination* (trans Barbara Johnson, London: 1981), pp. 61–172.

TOPSY

1. Williams, p. 115.
2. Scigliano, p. 196. In this section I draw on Scigliano's Chapter 15, 'Topsy was Framed', pp. 196–205.
3. The above narrative is taken from newspaper reports – rarely reliable at this

282

period. Susan Nance has come up with a significantly different account, which has to be quoted at length since there is no way of merging the two stories:

A year later, Topsy was in Brooklyn with the Forepaugh and Sells Brothers Circus. The papers, referring to her as 'Tops', said that at five o'clock in the morning that day Fielding Blount had crawled under the edge of the menagerie tent and 'staggered into the centre of the tent, where the long line of elephants stood, some of them standing stone still asleep, others rocking to and fro.' Blount was reported by a barn man to have offered an empty whisky glass to a number of the elephants, then approached the still sleeping Topsy and slapped her on the trunk. Another keeper awoke and from his cot warned Blount, 'You better keep away from her. She's ugly.' Blount seemed to be ignoring the advice when Topsy suddenly seized the man, threw him down and lowered her front right foot squarely on his chest. One keeper explained that he then heard a 'crushing, crunching noise and then everything was quiet'. (p. 184)

According to Nance it was Topsy's handler, Ault, who was in the habit of feeding her lit cigarettes.

4. Schroeder, Joan Vannorsdall. 'The Day they Hanged an Elephant in East Tennessee', 1 May 1993, https://docs.google.com/document/preview?hg-d=1&id=1WfN1oqrEz5NS-jlnp4CwNK-GLEjmeBik175_ZYkvb4c&pli=1. Subsequent reference and quotations are from Schroeder's account.
5. 'New York Honours Electrocuted Elephant', BBC News, 21 July 2003, http://news.bbc.co.uk/1/hi/world/americas/3083029.stm.

BUT SOMETIMES THE HOOF IS ON THE OTHER FOOT

1. Knox, op cit, Vol 1, pp. 246–7.
2. Rousselet, Louis. *India and its Native Princes: Travels in Central India and in the Presidencies of Bombay and Bengal* (India, 1882; reprint Asian Educational Services, 2005), pp. 134–5.
3. The authoritative account of Conrad's voyage to the interior of Africa is given in Sherry, Norman. *Conrad's Eastern World* (Cambridge University Press, Massachusetts, 1966).
4. Jean-Aubry, George. *Joseph Conrad: Life and Letters* (New York, 1927), 1: 141.
5. The most usefully annotated edition of *Heart of Darkness* is the 4th 'Norton Critical Edition' (Norton, New York, 2005). References here (as to other canonical texts cited in this book) can easily be located by word search in the free-access Gutenberg.org online editions.
6. Conrad's remark is found in 'Geography and Some Explorers', collected in *Last Essays*, ed. Curle, Richard. (J.M. Dent, London, 1926), p. 15.
7. Shakespeare, William. *Antony and Cleopatra* (1623), II.5.2–9.
8. Robbie Marsland, the UK Director of the International Fund for Animal Welfare (IFAW), *Sky News*, 5 January 2011, reproduced on http://news.sky.com/story/1033673/major-surge-in-ivory-smuggling-in-china.
9. Jane Goodall, quoted on 19 December 2012 on http://www.ecorazzi.com/2012/12/19/africas-elephants-facing-extinction-says-jane-goodall.

BIBLICAL JUMBOISM

1. http://answers.yahoo.com/question/index?qid=20100511192524AA3KVhl.

BIG GAME, BIG MEN

1. Theodore Roosevelt, *African Game Trails: An Account of the African Wanderings of an American Hunter-Naturalist* (London, 1910), p. vii. 'I speak of Africa and golden joys' is a quotation from Pistol, in Shakespeare's *Henry IV: Part Two*, V.3.101.
2. Ibid p. 283
3. Ibid p. 28
4. Ibid p. 445
5. Orwell's essay, 'Shooting an Elephant' was first published in the magazine *New Writing*, autumn 1936. Sonia Orwell's furious comment was recorded by her authorised biographer, Bernard Crick, some of whose research she felt was too punctilious. Crick tends towards scepticism about the shot elephant.

JUMBO DUNG AND JUMBO SEX

1. www.elephantsforever.co.za.
2. www.pbs.org/wnet/nature/elephants/trunk.html.
3. The Riesfeldt story originated in summer 1998 in the publication *Weekly World News*. Paderborn has no zoo. *WWN* subtitles itself 'The World's Only Reliable News'. Its issue for 8 August 2013 reports that sharks have been seen in the New York Subway system.
4. Guerrini, Dominic. http://www.chrisofiliprints.info/biography.php?cur=USD.

JUMBO EXILED

1. The *Evening Standard*, 12 March 2002, reproduced here: http://www.standard.co.uk/news/elephant-set-out-to-kill-keeper-6329871.html.
2. Virginia McKenna, reported on the BBC, 1 November 2001, http://news.bbc.co.uk/1/hi/england/1631128.stm.
3. Ann Grain, reported in the *Evening Standard*, 31 October 2001, http://www.standard.co.uk/news/elephants-to-leave-london-zoo-6312885.html.

EPILOGUE: ELEPHANT MISCELLANY

1. Sillar and Meyler, p. 141.
2. Williams, p. 115.
3. Bill Watterson, http://qi.com/infocloud/knees.
4. Emily Rothwell, 'Sleeping Giants', 17 June 2009, http://blogs.sandiegozoo. org/2009/06/17/sleeping-giants.
5. Jedd Akst, 'Ants Save Trees from Elephants', *The Scientist*, 2 September 2010, www.the-scientist.com/?articles.view/articleNo/29239/title/ Ants-save-trees-from-elephants.
6. See http://www.booksofzimbabwe.com/ahrs11.html. Sutherland published his autobiography, *The Adventures of an Elephant Hunter*, in 1912.

Index

Index

Index